A MURDER IN MUSIC CITY

A MURDER IN MUSIC CITY

CORRUPTION, SCANDAL, AND THE FRAMING OF AN INNOCENT MAN

Michael Bishop

Foreword by Richard Walter
Forensic psychologist, and consultant to law enforcement agencies

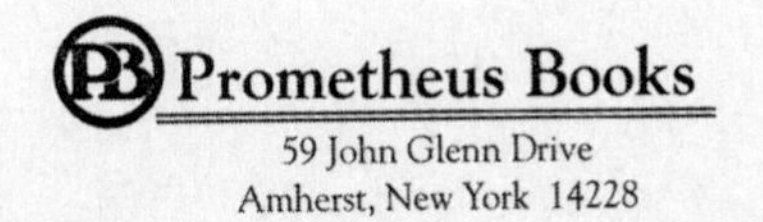

59 John Glenn Drive
Amherst, New York 14228

Published 2017 by Prometheus Books

Inquiries should be addressed to
Prometheus Books
59 John Glenn Drive
Amherst, New York 14228
VOICE: 716–691–0133 • FAX: 716–691–0137
WWW.PROMETHEUSBOOKS.COM

21 20 19 18 17 5 4 3 2 1

Library of Congress Cataloging-in-Publication Data

Names: Bishop, Michael, 1956- author.
Title: A murder in Music City : corruption, scandal, and the framing of an innocent man / Michael Bishop.
Description: Amherst, New York : Prometheus Books, 2017. | Includes index. | Identifiers: LCCN 2017013766 (print) | LCCN 2017031053 (ebook) | ISBN 9781633883468 (ebook) | ISBN 9781633883451 (pbk.)
Subjects: LCSH: Herring, Paula, 1945-1964. | Murder—Tennessee—Nashville—Case studies. | Murder—Investigation—Tennessee—Nashville—Case studies.
Classification: LCC HV6534.N18 (ebook) | LCC HV6534.N18 B57 2017 (print) | DDC 364.152/30976855—dc23
LC record available at https://lccn.loc.gov/2017013766

Printed in the United States of America

for Paula and Alan

CONTENTS

PART III: TRUE DETECTIVE

PART IV: HOUSE FULL OF HELL

FOREWORD

This book chronicles a web of debauchery and intentional wickedness that results in unapologetic murder, miseries, and the scapegoating of the innocent. How and why does this happen? The reader is advised that "man" is the only animal in the kingdom that has the ability to understand the past, present, and future and to make moral decisions of right and wrong.

Furthermore, inasmuch as choice is part of decision-making, it follows that "man" is the only animal that has the option of not living up to its full potential. Needless to say, there are many developing and full-blown scoundrels who exercise the latter option. For those who choose to improve their personal and social life through attitudes, mores, and ethics, however, laws exist to disapprove, judge, and punish those who violate the social codes of the society. As the reader will see in the forthcoming pages, there are those people who covertly attempt to have a foot in both crime and law. These moral chameleons are exploiters who deserve a special place in hell.

While exploring a murder case that was never intended to be understood, Michael Bishop intuitively understood that investigative skill means asking the right question rather than simply hearing the answers. Obviously, the answer is worthless if not responding to a poignant question. To ask that question is talent at its best. We can hope to get lucky, but luck is mercurial and a risky approach, often leading to a disastrous end. Instead, it is wisest to use skills and talent that lead to pattern development and recognizable motives, methods, and opportunities. Watch for the clues in this book, and the author will lead you from chaos into understanding. Ah, the journey should be fun. No, I will not be a storyline spoiler and tease out nuggets of gold for explanation. Instead, it is the work of the reader to participate in the process of understanding.

Finally, kudos to the author for writing a talented exposé on behalf of belated justice, with a provocative storyline and keen observations on the human condition that tends to limit truth to the perception of truth.

Hope you enjoy the book!

Richard Walter
Forensic psychologist,
and consultant to law enforcement agencies

PREFACE

In November of 2016, I made a road trip to the lovely mountains of northern Pennsylvania to have breakfast with my friend Richard Walter. Just after sunrise on the appointed day, I plotted a course over a two-lane blacktop road to the small village where the world's living Sherlock Holmes had taken up residence. Upon arrival, a warm greeting, and expressed astonishment by my host that I had so easily found him, I drove us to Richard's favorite breakfast eatery. On the way to the restaurant, I posed a simple question to the eccentric intellectual.

"Richard, does anyone in this town have any idea who you are, or that the living Sherlock Holmes resides here?" I asked.

"No, I don't think so," he said.

Moments later, I parked the car in front of the local diner he had chosen and we entered to the comforting aroma of coffee, bacon, and biscuits. Perhaps a full two seconds passed before my host was being hailed by the dozen or so locals having breakfast.

"Hey Richard! How are you man?"

"Hey Richard! Did you see that program on television last night, about JonBenét Ramsey? We need to talk!"

"Richard, is this the guy you said was writing a book? When does it come out?"

After being seated, and while reviewing the breakfast menu, I casually volleyed a dry comment over to my host. "So, you're pretty much anonymous here, is that what you were saying?"

An hour later, we sat down in Richard Walter's kitchen as a prelude to discussing the foreword needed for this book. I had previously broached the topic by phone with Richard, and he had graciously said he would be honored to write it. Over the course of the next few hours we discussed again the Paula Herring slaying and his insights into the murder. At midday, as I was gathering my papers and photographs, about to depart, the living Sherlock Holmes presented me with a batch of his freshly baked soft gingersnap cookies. I could not stop smiling and laughing at this surprising gift, and before I could back my rental car out of his driveway, I also learned that they were the best gingersnap cookies I had ever eaten.

A few days later, the foreword arrived, and I quickly realized that I had failed to ask Richard a few essential questions that a reader might find of keen interest. So, I called him on the phone to confess my oversight, and he bailed me out with the answers below. Enjoy.

MB: Do you get a lot of requests for help from wannabe detectives or novice investigators?

RW: A few, but mostly I decline the requests. The Vidocq Society members routinely tell people not to bother. I don't disagree with that assessment.

MB: How do you choose the ones you help versus the ones you decline?

RW: It helps if you're smart, and I find the case interesting, as in this murder. Most of the requests I get are from lazy fools with harebrained ideas, who've done no work, have no theory, and just want to exploit me. You can imagine my response to those inquiries.

MB: Which brings me to the Paula Herring story.

RW: In your story, you had innately asked the right questions long before you reached out to me for assistance, and I could tell you were determined to find the truth.

MB: If we could go back in time, to the night of the Paula Herring slaying, how would you have interviewed the person you deemed most likely to have committed the murder?

RW: You ask them to tell their story. Talk about their home life. You inflate their ego and note that they are a major player in the city. You ask about their friends, short-term goals, long-term goals, values, where they spend their time, but really you want to know where they spend their money. You try to identify their sexual orientation and friendship patterns. When you explore their group loyalties, you may find that instead of the local civic club, it's the guys at the local bar. By the time you switch gears and tell them what you are thinking, they are ready to lawyer up. Especially so if your analysis of the crime scene and the person most likely to have committed the murder are a match with the person you've just been interviewing.

MB: What's the secret ingredient in those soft gingersnap cookies?

RW: A half-cup of a particular brand of molasses. If it's not available, make a different cookie.

Some names and identifying details have been changed to protect the privacy of individuals. In certain instances, I have attempted to recreate events and conversations from my recollection, interview notes, and audio recordings.

PART I

THE BABYSITTER STORY

Lock the doors, or you'll end up like Paula Herring.
—Metro Nashville's first urban legend

CHAPTER ONE

SATURDAY NIGHT SLAYING

Paula Herring's murder had been predicted for months. That the victim was a pretty, blond coed wasn't all that surprising to authorities, especially since a number of young women in one of Nashville's newest subdivisions had been targeted by a rapist for more than a year. Metro Police had predicted that the activities of the rapist would eventually escalate to murder. It was just a matter of time and circumstance, they said, and on this Saturday night, February 22, 1964, it appeared that an eighteen-year-old babysitter had provided their tragic confirmation.

A few miles north of the crime scene, at the Municipal Safety Building in downtown Nashville, twenty-year-old Jim Squires was working his newspaper's graveyard shift, the uncoveted Saturday night assignment usually reserved for cub reporters.[1] Years later, Squires would oversee a Pulitzer Prize–winning staff of his own as editor of the *Chicago Tribune*, but on this night he waited patiently for the police dispatcher to alert him that a story was in the making.

Just ninety days after President Kennedy had been assassinated in Dallas, there were a number of stories that Squires could have covered. He could report on the frenzied activities of four young English musicians who had just taken the country by storm. But the Beatles had flown from New York City back to London on that very day, having completed their first American tour. Or he could focus on the trial of the inept men accused of kidnapping nineteen-year-old Frank Sinatra Jr., in December of 1963, or on the anxiously awaited prize fight in Miami Beach between heavyweight boxing champ Sonny Liston and a twenty-two-year-old challenger named Cassius Clay, a fight slated to take place in less than seventy-two hours.

But, as fate would have it, shortly after 11:00 p.m., the young journalist heard the voice of the night dispatcher from the wall-mounted speaker above his head directing cars forty-three and forty-four to an address on Timberhill Drive.[2] Squires had covered the police beat long enough to know that these were the car numbers assigned to Metro's homicide detectives. And on this night, wherever they went, he went.

It was a cold night, with daytime temperatures on Friday and Saturday barely reaching the freezing mark. By the time Squires arrived at the home on Timberhill Drive, the outdoor temperature had fallen to twenty degrees Fahrenheit, with a trace of snow in the air.

The address provided by the police dispatcher turned out to be a modest red-brick, ranch-styled home with three small bedrooms, a sloping front yard, and an attached, one-car garage. The home was fairly new—part of the Crieve Hall community, a group of houses only a short drive to the southeast from downtown Nashville, and one of the many new subdivisions that had sprouted up as part of the post–World War II growth era.

Jim Squires found almost a dozen uniformed officers, a couple of homicide detectives, and investigators from the district attorney's office already working the brutal crime scene. It didn't take Squires long to discover that it was as baffling as it was bloody.[3]

At approximately 11:00 p.m. that night, Jo Herring, a widow and a nurse at Vanderbilt University Hospital, had returned from a dinner engagement and entered the house with her two male companions. Jo's eighteen-year-old daughter, Paula, had volunteered to stay home and babysit her younger brother while she worked on a book report for school.[4]

According to one of the dinner companions, after parking the car the three made their way through the side door of the attached garage and into the den. That's where they found Paula; fully clothed, the blond girl was lying facedown and lifeless on a blood-soaked rug in front of the television set. Her pretty face was ghostly, bloodied, and bruised, and the entire front of her white blouse was stained a horrific crimson.

Jo Herring immediately dropped to her knees and attempted to find a pulse on her daughter's body. One of the men, the driver of the car, became nauseous and, without so much as a word, exited through the garage, got back into his car, and drove away. The other man grabbed the telephone in the den and placed an urgent call to the police. While he was on the phone with the authorities, Jo Herring's little blond son, six-year-old Alan, emerged unharmed from his bedroom. According to the trembling child, he had been put to bed earlier in the evening but had awoken to find Paula lying on the floor in the den. When she didn't respond to his pleas to "get up" he went back to bed until his mother returned home from dinner.

Hearing about this from the police on the scene, Jim Squires knew he was under pressure to phone in the biggest story of his young career. And since the *Nashville Tennessean*'s chief rival didn't publish on Sunday, Squires had the story all to himself, as long as he phoned it in on time. While the young reporter waited for additional details, the detectives and investigators reviewed the puzzling scene before them.

Paula Herring had been found lying facedown on the floor, legs spread, with one foot hooked around the front leg of the television set. And though her arms were close to her sides, her hands were in an awkward, palms-up position, as if someone had just removed her coat. Paula's medium-length blond hair, splattered with blood, obscured most of her face. In addition to the white cotton blouse she'd been wearing, Paula had on a gray wraparound skirt, penny loafers, and dark, knee-length socks.

Underneath Paula's body, the detectives found two spent bullets. One of them had to be pried out of the floor. The officers also noted Paula's matching gray wool sweater wadded up on the couch along with school books and papers. When the detectives took a closer look at the sweater, they found two bullet holes in the back, indicating that the killer had apparently used the sweater to muffle the sound of the gunshots. Jim Squires hastily made notes as bits and pieces of the puzzle came trickling in.

Just before midnight, the Metro Nashville coroner, Dr. W. J. Core, arrived at the crime scene to fulfill his obligations to the city and to the Herring family. As the detectives and investigators gathered around the elderly medical examiner, Core, a short, rotund man, provided confirmation of their initial assessment: Paula Herring had taken a brutal beating, been choked and strangled with bare hands, and, when that didn't finish her off, two gunshots in the back, apparently fired execution-style from a .32-caliber automatic, had done the deed.[5]

As Dr. Core carefully examined the body, he added that the victim also had been shot once in the upper left chest. And though initially it appeared no sexual assault had taken place, Core noted that he couldn't be completely certain of that fact until further examination took place at the morgue. As for time of death, the doctor could offer only an estimate, but based on the body's rigor mortis and the clotting of blood, he placed it near 10:30 p.m., in part because the hands of the shattered wristwatch Paula was wearing had stopped at 10:32 p.m. That the victim's younger brother had unknowingly slept through the tragedy was mind-boggling to everyone in the room.

A few moments before Paula Herring's body was removed from the home on Timberhill Drive, police allowed the *Nashville Tennessean*'s young journalist to make his way into the den and phone in his story, a story that sent the community into a panic on Sunday morning.

CHAPTER TWO

LEAVING TEXAS

A few days before Paula Herring came home to Nashville from the University of Tennessee in Knoxville, a winter storm developed in the southeastern United States. The storm moved northeast through the Smoky Mountains and dropped feet, not inches, of snow from East Tennessee and North Carolina on up the eastern seaboard into Virginia and New England.[1] In many areas, power lines were down, roads were closed, and citizens were nervous. But not Paula Herring; she loved it.

Paula was thrilled with snow skiing and was glad about anything that would produce more of the white powder on the ski slopes of Gatlinburg, Tennessee, where she was learning the sport. The Gatlinburg Ski Resort had been open for only two years when Paula and some of her University of Tennessee classmates formed the school's first Ski Club during the Winter Quarter of 1964.[2] With little Mount Harrison as its primary peak, the resort boasted 3,500 feet of elevation—approximately two-thirds of a mile altitude—and several easy runs for skiers to use while learning the sport. Less than forty miles from the university, the slopes were easily accessed by driving southeast from downtown Knoxville along Chapman Highway to Gatlinburg and then up Ski Mountain Road.

Paula was overjoyed with skiing and could not get enough of it. As a gifted athlete, the 5′5″, 110-pound blond was surprisingly strong, all muscle, with a body made for the fast-twitch jumps and turns and the tricky balance needed to use the edges of her skis to navigate the steeper runs of the little resort. As one of her dorm mates noted, "Paula would rather spend money on lift tickets than food."[3]

But skiing was by no means the only athletic endeavor at which she excelled. Jo Herring would describe Paula as having been her daddy's "tomboy," with basketballs, tennis balls, and her dad's golf clubs filling up her room at home. Part of the first graduating class of John Overton High School in southern Nashville, Paula had been captain of the girls' basketball team, had played tennis, and was an excellent bowler. She had more than a few trophies on display in the house on Timberhill Drive.[4] And, like the tomboy she was, and given her last name, she was always referred to as "Fish" rather than "Paula" by friends and classmates at Overton High.[5]

She also carried her father's love for the Baylor Bears football team, his favorite while growing up in Texas. If she hadn't grown to love the University of Tennessee in Knoxville, she would have given serious consideration to attending Baylor University, but she couldn't wait to get to the University of Tennessee after graduating from John Overton High in June 1963.

Paula's parents, Wilmer and Eva Jo, both had grown up in the hill country of Texas, forty miles east of Waco, near the working-class communities of Groesbeck and Mexia.[6] Near the time of Wilmer's birth, in December 1919, enormous fields of natural gas were found in the area, and the economy as well as the population swelled in response. However, by the time Wilmer was eighteen, the community had settled back to a population of approximately six thousand residents.

Mexia, with a reputation as a small Texas town you would enjoy no matter how you pronounced it, was where Wilmer Herring and Eva Jo Ainsworth graduated from high school. Decades later, Mexia would also be home to a future celebrity and Playboy Playmate named Anna Nicole Smith, who worked at a local fried chicken restaurant while sporadically attending Mexia High in the early 1980s.[7]

Wilmer was four classes ahead of his future bride. He was the oldest of six children and along with his family had been a regular churchgoer from an early age, in part because his grandfather, Napoleon Bonaparte "N. B." Sikes, had been an influential gospel preacher in the area, with the conservative protestant group known as the Church of Christ.[8]

After high school graduation, Wilmer worked at the local J. C. Penney company and then, in July 1941, was inducted into the

United States Army Air Forces, where he began study at the military's radio communications university.[9]

As a radio operator, Wilmer was responsible for monitoring changes in bomber flight plans, for record keeping, and for broadcasting to other planes, as well as for sending Morse code, at a minimum of twelve words per minute, when required. Three years later, in the summer of 1944, Wilmer Herring earned his silver wings as an aviator and received a commission as a second lieutenant.[10]

Eva Jo Ainsworth, born in October 1923, was the second child of a pipefitter and his wife and was thirteen months old when a prospector struck oil in Limestone County, Texas, near the little town of Wortham, where the Ainsworths were living at the time. Up until oil was discovered, the town had primarily been known for ginning cotton for local farmers. But when word of an oil gusher leaked out, the little town was transformed from a few hundred residents to more than 30,000 fortune hunters. Three years and millions of barrels later, the wells dried up, the fortune seekers departed, and the community returned to its former life. When the Great Depression began to impact the farmers in the area, cotton prices plummeted and money became scarce. Jo Herring's father, with a wife and two girls and two boys to support, was hit especially hard by the exit of the drilling operations and the onset of the Depression.

In September 1941, just weeks before she turned eighteen, Eva Jo Ainsworth embarked on a career as a nurse. The future could not have been brighter on such a path, as there was already a nationwide shortage of nurses when the Japanese bombed Pearl Harbor in December 1941. In July 1943, the dark-eyed brunette from Limestone County obtained her Cadet Nurse card and began a career as a public-health nurse. At around the same time, she married the handsome Wilmer Herring, and he soon went off to war in the South Pacific.[11]

Wilmer, meanwhile, served honorably as an Army Air Forces pilot and eventually earned a promotion to first lieutenant. At 5′10″ and 150 pounds, he carried his ancestors' handsome features and kept his wavy black hair combed back from his forehead. In August 1945, while Wilmer dreamed of returning home from the Philippines, where he was serving with the famous Bomber Barons, his daughter, Paula, was born in Texas on Tuesday, August 21. It was twelve days after the United States dropped an atomic bomb on Nagasaki, Japan, and twelve days before Japan formally surrendered to General MacArthur on the deck of the USS *Missouri* on September 2, 1945.[12]

After the war ended, Wilmer took advantage of the GI Bill to enroll in Baylor University, where he continued his radio studies, combined with a surprising focus on a foreign language—French—and graduated in the class of 1948. With the advantages of good looks, a college diploma, and a prestigious military career, Wilmer Herring accepted a job with Life and Casualty Insurance of Tennessee, housed in one of the tallest buildings in the South, in downtown Nashville. And in 1949, with the promise of rapid career advancement, the Herrings moved from Texas to Gallatin, Tennessee, just north of Nashville, and Jo Herring took a job as county nurse for Sumner County, as the family settled into postwar life.

For the next ten years, the Herring family built a life in Gallatin, and Paula enjoyed the undivided attention of her parents. In 1958, the family welcomed a newcomer into the mix, baby brother Alan, and a year later they departed Sumner County and moved into a rental house on Elysian Fields Road, near an area south of downtown Nashville that would one day become the Nashville Zoo. While Wilmer continued his work with Life and Casualty, Jo Herring transitioned from her role as county nurse to working as a full-time nurse for Vanderbilt University Hospital. But tragedy struck in September of 1960, when forty-year-old Wilmer Herring was found dead in one of the guest rooms of the Noel Hotel, located in the heart of downtown Nashville.[13]

The Noel Hotel was mere steps to Nashville's illegal entertainment mecca, Printers Alley, home to gambling, free-flowing liquor, and adult pleasures. As a conduit to the Alley, the Noel provided twenty-four-hour free parking, twenty-four-hour food service, and a radio and television in every air conditioned room of its building.[14]

By all accounts, the loss of her father was especially hard on Paula. Friends said she kept quiet about the tragedy, and focused her energy, talents, and especially her anger on athletic endeavors at her new high school. When the Herrings had moved from Gallatin to Nashville in 1959, John Overton High had just added a ninth grade class to the seventh and eighth grades it had opened with in the fall of 1958. Sadly, on the same day that Wilmer Herring was buried in Mexia, Texas—Tuesday, September 6, 1960—Paula Herring was scheduled to begin the newly added sophomore class at John Overton High School. Years later, many of Paula Herring's closest friends would state that they had not been aware of the circumstances surrounding Paula's father's death, nor even that he had died.[15]

A few weeks after Wilmer's funeral, Jo Herring took the life insurance money from Wilmer's policy and purchased a one-year-old home on Timberhill Drive in the Crieve Hall community as an attempt at a fresh start for the little family.

In time, Paula's classmates would describe the athletic teenager as "bright, clever, and a jokester," as well as a tough basketball player. She also took on the enjoyable challenge of being the society editor of the school's newspaper for all four years of high school.[16]

Two years later, in September of 1962, seventeen-year-old Paula was one of a several Nashville citizens reporting strange black circles and semicircles in their yards. The *Nashville Tennessean* described the story in their Saturday, September 22nd edition as "A Dark Whodunit," and then quoted Paula as claiming to have found a ten-foot-wide circle in her own yard: "My science teacher told me it was probably some kind of mushroom or mold. Whatever it is, it sure is weird."[17] And a few weeks later the seasonal change in the weather caused the circles to simply vanish as if they had never appeared.

During her final year at John Overton, Paula switched from wearing eyeglasses to contact lens and then lightened her brown locks to accentuate her new look, as she began leaving her tomboy phase behind.[18] Male classmates described Paula as "playful and likeable, but not flirtatious, or coquettish." Her high school graduation photo reflected an attractive young woman with a Mona Lisa smile, a smile that seemed to suggest she had plans for the future.

A few weeks after Paula's murder, in an interview with Julie Hollabaugh of the *Nashville Tennessean*, a grief-stricken Jo Herring described her eighteen-year-old daughter as "a girl full of the joy of being alive."[19] Paula was "warm, lovable, intensely energetic, and full of plans for the future. She was an ambitious girl and could achieve anything she wanted to achieve," recalled Mrs. Herring. "After she outgrew the tomboy stage she thought for a while of going into journalism."

Talking about Paula's athleticism and her being captain of her high school basketball team, Jo Herring said, "We used to go to all the basketball games and whenever she'd have a free throw and the gym would get quiet, her little brother would look around and say, 'that's my sister, hit it, Sister!'"[20]

That Alan Herring was proud of his big sister was obvious to anyone who saw them together. And Paula adored her little brother, as well. She nicknamed him "Sputnik" a year after Russia launched the space age in October 1957 by putting their Sputnik satellite into orbit. Paula and her mother later shortened the nickname to "Sput."

"Paula was a gregarious extrovert," said Mrs. Herring, "who made friends easily and rapidly. Within weeks of her enrollment 'on the Hill' [University of Tennessee, Knoxville campus] she'd made scores of friends, her room became headquarters for card games and gab-fests and hairdos and she'd been elected president of the dorm floor." According to Jo Herring, Paula called just before she came home for that fateful weekend in February, saying she'd decided to change her major from biology to pre-law. It was the girl's first visit home since Christmas, Mrs. Herring added.

Later in the same interview, Jo Herring said that she and Paula "had been close since the death of Paula's father, and that it was at Paula's suggestion that she went to dinner that Saturday night. She said, 'why don't you take the evening off? I have to read a book and make a report.'"

Decades later, an amateur researcher would pause to wonder why Paula Herring, who clearly was having the time of her life at the University of Tennessee, would choose to leave the ski slopes and the biggest snowfall in years, as well as her sorority friends, just to come home to Nashville to write a book report on a Saturday night in February 1964.

As for her feelings about the murder, Mrs. Herring said, "I'll never get adjusted to it. I just can't believe it or realize it's happened. I'm living one day at a time. Somehow with friends and help of God, I've managed to survive it this long. But I just keep thinking it's a dream, Paula's still at school."

But Paula wasn't at school, and the citizens of Nashville were up in arms over the coed's murder.[21] They also felt betrayed and abandoned by the sheriff and other Metro policemen, who had been indicted for taking payoffs to maintain the corrupt lifestyle of Printers Alley. So much so that many of those living in the suburbs decided they were better off banding together in neighborhood watch groups where men would walk nightly patrols while armed with guns and walkie-talkies.

CHAPTER THREE

1964 INVESTIGATION

After visiting the Paula Herring crime scene early Sunday morning, the chief of police, Hubert Kemp, ordered every available man on the police force to be involved in an around-the-clock investigation of the girl's murder. In Kemp's view, "the Herring case takes priority over all other police work."[1]

As for suspects in the Herring case, detectives immediately thought of Boston.[2] From June of 1962 through early 1964, the city of Boston had been on a desperate hunt for a man simply known as "the Strangler." It was said that the strangler had been responsible for as many as thirteen sexual homicides in the area, and he was still on the loose.

With unfortunate parallels to Boston, in the Crieve Hall area of Nashville there had been many reports of a man prowling the neighborhood. And all the reports had a similar description: a young man with dark hair, fast runner, early twenties, around 5′11″ with a light build, and usually seen late at night on weekends, always targeting houses where there was no man at home at the time.[3]

In September 1963, a young pregnant mother of two had been raped in the living room of her home by a man fitting the description. Her husband had been away at the time, and her two small children had been asleep in nearby bedrooms.[4]

Seven weeks later, a seventeen-year-old girl who was babysitting for a neighbor in Crieve Hall heard someone rattling the locked front door. When she saw a man through the window of the door, she ran to another room and called her father at their home two streets away. When the father arrived at the house, the young man had disappeared into the night.

These episodes were behind the formation of a group of vigilantes made up of approximately 250 residents of the new suburb.[5] The primary catalyst for their formation was the group's feeling that the area "was not getting proper police protection. And when called, the police were taking too long to arrive and when they did they trampled upon whatever evidence was left behind." The group paired up in twos starting around 9:00 p.m. each night; armed with walkie-talkies provided by the new Metro government, they patrolled the area in hopes of catching the rapist and providing some much needed comfort to area residents.

Residents of the area didn't allow children to play outside, and under threat of corporal punishment forbade them from answering any knock at the door. Area hardware stores couldn't keep up with the demand for door locks, door latches, and guns of every make and model. In many households, the mantra was to shoot first and ask questions later, and the terrorized residents were deadly serious about following this plan.

On March 4, 1964, ten days after the murder of Paula Herring, one of the Herrings' neighbors left his home on Timberhill Drive at around 3:00 a.m. to manage a group of newspaper carriers for the *Nashville Tennessean.* About fifteen minutes later, the man's wife heard a car pull into the driveway and then someone whistling as they approached the bedroom door, which opened to the backyard. The woman assumed that her husband had forgotten something and had returned home. She heard the doorknob turn and rattle. Before opening the door, she decided to look outside. A lightning flash at that moment illuminated not her husband but a thin young man, in his early twenties. Her screams brought her father from another part of the house with a pistol in his hand, but the prowler had driven away by the time the father had gotten to the door.

The additional manpower on the Paula Herring murder case immediately produced results. A neighbor of the Herrings, living two blocks south, noted that, on Saturday night, he and his wife had retired for the evening at 9:30 p.m. Within five to ten minutes of going to bed, they heard a loud noise at the juncture of the two streets in front of their home. The neighbor described the noise as a car taking off with a sound like a fan turning and metal hitting against metal. By the time the man looked out his bedroom window, the car was out of sight, headed north toward Nashville.

On Sunday, a local television station reported that the police had arrested two Vanderbilt University students on suspicion of murder just hours after the Paula Herring slaying. A WLAC-TV cameraman photographed one of the police officers involved holding a .32-caliber pistol taken from the students and identified it as a possible murder weapon in the Paula Herring case. While police held the students, a ballistics expert from the Tennessee Bureau of Investigation quickly ran comparison tests against the bullets recovered in the den on Timberhill Drive. But the suspects were released when the ballistics didn't match and the students produced an airtight alibi for their whereabouts on Saturday evening.

As disappointing as this news was to Nashville law enforcement, they caught a solid break when a night manager at the Krystal hamburger restaurant on Franklin Road contacted the district attorney's office about a bloody guest who had visited her establishment on Saturday night, apparently not long after Paula Herring had been murdered. In addition to the obvious significance of a bloody customer, the proximity of the restaurant to the crime scene was especially noted, a distance of less than three minutes by car.

According to the night manager, the bloody man entered the restaurant and began looking through the phone book, at which point she asked if she could assist, and the customer requested her help in finding the phone number for Rhea Little's service station, noting that he was having car trouble. At this point, the night manager pointed out that Rhea Little's station was directly across the street from the Krystal but had already closed for the evening. According to the restaurant manager, the bloody man then quickly left the restaurant.

MONDAY—FEBRUARY 24, 1964

Just after daybreak, patrolmen noticed a young man traveling on foot not far from the Herring neighborhood. When the suspect realized he was being followed, he bolted.

By the time the officers caught him and delivered him to police headquarters, their suspect was readily admitting to peeping into houses and prowling around homes at all hours of the night.

However, shortly after detectives began their interrogation, someone noticed that their talkative guest was wearing some unusual footwear. After further questioning, it turned out that their prime suspect was actually a twenty-five-year-old mental patient who had walked off the property of the nearby Central State Psychiatric Hospital.[6]

While investigators were looking for their killer, Jim Squires was adding even more intrigue to the slaying with his second story of the week. The story described a book missing from the crime scene, which the detectives assigned to the case deemed to be a clue to the killing. The detectives, however, did not yet want to name the missing paperback book, and the young reporter dutifully withheld that information in his article.

On Monday afternoon, twenty-seven-year-old Al Baker of Nashville finally met up with a friend he had been trying to reach. The friend was a Metro policeman, and over coffee Baker told the officer a story. What he said put Baker in a position to collect $7,480.00—more than a year's salary—in reward money offered by Governor Frank Clement, the Metro Council, and the *Nashville Banner*.[7]

Baker's story was so helpful that he was taken to downtown Nashville, to the Municipal Safety Building, and asked to repeat it. There, he told the attentive police officers that, for the past three years, he'd been acquainted with a man named John Randolph Clarke. Baker said that he knew the thirty-nine-year-old as "Red" Clarke, a moniker denoting Clarke's hair color, and that they had gotten to know each other because they had previously dated women who happened to share adjoining apartments, notwithstanding the fact that John Clarke was a married man. After this shady beginning, Baker and Clarke began to meet from time to time at various watering holes around the Vanderbilt University area.

On the most recent Saturday night, Al Baker said he had gone to Ruth's Diner, and when he got there Red Clarke was on the phone but later joined him at the counter. According to Baker, Clarke told him that "he had just been talking to a UT freshman who was home visiting her mother, and that Clarke had invited himself over with some beer." Clarke said that he "phoned with the idea of seeing the girl's mother," with whom he had struck up a conversation at Ruth's Diner a few days earlier, but since the girl's mother wasn't home, Clarke planned to go on over to the house and make advances toward the daughter instead.

Baker noted that Clarke then finished his drink and left the restaurant a short time afterward. Deeply troubled by his knowledge, Baker said that he sure hoped it wasn't his friend Red Clarke who had committed this awful crime, but after reading the newspaper headlines on Sunday, his conscience had begun to torment him.

The police asked Baker if Clarke owned a gun, and Baker said Clarke owned a .32-caliber Beretta, usually carried in a shoulder holster. At this news, the chief homicide detective dispatched two officers to pick up Clarke for questioning. It was a short ride for the officers, since the Clarke home was located near the Vanderbilt University football stadium.

Around 5:45 p.m. Monday afternoon, police officers knocked on the door of the Clarke home, and after a brief discussion the redheaded man agreed to ride down to the Municipal Safety Building to answer a few questions. Callie Clarke, John's wife, who was ten years older than her husband, followed in the family car in order to bring John home when the police were finished. What no one knew at that point was that the questioning would continue for over eleven hours.

Unknown to the policemen who had been sent to retrieve Red Clarke, their suspect was from a prominent family. John Clarke's father had been a general sessions judge in East Tennessee, and at one point the Republican floor leader in the state senate. Clarke's siblings were all successful, with career paths that included the CIA, the Air Force, real estate, and education. But John Clarke's contribution to the family legacy was less noteworthy, having changed jobs five times in five years. Worse yet, he had been mostly unemployed for the previous eighteen months.

In 1943, Clarke entered the Navy after graduating high school in Livingston, Tennessee. On D-Day, his ship had been torpedoed during landing exercises, and Clarke was found unconscious on Omaha Beach. In 1945, he received an honorable medical discharge from the Navy, and a few months later Clarke used his military benefits to enroll at Tennessee Tech as a social science major. The college, based in Cookeville, Tennessee, was then known as Tennessee Polytechnic Institute, or TPI.

Apparently Clarke enjoyed his short stint as a college student, based on an article Bob Wilson wrote for the *Knoxville News Sentinel* following a football game between the University of Tennessee and TPI, a game won 49–0 by the University of Tennessee in front of 12,000 adoring fans:

> One of the highlights at the VOL–TPI game was the Tennessee cheering section, or maybe I should say a red-headed character by the name of John Clarke, who happened to be a Tennessee Poly student. When Clarke, attired in dungarees, took over as guest cheerleader of the Volunteers, the Tennessee rooting section sounded off as never before. The UT rooters enjoyed Clarke's antics in leading the cheers so well that they wanted to keep him the remainder of the game. When the regular UT cheerleaders took their positions in front of the stands, the rooters booed them down and Clarke did an encore. I'll say this for him, he had plenty on the ball in getting the rooters into action and keeping them going.[8]

After the cheerleading incident was reported in the Knoxville newspaper, John Randolph Clarke was asked to leave the Cookeville school.

Upon making the short ride downtown, detectives escorted the 5′11″, 200-pound redhead to a room with some privacy and began the formal interview regarding his whereabouts during the previous Saturday night. Clarke's alibi centered upon visits to friends, taverns, and liquor stores, all in the Vanderbilt area. Clarke added that he was home by 9:30 p.m.

On Sunday, Clarke said he and his wife went to visit her family in Tullahoma, a small town about seventy miles southeast of Nashville. While there, Clarke noted that he had picked up a large number of paperback books that his brother-in-law had been trying to sell for him at a drive-in theater.

At the mention of books, the detectives in the room made eye contact with each other. One of the officers asked Clarke if he owned a gun. The answer was yes, a .32-caliber automatic, but it had been stolen about ten days prior. The detectives wanted to know if Clarke had reported the theft. No, came the response.

Clarke would later testify at the criminal trial that he was questioned the entire night by never less than two interrogators and by as many as fifteen policemen at once. He noted that he was not given food, access to a lawyer or a doctor, or his medication. When he asked to use the restroom, Clarke said he was told, "You're stuck to that chair!"[9] In return for the hospitality, Clarke refused to participate in all tests, including ballistics, paraffin, fingernail scraping, and polygraph, though he did submit to a full body search that revealed no scratches, bruises, marks, or cuts of any kind.

While this vignette was being played out within the confines of the Municipal Safety Building, news that it was taking place began to spread. Before long, the hallways in the building were filled with photographers and reporters, hoping not only for a photograph of the suspect but for any inside scoop or bit of detail that might provide an edge over their newspaper and television rivals.

At around 1:00 a.m. on Tuesday morning, the Krystal manager was brought into the police station to identify her "bloody" customer from Saturday night. She had been whisked from the restaurant, still wearing her all-white outfit and food-stained apron, as Red Clarke was inserted into a lineup along with four other stocky white males. After the lineup, the restaurant manager was led to the office of an assistant police chief, where in his presence, and the presence of a detective, she could not settle on a firm conviction that it had actually been Clarke in a bloody condition inside her food establishment.

Given the unusual access of their newspaper reporter, the *Nashville Tennessean* held its morning press run for most of the night in hopes of breaking news in the sensational case, especially with a lineup hanging in the balance. Just around daybreak on Tuesday morning, at a time when the *Nashville Tennessean* normally would have delivered fresh newspapers to its carriers, the authorities made one last attempt to tie Clarke to the slaying, asking to listen to his car for any sign of the "noisy vehicle." But hearing nothing out of the ordinary, they decided they did not have enough evidence to hold Clarke and released him. With citizens desperate for news, the morning paper did finally arrive, albeit several hours later than usual.

TUESDAY—FEBRUARY 25, 1964

After Clarke's long night with detectives, he spent the day sleeping, and in the early evening felt well enough to listen to a radio broadcast of a heavyweight boxing match out of Miami, Florida, where twenty-two-year-old Cassius Marcellus Clay Jr. was about to shock the world with his technical knockout of heavyweight champ Sonny Liston. The following day, Clay announced his membership in the Nation of Islam, and changed his name to Muhammad Ali.

At the Harris-Donoho funeral home in Gallatin, Tennessee, mourners arrived early for a 10:00 a.m. memorial service. They offered sad condolences to Paula's grief-stricken mother. A number of Overton High School students, classmates, teachers, and neighbors paid their respects, as did several heartbroken girls from the New West Dorm at the University of Tennessee. To every well-wisher who came through the line, more than one remembered that Jo Herring offered a strange yet simple challenge: "Just find who did it."

Just before noon, when Paula's casket was lowered into a grave at Crestview Memorial Gardens, the weather was cold but sunny, and Jo Herring still seemed to be in shock.[10] Dressed all in black and wearing dark sunglasses, she sat motionless during her daughter's last rites. Alan Herring was nowhere to be seen. Less than two hundred miles away, in Knoxville, flags were flown at half-mast across the University of Tennessee's campus in honor of the murdered student.

CHAPTER FOUR

THIRD BULLET

WEDNESDAY–FEBRUARY 26, 1964

Wednesday morning's *Nashville Tennessean* detailed how fifty cops and workhouse prisoners had spent the day on Tuesday walking the Radnor Rail Yards near Timberhill Drive, unsuccessfully searching for the missing paperback book.

Later that morning, however, the same man who had reported hearing a noisy car on Saturday night discovered the missing book at the edge of a field across from his home.[1] The book turned out to be a seventy-five cent paperback version of *All the King's Men,* the Pulitzer Prize–winning novel by Robert Penn Warren, himself a former Vanderbilt student and literary legend.

Warren's book involved a fictional character named Willie Stark, who many said was actually based on the controversial Huey Long. Long, nicknamed Kingfish, was governor of Louisiana and then US senator in the early 1930s, around the time that Warren had taught at Louisiana State University. The book became an Oscar-winning film, with Broderick Crawford in the lead role as Willie Stark.[2]

On Wednesday, detectives and investigators were surprised to learn that Al Baker had yet *another* story to tell about his drinking buddy John Randolph Clarke, and this time it was a story that would ultimately seal Clarke's fate.[3]

Baker told detectives of an incident that had happened two months prior, on Christmas Eve 1963. According to Baker, on that night he had also crossed paths with Red Clarke at Ruth's Diner. It was at the tavern that Al Baker talked Clarke into going with him to a Christmas party near Music Row. At the party, Clarke got into an argument with another man, and, after tempers flared, Clarke pulled his pistol and threatened to use it if necessary. Clarke's opponent took the threat seriously and left.

After the party, Baker and Clarke dropped off a couple of their friends, a man named Murray Cook and one named Jesse Henderson, at an apartment on 18th Avenue. While Baker drove the foursome to the apartment, the other passengers began teasing Clarke about carrying a pistol loaded with blanks. When they arrived at their destination, Clarke unholstered his .32-caliber pistol and fired one round into a pile of snow next to the sidewalk. Baker said he remembered seeing a little white puff rise from the ground when the gun went off.

Upon hearing this story, two Metro detectives, Al Baker, and a metal detection expert made a quick trip to the 18th Avenue apartment on Wednesday night. After receiving permission to conduct the search, the digging began just after 10:00 p.m., in a space less than ten feet by ten feet, using a searchlight and a metal detector. After working until 2:00 a.m. Thursday morning without success, the group decided to quit and try again during daylight hours. The search area was left unguarded, and when the men returned the next day one of the detectives immediately spotted a bullet lying partially uncovered next to the sidewalk.

A few hours later, a specialist with the Tennessee Bureau of Investigation noted that the two bullets recovered from the murder scene and the bullet from the sidewalk on 18th Avenue were indeed a perfect match and had been fired from the same weapon.[4] The question for the local authorities, however, was whether the spent bullets, without the gun, would be enough to charge their chief suspect with the murder of Paula Herring.

In the meantime, John Randolph Clarke quietly checked into Park View Hospital in hopes of obtaining help for blackout spells and high blood pressure. While Clarke received medical care, his clothing, retrieved from a local laundry, Paula Herring's bloody garments, and the recovered paperback book were all personally escorted to Washington, DC, to the FBI, by officials from the Metro Nashville Police Department and the district attorney's office. J. Edgar Hoover's FBI promised a preliminary report of their analysis within twenty-four hours.

THURSDAY–FEBRUARY 27, 1964

Buoyed by the knowledge that the bullets matched, the mayor, the district attorney general, and the chief of police were in a much better mood; the authorities in Nashville felt with a high degree of certainty that they had found their killer and that his name was John Randolph Clarke.

Early in the evening on Thursday, February 27, WLAC-TV began to break into their programming with dramatic news bulletins announcing that the mayor of Nashville, the Honorable Beverly Briley, would appear on the "Big News" at 10:00 p.m. and would, at that time, reveal the name of Paula Herring's killer. The bulletins were repeated at intervals throughout the primetime viewing hours, which caused great excitement and anticipation in Middle Tennessee, as word passed that the case was to reach a climax that evening. When the newscast began, the mayor appeared and dramatically announced to as many as one hundred thousand households that he knew the name of Paula Herring's murderer, and that the guilty man's arrest was imminent:

> We know who's guilty of this crime, we are certain. . . . The man is under surveillance and he's not under arrest, but we know what's going on.[5]

Within an hour of the mayor's pronouncement, a telegram was delivered to Metro's chief of police, Hubert Kemp from the FBI. The message read:

> Reference Paula Herring murder case and evidence delivered to FBI laboratory on February twenty-six. Victim's sweater composed of blue orlon fibers and white orlon fibers. Orlon fibers of both colors were found on front of suspect's coat and trousers. Victim's skirt contains coarse white woolen fibers used for novelty effect in certain fabrics. One such fiber found on front of suspect's coat. Above fibers found on suspect's clothing could have come from victim's sweater and skirt. No blood found on book or on suspect's clothing. Latent fingerprints and palm prints developed on book. Comparisons are being made. Will advise upon completion. No

palm prints available for suspect. Confirmatory report will be furnished when all laboratory examinations completed. HOOVER.[6]

Shortly before midnight on Thursday the 27th, Mayor Briley gathered with Attorney General Harry Nichol, Chief of Police Hubert Kemp, detectives, and other law enforcement members to consider the evidence in the Paula Herring slaying. The joint decision was to swear out a warrant charging John Randolph Clarke with first-degree murder, and that it be delivered as soon as hospital doctors allowed.[7]

The Saturday morning edition of the *Nashville Tennessean* reported another prowling episode from Thursday evening. Worse yet, it was another Crieve Hall address near Timberhill Drive. The front-page story noted that a frightened homeowner had been awakened in the middle of the night by his wife, who had heard a prowler in their kitchen. Taking no chances, the armed citizen fired six shots from his .22-caliber pistol into the darkened room. After turning on the lights, the man discovered that he had killed the intruder—a mouse—and had also mortally wounded his electric stove.[8]

FRIDAY—FEBRUARY 28, 1964

Early on Friday morning, a lieutenant from the Metropolitan Police Department served the first-degree murder warrant on John "Red" Clarke. Metro's public defender, Charles Galbreath, was in the hospital room at the time with his new client. The lawyer proclaimed to anyone who would listen that his client was innocent, saying that the Metropolitan Police Department had "covered up a whole lot of evidence that points away from Clarke to another person" and that "a lot of people in this county are under protection of the police."[9]

The *Nashville Tennessean* continued to write stories about the murder. One reporter asked Jo Herring about rumors that she was an acquaintance of Paula's accused killer. "Absolutely not true," was the reply.[10] And on Sunday, one week after the morning daily delivered the bombshell news of Paula Herring's murder, the paper published a story by Frank Ritter describing the "Sherlock Flair Shown by Lawmen" in bringing Paula's killer to justice.[11]

A few days after Clarke was served a murder warrant, the local grand jury called twenty witnesses to hear testimony in the Paula Herring case. Three of the witnesses testified together—Jo Herring and the two men who brought Jo Herring home from dinner on the night of the murder and were with her when Paula's lifeless body was discovered in the Timberhill den, Billy Vanderpool and A. J. Meadows Jr. Little Alan Herring was not subpoenaed for testimony, but sixteen police officers and a couple of investigators from the district attorney's office appeared before the panel.

On March 13, the Davidson County grand jury charged John Randolph Clarke with premeditated murder and murder while attempting to commit the felony of rape. Attorney General Harry Nichol promised to fight any effort by Clarke to obtain bond. In addition, Nichol planned to push for the death penalty or, at a minimum, a prison sentence of at least fifty years. A local judge also ruled on a request by Charles Galbreath to move the criminal proceedings out of Nashville due to concern that negative publicity would impact Clarke's ability to receive a fair trial. The judge agreed, and the trial was moved to Jackson, Tennessee, and slated for September 1964.

Both the *Nashville Banner* and the *Nashville Tennessean* were also screaming with headlines that Metro's sheriff, Leslie Jett, some of his top men, and a few high-ranking Metro police officers were being indicted by a federal grand jury for accepting payoffs from Printers Alley business owners.[12] Printers Alley, a literal cobblestone alleyway running between 3rd and 4th Avenues and Church and Commerce Streets in downtown Nashville, had been home to publishers and printers in the early 1900s. But decades later, it had evolved into one of America's premier illegal entertainment havens, with a winning trifecta of booze, gambling, and pleasures of the flesh. Numerous gambling casinos and strip clubs in the alley posed as dinner clubs and music venues, with names such as the VooDoo Lounge, the Rainbow Room, the Black Poodle Lounge, and the Uptown Dinner Club. By the early 1970s, world-famous exotic dancer Miss Heaven Lee began to draw sold-out crowds to Printers Alley to watch her performances at the Black Poodle and the Rainbow Room.[13]

During most of the 1950s and 1960s, liquor by the drink was illegal in Nashville, but patrons could bring their own bottle with them, and the mixing bar business became a profitable enterprise in Music City. It was especially so when a patron could depend on being served liquor whether they had brought their own bottle or not. And local law enforcement was leery of arresting anyone, especially in Printers Alley, for fear of arresting a local politician, someone from the legislature, or perhaps a popular country music star. When it was all said and done, the sheriff's payoff system ensured uninterrupted business for club owners, not only in the alley but also in the suburbs.[14]

Another reason to forego an arrest was the risky element of unknowingly arresting a mobster, such as Little Mickey Cohen of Los Angeles, who visited Printers Alley on several occasions. To no one's surprise, in the mid-1960s, a Nashville police sergeant, as well as one of the Printers Alley club owners, ended up in Los Angeles to testify in front of a federal grand jury regarding their ownership of guns used in a mob slaying involving one of Mickey Cohen's rivals.[15] The guns were all .38-caliber revolvers, and one happened to have been owned by a Nashville police sergeant who was one of the men indicted for accepting payoffs in Printers Alley."

Eventually, the corruption angle was the undoing of Sheriff Jett and other high-ranking police officials. Their willingness to accept monthly payoffs from the Printers Alley club owners led to their downfall. The indictments were aided by new federal antiracketeering laws, which were written to cover interstate transactions. With chips for the gambling enterprise being shipped from out-of-state manufacturers to Printers Alley clubs, the Feds moved in with their indictments. Ultimately, a tax evasion charge crumpled Leslie Jett's career plans: a key piece of evidence in the indictment revealed that a large boat the sheriff had purchased from country music star Faron Young was worth far more than Jett had reported on his income tax return.

If these indictments didn't provide enough confirmation of corruption in Metro, the fiery labor leader with the prophetic middle name, James Riddle Hoffa, was also on trial at this same time for jury tampering in an earlier Nashville criminal trial. Bobby Kennedy, the US Attorney General, had been pursuing Hoffa in court for years, and after the trial was moved to Chattanooga, Tennessee, he finally got a conviction in March 1964, via Jim Neal, the prosecutor assigned to the case. Hoffa was sentenced to eight years in prison.[16]

From a public relations perspective, America's biggest small town had become one of the most corrupt cities in America.

CHAPTER FIVE

CRIMINAL TRIAL

The trial of John Randolph Clarke included three sensational elements guaranteed to create a following wherever it was held: murder, sex, and mystery. But in a bit of pretrial maneuvering, Charles Galbreath had removed one aspect of the sexual element; he was able to get his client's charge of rape removed from the Nashville grand jury indictments because the medical examiner confirmed that no physical evidence existed to support such a charge.

Against this background, the week of September 21, 1964, marked not only the first day of the criminal trial in Jackson, Tennessee, but also the official arrival of fall—which was hardly noticed by the locals as temperatures in western Tennessee hovered near ninety degrees both before and after the autumnal equinox. The other arrival was a carnival of attorneys, television and newspaper reporters, photographers, and witnesses for both the prosecution and the defense.[1]

Jackson, a two-hour drive west of Nashville, had been settled in the 1820s as a cotton port town on the Forked Deer River. It was named for Andrew Jackson, famous military general and US president. In 1964, the area economy depended largely on agriculture, manufacturing of cotton products, and paper. The little town had an impressive history: Davy Crockett had represented the district in Congress in the early nineteenth century and General Ulysses Grant had headquartered on East Main Street during the Civil War. John "Casey" Jones had also made Jackson his home, prior to becoming the only victim of his infamous train wreck.

The site of the trial would be the Madison County Courthouse, built in 1937 and also located on East Main Street. From the start, the trial of *State of Tennessee v. John Randolph Clarke* had a strange aura to it.

Instead of Nashville's district attorney general Harry Nichol leading the prosecution, it was led by two of his assistants, John Hollins and Howard Butler. Stranger still, the plan to seek the death penalty had been abandoned. In an unusual proclamation, the judge hearing the case let it be known that the trial would last exactly five days and that the jury would be sequestered for the duration. Oddly, neither the defense team nor the prosecution objected to such an abbreviated timeline. And as if spoken by a true prophet, at 5:15 p.m. on Friday afternoon, five days after court was gaveled into session, the jury would return with a verdict.

In the meantime, twelve of Jackson's citizens, plus one alternate, became the jury that would decide the fate of John Randolph Clarke. The jury included two women, both housewives. The husband of one was a vice president of the local electric company, and the husband of the other was a revenue officer with the IRS. The ten men included six salesmen, an account manager for the Federal Land Bank Association, a manager of Pittsburgh Plate Glass, and a Health and Sanitation Department employee. The lone alternate, a man, was an accountant.

Nearly everyone who came from Nashville to Jackson for the trial lodged at the New Southern Hotel. One visitor would recall years later that the hotel may have been southern, but there wasn't anything new about it. New Southern had been the major downtown hotel in Jackson, Tennessee, since its opening in the 1920s and was less than two blocks from the courthouse. It was also air conditioned, and the lobby contained a barber shop, cigar stand, and shoeshine station, along with a coffee shop and a popular tap room where the beer was kept cold.

After the jurors were seated in the jury box, Judge Andrew "Tip" Taylor gaveled court into session as he always did in his own unique style, with the palm of his hand rather than with a wooden gavel, and on Monday morning at 9:30 a.m., September 21st, the criminal trial of John Randolph Clarke began. Taylor was well known to Tennesseans and had graduated from Union University in Jackson, and then Cumberland Law School in Lebanon, Tennessee. In 1958, he had made an unsuccessful run for governor.[2]

Leading the prosecution from Nashville were Assistant DA John

Hollins and Executive Assistant Attorney General Howard Butler. They were joined by Whit LaFon and David Murray, both from the Jackson District Attorney's Office. Defense attorneys representing Clarke were Charles Galbreath of Nashville, James P. Diamond and Carmack Murchison of Jackson, and John Goodlin, a friend of Clarke's father, from Johnson City, Tennessee. After a plea of not guilty was entered into the record, Judge Taylor quizzed the attorneys: "Is the rule called for in this case?" Assured that it was, Taylor described the rule by instructing both sides that any potential witness could not be present in the courtroom for any testimony prior to their own testimony. Taylor also told the sheriff that the jury, although sequestered for the evenings, could have the local newspaper as long as the articles about the trial were removed, and they could have radio and television privileges except during newscasts. With ground rules out of the way, Taylor instructed the state to call their first witness.

Wasting no time at all, Assistant DA John Hollins called his first witness to the stand: forty-year-old Jo Herring, the mother of Paula Herring. Hollins led his witness through biographical questions to explain that she was a widow and had become a registered nurse in 1944 after training at the University of Texas. She had one living child, a six-year-old boy, and she held in her hands a picture of her slain attractive, blond, eighteen-year-old daughter.

Under examination, it took Hollins less than fifteen minutes to get to the biggest surprise of the day: Jo Herring admitted that she'd had a one-night stand with John Randolph Clarke less than two weeks before her daughter had been brutally murdered. Her admission was nothing less than explosive, completely unexpected by the reporters covering the trial for television and newspaper outlets.[3]

Jo's explanation was that she'd been at Ruth's Diner in Nashville about seven months earlier.[4] Ruth's, a popular stop for many, was located within walking distance of Vanderbilt Hospital. On Monday night, February 10, Jo Herring was having dinner at Ruth's, sitting in a back booth with her six-year-old son and a man named Alan Prewitt. At the same time, Red Clarke had been sitting on a stool at the bar. When Prewitt and Jo's little boy went to play an arcade game, Jo said Clarke made the first approach and asked for her phone number. As she told him the number, he wrote it on the back of his hand.

Later that night, Clarke telephoned her at home and said, "This is the old redhead you saw down at Ruth's Diner." He got directions to her house and told her he would stop on Franklin Road and get a six-pack of beer. Jo suggested he bring Budweiser. Clarke arrived at the Timberhill Drive home at approximately 10:00 p.m. that same night. Jo testified that her young son was already in bed when Clarke arrived.

When John Clarke had a chance to testify, he noted that Alan Herring was actually still awake at 10:00 p.m. on February 10, and that he himself had given Alan a "horsey back" ride to bed, after placing the six-pack of beer in the refrigerator.[5] Clarke told Jo that he was a salesman for Westinghouse (a lie) and that he was married (the truth). Not long afterward, the two began to get intimate while sitting on the couch in the den.

When it came time for Clarke's attorney, Charles Galbreath, to cross-examine Mrs. Herring, he focused on the lover's tryst.[6]

Galbreath: How many times did you have intercourse with Mr. Clarke that night?
Mrs. Herring: Once.
Galbreath: Just one time, was it normal intercourse?
Mrs. Herring: I guess you could say "fair."
Galbreath: Fair!

For a trial focused on a heinous crime, it was a moment of levity that Galbreath could not resist, as he and others in the courtroom began laughing. After more questioning, Jo Herring said Clarke saw a picture of Paula, her high school graduation photograph, and she told him that her daughter was away at college. Jo claimed that there was no way John Clarke could have known her daughter. Charles Galbreath asked her why she had given her phone number to the redhead, and she responded with two words: "Just stupid."

With the prosecution wanting to move along, Jo Herring was prompted to tell about Paula's final day in Nashville. Regarding the day of the murder, Jo said she had worked at the hospital that Saturday and arrived home in the early afternoon. Given that Paula had gotten home the evening before, on Friday, it had been the first real opportunity for mother and daughter to sit and talk about school. Jo said Paula was as happy as she'd ever seen her.

According to Jo Herring, after their conversation, Paula showered, changed from her jeans into the gray skirt and sweater combination, and left to go shopping, have the car serviced and washed, and get her sunglasses repaired. When Paula returned two hours later, Jo informed her daughter that she had been invited to have dinner with two gentlemen she'd met the night before, and Paula insisted that her mother go on the dinner date and that she would stay home and babysit her little brother. "Besides," she quoted Paula as saying, "I've got a date with *All the King's Men* and a report to finish by Monday for school." According to Jo Herring, Paula had waved the paperback book at her mother as she made the declaration.

Jo Herring's dinner companions were to be the two men she'd met the previous evening at Wedgewood Diner, with one of her nursing friends from the hospital. The men, Billy Vanderpool and A. J. Meadows, picked her up around 6:00 p.m. Saturday evening, and the trio made a repeat trip to Wedgewood Diner where they stayed until returning to Timberhill Drive around 11:00 p.m. that night. During Charles Galbreath's cross-examination of Jo, he tried to portray Paula's mother as a cold woman who had profited from her husband's death:

Galbreath: Now then, again not wanting to unduly bring back unpleasantries, your husband, he died a tragic death, did he not?

Mrs. Herring: Yes, that's right.

Hollins: May it please the court, her husband's death has got nothing to do with this case.

Judge Taylor: No, something that occurred four years ago, I don't believe that would be material to this matter.

Galbreath: If the court please, I want to connect it up, to try to show a relationship between the two deaths.

Judge Taylor (to the bailiff): Take the jury to the jury room.

Galbreath: We'd like to inquire about the insurance of her husband, how it was left, and who stood to profit by this girl's death.

Judge Taylor: Who stood to profit by her daughter's death?

Galbreath: Yes, we want to establish a motive or a lack of motive.

Mrs. Herring: My husband's insurance was left solely to me. Paula was fifteen years old at that time, and my little boy was two and a half. He left no will; everything was mine.[7]

With the jury back in place moments later, Charles Galbreath homed in on the character of Jo Herring and inquired about her leaving Vanderbilt Hospital between the time of the murder in February 1964 and the trial in September 1964:

Galbreath: Do you know who killed your little daughter?

Mrs. Herring: Yes, there is no doubt in my mind.

Galbreath: Is this of your own knowledge?

Mrs. Herring: It's from the evidence.

Galbreath: Do you know where the gun is?

Mrs. Herring: No.

Galbreath: Was your daughter robbed?

Mrs. Herring: No.

Galbreath: Was she sexually assaulted?

Mrs. Herring: No.

Galbreath: Mrs. Herring, you at one time were employed by Vanderbilt Hospital, were you not?

Mrs. Herring: That's right.

Galbreath: Were you asked to leave your employment there?

Mrs. Herring: No, I wasn't.

Galbreath: Did you have any difficulty over the use of drugs?

Mrs. Herring: No.

Galbreath: Are you addicted to any type of narcotic drug?

Mrs. Herring: No, sir. I had major surgery, and Paula left to go to college, and I could no longer work weekends, and I had to find a job where I could be home with my little boy on weekends.[8]

Around 3:30 p.m. on the first day of the trial, one of the youngest witnesses in a criminal court proceeding in Tennessee took the witness stand: blond, six-year-old Alan Herring. Over the next few minutes, Hollins led the little boy through a series of forty-five questions, beginning with Alan's full name, age, school attended, grade in school, and church attendance, before moving on to the more serious matter at hand:

> Hollins: Son, do you know what it means to tell the truth? Do you know that you're supposed to tell the truth?
> Alan: Yes, sir.
> Hollins: What happens to you if you don't tell the truth?
> Alan: You get punished.[9]

Alan described how his sister had given him the nickname "Sputnik" and told of watching television that evening. He told of the two phone calls that he remembered the night of his sister's murder. The first came while he was watching television and Paula was reading a book. The call was answered by Paula with "Hello?" and after a short interval, "Goodbye." As to Paula's tone on the call, Alan said, "It sounded like she was a little bit friendly."

The second call came later, with no way to tell exactly how much later. Alan had gone to bed. He got up to answer the ringing phone in the den, and a man's voice asked if Jo was there. Alan answered no, and the man disconnected. Alan said to Paula, "Wake up sister, wake up." He then returned to his bedroom and stayed there until he heard his mother and the two men enter the house at 11:00 p.m.

James Diamond then took the turn for Clarke's defense team and asked the little boy forty-four questions, which, oddly enough, were basically the same questions that John Hollins had already asked regarding nickname, age, school topics, and phone calls. No questions regarding whether Paula had seemed happy or angry that fateful evening. No questions about any activities that Paula had engaged in on Saturday. No questions about any activities that Paula and Alan had engaged in together. No questions as to whether any of Paula's friends had stopped by to visit. No questions about hearing other voices inside the house after he went to bed. No questions about hearing gunshots in the house. No questions about Alan's memory of the earlier visit by John Randolph Clarke. Not a single question posed that could have pointed toward someone other than John Randolph Clarke as the guilty party in his sister's slaying.

On a Saturday in 1964 Nashville, a child might spend his morning watching cartoons on television, while being entertained in the evening by any of the three local television stations.[10] Oddly enough, as if completely unaware of the typical day of a six-year-old, neither side of the legal aisle asked a single question of Alan Herring about what surely must have been a regular Saturday spent on Timberhill Drive.

James Diamond finished his examination by asking two questions that may have provided the most overlooked clue in the courtroom as to Paula's condition when her little brother found her on the floor on the night of the murder:

> Diamond: Did you observe your sister when you said it looked like she had tomato juice on her?
>
> Alan: I thought that was really tomato juice.
>
> Diamond: Did you see any marks on her, other than this tomato juice?
>
> Alan: No, sir.[11]

Following the little boy's testimony, the attorneys agreed to let Alan return to Nashville and continue his schooling at Norman Binkley Elementary School in the Crieve Hall neighborhood.

The Herrings' next-door neighbor, Catherine Wexler, followed Alan Herring on the witness stand and testified that Paula had called her from the Nashville Airport when she got in on Friday evening, February 21. Since no one was home at the Herrings', the cab driver delivered Paula to the Wexlers' home.

The Wexlers had lived next door to the Herrings for five years, and Mrs. Wexler was a good friend to Paula. Paula had babysat for the family numerous times, most recently when she had been home from Knoxville during the Christmas holidays. Mrs. Wexler confirmed that Paula kept her watch on "University" time, the Eastern time zone, during her return visit to Nashville's central time zone. The attractive next-door neighbor also volunteered that she personally had written a check for Paula's cab fare on Friday evening.

Another witness for the state was Dr. W. J. Core, the Metro Nashville medical examiner.[12] Dr. Core was a kindly old gentleman who had graduated from Vanderbilt Medical School in 1915, almost a half century before the trial. Core told the jury that his job was to check all deaths from violence, all deaths where the deceased had not had medical attention within twenty-four hours, and all rapes.

Dr. Core estimated the time of death to be 9:30 p.m. on February 22, 1964. At the time of his initial assessment, the physician had stated that Paula Herring had been shot three times, once in the front and twice in the back. But in open court in Jackson Core simply noted that Paula Herring had died as the result of two gunshots from close range and that the bullets had entered the girl's back and passed through her heart, ultimately ending her life.

In a grandfatherly voice, the old doctor described the physical results of the terrible crime: multiple contusions of the face, a severe bruise on the left jaw below the ear, deep scratches in the middle of the neck, and four contusions on the right side of the face, possibly caused by a fist. The victim's clothing was in place, and she definitely had been facedown on the rug when the killing shots had been fired.

On the question of intercourse, Core said no. Nor was seminal fluid present at the time of his examination.

Following the elderly physician on the witness stand were the analysts from the FBI and the TBI. They described in detail their findings regarding the fibers found on Clarke's clothing and also the matching of the three bullets that had been linked to the slaying. The prosecution's last witnesses were the detectives who had been involved in Clarke's all-night interrogation.

One detective after another took the stand and told similar stories about their observances of the crime scene on Saturday night, as well as their part in the grilling of John Randolph Clarke two nights later.

Each detective described how they all had arrived at the Timberhill Drive home within minutes of the call that Billy Vanderpool had made to the police dispatcher. Each said that, other than policemen, the only living people at Timberhill Drive when they arrived were Vanderpool, Paula's mother, and little Alan Herring. Vanderpool and Jo Herring gave the officers the definite impression that they had been drinking. Jo was described as being hysterical and in a state of shock.

When it came time for the defense team to present alternate theories to the state's case against Clarke, Charles Galbreath seemed without direction. His initial plan had been to sully Jo Herring's reputation, but, with the help of the prosecution, Jo already had taken care of that aspect; Galbreath instead spent some time cross-examining Jo Herring's dinner companions from the night of Paula's murder. Billy Vanderpool had operated a wrecking company in Nashville for several years, and gathered materials from the tear-downs to build houses.[13] In the courtroom, Vanderpool testified that he first met Jo Herring on Friday the 21st at the Wedgewood Diner, and that he and Meadows had delivered Jo home to Timberhill Drive, where they were introduced to Paula, who had just flown in from Knoxville.[14]

The following afternoon, Saturday the 22nd, Vanderpool arrived with Meadows to pick up Jo Herring for a dinner date, and the men testified that they all had returned to Timberhill Drive just before 11:00 p.m. The other dinner companion, A. J. Meadows Jr., offered more detail, and Charles Galbreath bored in on his relationship to Billy Vanderpool and the evidence that investigators had discovered at the Herring home:

Galbreath: How well do you know Billy Vanderpool?

Meadows: He used to tear down a few houses, Charlie, and I was in the process of buying a little material from him where I could make me a little money building a house with used material.

Galbreath: Did you know anything about Mr. Vanderpool's illegal activities?

Meadows: Well, I mean, he had a massage room, and I found out later that's kind of outlawed.

Galbreath: That's a house of prostitution, isn't it?

Meadows: Well, I wouldn't say that, I mean, I don't know, I never have seen any activity.

Galbreath: Do you drink Sterling beer or know anyone who does?

Meadows: No, sir. I drink Budweiser or Blue Ribbon. Sterling gives me a headache, and I don't know anyone who likes Sterling.

Galbreath: Did you see a quart bottle of Sterling beer sitting there in the garage that night, broken?

Meadows: I did not see a Sterling beer. I mean the lights were off in the garage when I walked through. The only thing I remember is just barely getting through there and barely getting out.[15]

Charles Galbreath clearly had adult beverages on his mind, as over the course of the next hour, Galbreath elicited a steady stream of facts that had not been well known prior to the trial. Per A. J. Meadows and Billy Vanderpool, the night of the slaying turned out to be a beer-drinking marathon at the Wedgewood Diner. For approximately four hours, Vanderpool, Meadows, and Jo Herring sat and drank. Meadows testified that no one left the diner at any time, and certainly not to run to Timberhill Drive, commit a murder, and return to the diner.

Around 11:00 p.m., when the trio got to Timberhill Drive and the gruesome discovery was made, Meadows said he heard no cry or scream from Mrs. Herring. Meadows said he began to get sick and quickly decided to leave.

Galbreath's next step was to go after Clarke's conscience-stricken friend, Al Baker. The defense attorney took Baker through a series of questions related to Clarke's missing gun. He was able to get Baker to confirm that he had tried to purchase Clarke's pistol on more than one occasion, most recently just days prior to Paula's murder. Galbreath was able to elicit testimony that Baker had told mutual friends that the gun was his, though he hadn't actually paid Clarke for the weapon. It was clear that Charles Galbreath was suggesting to the jury that Al Baker might have taken Clarke's gun and used it to commit murder. At a minimum, it was an attempt to raise the question of reasonable doubt.

Before he allowed Baker to step down from the witness box, the defense attorney caught Baker off guard with a question regarding his whereabouts on that fateful Saturday night in February. Baker coughed up a rather disjointed reply: he had left Ruth's Diner at about the same time Clarke did, and then he had visited a string of beer joints and night-owl locations until just after midnight.

After Galbreath finished with Baker, the defense attorney seemed content to parade a series of character witnesses in front of the jury. Most of them provided little that could be described as helpful to his client.

When the time came to try the physical evidence in the case, Galbreath turned deadly serious and wasted no time getting down to business, especially with the investigators who had worked the case:

Galbreath: What were the results of the fingerprints found near the murder scene?
Investigator: We didn't get any.
Galbreath: You didn't get any fingerprints?
Investigator: No, sir.
Galbreath: Did you make any effort or do you know anybody that did make any effort to find any fingerprints?
Investigator: No, sir.
Investigator: Well, what were the results of the fingerprints found on the broken beer bottle in the garage?
Investigator: Didn't get any.
Galbreath: Well, how about on the cigarette butts you found there?
Investigator: I don't know what happened to those, Counselor.
Galbreath: Did you examine my client physically down at the police station?
Investigator: Yes, sir.
Galbreath: And what did you find? Did you find any scratch marks on him, any bruises, any cuts of any kind?
Investigator: No, sir.
Galbreath: But you knew you were supposed to be looking for someone who'd been scratched and was bleeding, didn't you?[16]

The next-to-last witness for the defense was Callie Clarke, John's wife, a meek school teacher. She testified under oath that her husband has gotten home on the night in question around 9:30 p.m. and that she observed nothing suspicious in his demeanor to suggest knowledge of any crime. The woman also said that there had been a few disagreements with John in the past concerning his tendencies to stay out too late, but she claimed that she'd never even heard of the Herring girl or her mother.

As his last witness, Galbreath brought John Randolph Clarke himself to the stand. Though he was under no obligation to testify on his own behalf, Galbreath wanted the jury to hear Clarke say that he didn't commit the awful murder, and along the way he took Clarke through a steady stream of denials.

Clarke denied that he'd seen Al Baker on the night of Paula's murder. He further denied that he had made any telephone calls to anyone from Ruth's Diner on the night of February 22. He had no recollection of shooting a bullet into the ground on the previous Christmas morning. And he stood by his alibi regarding a series of stops among local diners beginning with Ruth's, then Brown's, Chico's, and a liquor store on West End at the corner of 16th and Broadway, before arriving home around 9:30 p.m. that Saturday night.

But Clarke *was* able to lay out in detail the arrangement of the Herring home. He sketched the floor plan of the den with its entry into the garage, the bedrooms, bathrooms, and living room, as well as describing the furniture. Galbreath's final questions were simple and to the point:

Galbreath: Mr. Clarke, had you ever seen this poor little girl in your life?
Clarke: Never.
Galbreath: Did you know her name, Paula?
Clarke: No, sir.
Galbreath: Did you telephone the Herring house and speak to this little girl the night of this murder?
Clarke: No, sir.
Galbreath: Did you have a quart of Sterling beer with you?
Clarke: No, sir.
Galbreath: Did you have any Winston cigarettes or Lark cigarettes with you that night?
Clarke: No, sir.
Galbreath: Were you on the premises of that place at all on

the night of the murder or even in the Crieve Hall area that night?

Clarke: No, sir.[17]

Before the defense rested, the district attorney general for the Jackson, Tennessee, area, David P. Murray, requested just a few moments to cross-examine the defendant and ask a few questions of his own. With a rafter-raising voice, Murray posed over 950 questions to the accused man, and, five hours later, he was satisfied that he had enlightened the jury regarding the defendant's less-than-exemplary lifestyle. He had exposed Clarke's womanizing, heavy drinking, and ragged employment record for everyone in the courthouse to see. After Clarke realized what was taking place, he settled in for Murray's onslaught and answered almost every question with three simple words: "I don't remember."

On the same day that Clarke was enduring the grilling by David Murray, a report commissioned by President Lyndon Johnson was being delivered to the White House. A team led by Chief Justice Earl Warren concluded that Lee Harvey Oswald had acted alone and the Warren Commission Report detailed the intensive review that had begun some seven days after JFK's assassination in Dallas during the previous November.

In a bit of irony, on this same Thursday night in Jackson, Tennessee, Al Baker had been drinking in the taproom of the New Southern Hotel bar, while carrying on a conversation with one of the reporters covering the trial. The details of the conversation so stunned the reporter that he later provided a deposition of the event to a notary public in hopes that it might influence the outcome of the trial. According to the reporter, Al Baker had been standing at the bar drinking a Sterling beer and then had approached the reporter to compliment the way the reporter's newspaper had covered Baker's testimony of the previous day. In the course of the conversation, Baker mentioned that one of the most damaging pieces of evidence against Clarke was the bullet "that I fired, I mean that Clarke fired on the night of the Christmas Eve party." The deposition eventually made its way to Clarke's attorney in hopes that it might help with an appeal.[18]

It was midmorning on Friday, September 25, when the closing arguments from both sides were presented to the jury. John Hollins implored the jury to convict Clarke of murder, and suggested that Miss Herring had chosen "to die rather than have her body defiled by a half-man, half-animal."[19]

Following a recess for lunch, Judge Tip Taylor charged the jury and explained the range of possible outcomes: murder in the first or second degree, manslaughter, or not guilty.

Taylor informed the jury that, if they convicted the defendant, they also were required to set the sentence. If murder in the first degree was the choice, then the punishment was death by electrocution, unless there were mitigating circumstances, in which case they could reduce the sentence to not less than twenty years in the penitentiary.

On Friday afternoon at 5:15 p.m., the jury sent word to the judge that they had a verdict. With Clarke standing to face the jury, the foreman reported that they had found Clarke guilty of murder in the first degree, and, rather than send him to the electric chair, they had fixed his punishment at thirty years in the state penitentiary.

As the sentence was announced, Clarke appeared to black out, and he would have fallen to the floor if not grabbed by one of his defense attorneys. A few moments later, Clarke came to and asked, "What happened?" He then said that all he had heard was "Guilty."[20]

CHAPTER SIX

JO HERRING'S LETTER

Exactly one week after the verdict in Jackson, Tennessee, Jo Herring penned a handwritten note to Chief Hubert Kemp, lauding the work of Metro police officers, detectives, and investigators in her daughter's murder case, and Kemp passed the letter to the *Nashville Tennessean* for publication. Two days later, on Sunday morning, October 4, the newspaper buried the note in the Want Ads section on page fifty-four. However, by the time the note was published, someone at the *Tennessean* had added the district attorney general's office to the list of those being thanked and also included the prosecutors in the headline: "Mrs. Herring Lauds Police, Prosecutors." What caught my eye was that Jo Herring had not included the DA's office in her original note. Perhaps it meant nothing, but it seemed to me an unusual edit.

On the same day that Jo wrote her letter, the afternoon paper, the *Nashville Banner,* was noting an offer of reward by one of its subscribers. The subscriber was attorney Charles Galbreath, who said that he would pay $250 to anyone with information leading to the identity of the bloody man seen at the Krystal hamburger restaurant on Franklin Road on the night of February 22, 1964.

In what must have been a shock to the citizens of Nashville, four days after Clarke's conviction, two of his family members in East Tennessee posted a $25,000 property bond to allow Clarke to remain free while his conviction was being appealed by Charles Galbreath. The family members, whom Galbreath described as two "spinster aunts" had put up their twenty-six room home as surety.[1] Allowing a convicted murderer to remain free on bond was quite unusual and required the agreement of a willing trial court judge who was convinced that the defendant would reappear in court as requested. Perhaps the fact that Clarke's father was himself an East Tennessee judge played a role in this unusual act of freedom.

Meanwhile, Galbreath was hoping for someone to take the reward bait, while he filed motions and appeals on his client's behalf. Eventually, Charles Galbreath would appeal Clarke's murder conviction all the way to the US Supreme Court, but he had to exhaust each stage of the lower appellate courts before he could be heard by Chief Justice Earl Warren and his eight influential friends.

While Galbreath worked the legal angles, John Randolph Clarke continued to walk freely around Music City. This included helping his wife chaperone high school students, including teenage girls, to school activities in and around Nashville. All the while, Clarke continued to declare his innocence in the Paula Herring slaying and personally offered a $5,000 cash reward for anyone who could help him identify the guilty party.[2]

PART II

THE HERRING FILE

He that troubleth his own house shall inherit the wind.

—Proverbs 11:29, Old Testament

CHAPTER SEVEN

FORTY STORIES

Decades later, in August 1997, I was having lunch at a local restaurant near the Sylvan Park area of Nashville, not far from Vanderbilt University. The day was so hot the shade was looking for shade, and my friend Clayton began to tell me about his project to catalog major crimes and mysterious happenings that had taken place in Nashville over the previous hundred years. It wasn't the topic of conversation I had expected, but, given that I was still a relative newcomer to the Athens of the South, he had my full attention.[1]

As we waited for the food to arrive, Clayton began to reel off names and dates of events, such as the search for country music star Jim Reeves after his small airplane crashed and disappeared south of the city in the summer of 1964, the train wreck that killed 118 people in one of the worst railroad accidents in US history, and the 1973 slaying of *Hee Haw* star David "Stringbean" Akeman and his wife, Estelle. When I asked how many stories were on his list, he replied, "Oh, about forty of them." What I failed to realize was how much time he had already invested in the project, primarily at the main Nashville library and also at a place described as the Metro Archives.[2]

One of the reasons I was interested in the project was because of my previous history of research experience at the University of Tennessee in Knoxville. A decade earlier, I had just finished working my way through graduate school when the personal computer boom took off. And instead of continuing the path I had chosen, which is to say instead of continuing to be mostly unemployed save for a few hours a week fundraising for a local nonprofit organization, I went to work in one of the first computer retail stores in Nashville.

During this leisurely meal, I also learned how the city of Nashville and Davidson County had merged in 1963 to become the first "Metro" government in the United States. With consolidation, better schools and additional police and fire protection were promised to the suburbanites. In the pre-Metro world, it could take more than an hour for a sheriff's deputy from Davidson County to respond to a call, but the "Metro" promise was a law enforcement officer within five minutes of every home, notwithstanding the fact that the move to a metropolitan government meant an increase from 71 square miles of oversight to 533 square miles. When the consolidation vote received a green light, at the stroke of midnight on April Fools' Day 1963, a former county judge, Clifton Beverly Briley, became the mayor of the Metropolitan Government of Nashville and Davidson County.[3]

After the lunchtime conversation, and armed with directions and a list of forty crimes and mysteries, my curiosity got the better of me, and I made a quick trip to the archives to see if I might enjoy helping out with the project. After finding my way to a one-story brick building on Elm Hill Pike, I signed a visitors' register in the small lobby and was greeted by a young woman, who listened patiently to the reason for my visit and then ran through a concise history of the archives and its current role in Nashville government and told me that most of the day-to-day work was spent cataloging records and artifacts and warehousing any new arrivals until they could be processed.

It was at this that point that she casually mentioned that the archives had just received a number of boxes that were the effects of former Nashville chief of police Hubert Kemp. They had not yet cataloged the records, but she told me I was welcome to look through them if I was interested. My answer was a solid, "Yes, I would love to review them. Don't laugh, but when was Hubert Kemp the police chief?"

"That would have been when Metro Nashville Government was formed, back in the early sixties. The Metro Police Department sends their records to us after a few decades have passed. These are the latest ones."

A few moments later, I heard squeaky wheels drawing closer as the clerk returned with a stainless steel cart so large it barely fit through the doorway. After the clerk left the room, I stared at the stack of cardboard boxes. The only sound to be heard was the steady rain pelting the roof of the windowless building.

I grabbed a container and placed it on the table. The boxes themselves were so tall that it was easier to stand and explore them than make the attempt while seated. After removing the lid of the first box and glancing down inside, I froze.

"That's a brown recluse spider," I said to myself. "No, make that two of them." I had never seen a live one before but knew from photographs that the spider could be identified by a small "fiddle" neatly etched into its back. Both spiders were the size of a quarter, perched on top of the neatly arranged files inside the box.

Keeping a close eye on my new friends, I quickly stepped across the hallway to announce my findings to the clerk, who punched a line on her desk phone and asked one of her associates to "bring the spider spray." While waiting for the in-house exterminator, I reviewed the labels of the folders inside the open box at arm's length. Most were tagged as Attendance Reports, Complaints, and Training Logs. Not exactly my cup of tea. But for the rest of the week, every day at lunchtime, I signed in and reviewed box after box of Hubert Kemp's records.

On my third visit, which occurred during a heavy summer storm, I reviewed one of the final boxes in the stack. After a quick scan for spiders, I retrieved a file that seemed to be out of place among the attendance reports. Inside a manila folder labeled "Paula Herring," I found a disturbing set of black and white photographs, along with telegrams, personal notes, and letters to Hubert Kemp, chief of police, Metropolitan Nashville.

The photographs were eight-inch by ten-inch, and several appeared to have been taken inside the den of a 1960s-era home. In one photograph, a sofa, china cabinet, and television framed the figure of a young woman lying facedown on the floor. She was lying in a pool of what I could only assume was her own blood. Another photograph showed a detective, dressed in plain clothes and wearing an overcoat, black shoes, and white socks, squatting down in an empty garage pointing at a broken bottle of beer and the resulting splatter on the garage floor. The remainder of the photographs in the file appeared to have been taken on an autopsy table. They were brutal and disturbing. It was obvious that the pretty blond girl in the photographs had been violently slain.

And now I felt queasy. My little adventure to the archives had taken a dark turn for the unexpected. I glanced at the back of one of the photographs and saw the date: February 22, 1964. A few minutes later, after using the copy machine in the adjoining room, I said goodbye to the clerk and dodged puddles of water on the way back to my car. I sat there for several minutes, staring motionless through the rain-covered windshield, as I wondered why a crime scene file had been shipped to the Metro Archives with a box full of administrative records.

With some reluctance as to what I was getting myself into, two days later I opened my worn leather portfolio, and carefully organized the copies I had made into two stacks on a work table. In one pile were the horrific crime-scene images of Paula Herring and in the other pile I placed a copy of a postcard from a physician in Carthage, Tennessee; a letter from Mrs. Eva Jo A. Herring; a letter from then mayor of Nashville Beverly Briley; a couple of witness statements; telegrams from J. Edgar Hoover to Hubert Kemp; and other documents.

While sifting through the file, I made a call to my friend Clayton, asking if he remembered the murder of a blond University of Tennessee student named Paula Herring, from February 1964.

"You bet I do," he said. "That's one of the stories on the list. Why are you asking?"[4]

When I explained what I had stumbled upon at the archives, he recalled that Paula Herring had been babysitting her little brother on the night she had been killed. "I remember for years after her murder, parents would always tell their kids and babysitters to lock the doors while they were gone or they'd end up like Paula Herring."

Clayton had been a newspaper carrier at the time, and he remembered that the morning paper, the *Nashville Tennessean*, was held so late on a school day during the murder week that he had to get a written excuse from his dad to get into class. "By the way, who killed the babysitter?" he asked.

"I don't know, but I'll look it up. Oh, and I think the babysitter's six-year-old little brother was spared. The kid apparently slept through his sister's murder," I said.

"Maybe the killer didn't know the little boy was in the house?"

"Maybe, but it sounds like the makings of an urban legend if you ask me," I replied.

CHAPTER EIGHT

NEIGHBORS

I initially began researching the babysitter story with hardly a thought as to whether I should actually be engaged in such an activity, and more because the urban legend of a boy sleeping through his sister's murder had hooked me hard from the moment I first discovered it. From this unusual beginning I attempted to reach out to the 1964 neighbors of the Herring family, especially those who lived on either side of Paula Herring. My assumption was that the neighbors would be more than willing to share their remembrances of the old tragedy, and the timeline would have been seared into their consciousness, given that the slaying had taken place exactly ninety days after President Kennedy's assassination in Dallas, Texas.

I was so convinced of this naive point of view that I asked the Ben West Public Library staff to show me their collection of ancient city phonebooks so that I might find the names of neighbors who had lived on Timberhill Drive near the Herring family at the time of the 1964 murder, in hopes of tracking them down and asking about the slaying.

Me: I'm researching the Paula Herring murder from 1964.
Neighbor: I wouldn't have anything to say.
Me: But you were her neighbor at the time?
Neighbor: I'm sorry, I wouldn't.
Me: You don't care that she was murdered?
Me: Could you help me understand?
Neighbor: I wouldn't be interested.

The next call will be better, I assured myself. I just need to set it up with a little more finesse and not be so eager and direct with my questioning.

Me: Hello, we haven't spoken before and I'm hoping you can help me with an old event from your neighborhood in 1964. It involved a girl named Paula Herring.

Neighbor: I don't know anything, OKAY? And I don't have an opinion one way or the other, so, don't ever call me again.

After adjusting my introduction yet again, my third attempt was a bit more productive.

Me: Good afternoon, I'm trying to do some research into a story from the 1964 era that involved the Crieve Hall community and your former neighbor, Paula Herring.

Neighbor: Well, it electrified the whole community, I can tell you that.

Me: I bet so. What happened on the night of the murder? You must've known the victim, right?

Neighbor: What's the reason for the inquisition?

Me: Oh, no formal inquisition, I'm just trying to get a better understanding of that February timeline back in 1964.

Neighbor: Well, I'd direct you to the newspapers, and like I said, it certainly electrified the community, but other than that I wouldn't have anything to say to you.

Though I had a full-time job selling computer-based services and products to corporate America, I was still attempting to use my lunch hour to research the Paula Herring story. Initially, I attempted to find Paula's mother, thinking she might still be residing in Middle Tennessee. After a week of dialing "Herrings" and repeatedly striking out, though, I came to the realization that, over the course of several decades, Paula's mother could have gotten married and divorced multiple times or be living with relatives and have no personal phone, and, either way, she would now be in her mid-seventies.

So I switched my focus to Paula's father and after some digging I discovered Wilmer Herring's sad demise on September 1, 1960, noted in the *Nashville Tennessean* newspaper. According to the Davidson County Medical Examiner, Dr. W. J. Core, forty-year-old Wilmer had been found in a hotel room on Friday, September 2, with time of death estimated to have been at 10:00 p.m. on Thursday evening. Dr. Core ruled the death as suicide due to poison that Wilmer Herring had swallowed.[1]

A few days later, I stumbled upon one of Wilmer Herring's family members via telephone, and I learned that Jo Herring had returned to Waco, Texas, with her young son not long after Paula had been murdered, in part so she could be closer to her family, and in part to take a job as a nurse at a Waco hospital.[2] Over the next decade, Jo Herring's chronic alcoholism eventually caught up with her and took her life due to liver failure at the relatively young age of fifty-two in 1976.[3]

When I inquired as to the circumstances surrounding Wilmer's death at the Noel Hotel, the family member said, "We were told that he had committed suicide, but we had serious doubts about that. Jo told us that Wilmer had been devastated when he lost his job, but he was a college graduate, and he had been a pilot during World War II. He could've gotten a job. It just didn't make sense to us. I remember when Jo brought Wilmer's body to Texas for the burial that Labor Day weekend in 1960, she told us that he had left a suicide note but, she never showed it to us. We just never understood it."[4]

As I thought through the timing of this tragedy, it dawned on me that public schools in Nashville would have started back on the Tuesday after the Labor Day holiday. On Monday, kids and families would have been enjoying the last rites of summer, with a focus on picnics, grilling out, and swimming pools, before being sent back to school. Paula Herring, however, would have celebrated her fifteenth birthday about ten days prior to Wilmer Herring being found dead on the Friday of Labor Day weekend. Then, instead of looking forward to obtaining her learner's permit to drive the family car, she would have been burying her father on the same day that the new school year was to begin.

As for her younger brother, by the time Alan Herring had turned eighteen, he had lost his father to suicide, his sister to murder, and his mother to an early death. If I had been Alan Herring, I might have wondered for a lifetime why I was spared on the night my sister was murdered, while I had slept within a few feet of the tragic event.

A week or so after I received the update on the Herrings, I surprised myself by locating the boy who had slept through his sister's murder and was now living hundreds of miles away from Nashville. In all of my searching and thinking about searching, I had spent little time actually preparing for a conversation that might transpire if I ever did find Jo Herring's son.

I reached Alan Herring on a warm September day and quickly realized just how intrusive my phone call might have been to the man on the other end of the telephone line.[5] But he was considerate, and curious that anyone would be reaching out to him decades after losing his family. My disjointed explanation for the call was to walk him through the Nashville stories project and the potential inclusion of the babysitter legend as a cornerstone element of the future work.

As I fumbled through the details, I wondered how long it had been since Alan Herring had last spoken with anyone about Paula's death. Near the end of our discussion, I made a feeble attempt at empathy, noting that in the early 1960s, about the time I had also been six years old, my eighteen-year-old Aunt Mae had vanished from our home in northeast Alabama and had not been seen or heard from since. The only other comment I could muster, in an attempt to build rapport, was to note that I had completed a graduate degree at the University of Tennessee in Knoxville, though it had been several years after his sister Paula had been there.

Finally, I asked about the tragic night of February 22, 1964. It came as no surprise to me when I learned that Alan Herring didn't remember that night at all, and had lost that entire weekend in his conscious memory.[6] But he did have two questions that had haunted him for decades: Why hadn't Clarke killed him on the night of his sister's murder? And where was his father's suicide note? His mother had told him she had it and would let him see it at some future point in time, but she had never produced the note, and he didn't find it in his mother's personal effects after her death.

CHAPTER NINE

INMATE #62250

After reading in the 1964 Nashville newspapers that John Clarke had indeed been indicted and convicted, I made the simple deduction that perhaps a visit to the Tennessee Department of Corrections might be enlightening. So I made the trek from my West End Avenue office to the Rachel Jackson building on Dead-erick Street in downtown Nashville, and then rode the elevator to the operations group of the TDOC.

I knew that my initial plan to track down John Randolph Clarke and ask him point blank, "Why didn't you kill Paula Herring's little brother while you were taking Paula's life?" was foolish at best, and perhaps dangerous at worst; but frankly, I was willing to pursue the answer, even at some real or imagined peril. The problem, however, wasn't asking the question but rather finding the convicted felon some thirty-five years after his Murder One conviction.

Just before the elevator door opened, I mentally confirmed what I had been thinking for much of the morning: I'm out of my element here. I'm not a lawyer; I'm not a court reporter; I'm not a journalist; and I'm not a paralegal on an errand. This could go badly. But much to my surprise, when I exited the elevator, the first person I encoun-tered was a middle-aged, raven-haired woman with a smiling face and helpful disposition.

"I'm hoping you can help me," I said. "I'm trying to find informa-tion on a Davidson County resident who may be in the care of the Department of Corrections."

The response behind the desk could not have been more helpful: "Sure, we just need you to fill out this form. If you're looking for records, the cost for the search and printing of files is ten dollars.

We'll need a check with the application form and your personal information completely filled out." As she handed me a clipboard, she motioned toward a chair in the empty waiting room. Ten minutes later, after I had completed the form and returned it to the desk, the helpful clerk explained that they would contact me when the report was available.

In the last days of the nineteenth century, circa 1898, the state of Tennessee had built a new penitentiary near the Cumberland River, bordering the city of Nashville. It was a striking example of gothic architecture, but its usefulness would last less than a century for housing inmates. In fact, after its correctional use was finished and the prison closed in 1992, the abandoned structure became famous when the 1999 Oscar-nominated movie *The Green Mile*, based on Stephen King's novel, was filmed there with superstars Tom Hanks and Michael Clarke Duncan.[1] In 2001, *The Last Castle*, with Oscar-winning actor Robert Redford and *Soprano*'s star James Gandolfini, was also filmed at the prison.[2]

A few days after my document request, I was back at the TDOC office picking up a large manila envelope from the helpful clerk.[3] I sat down in the first available chair and proceeded to bend back the two metal clips securing the TDOC record of John Randolph Clarke. Inside the envelope, I discovered that my ten dollars had purchased several photocopied pages of Clarke's tenure with the Tennessee Department of Corrections.

In November 1966, when the prison was almost seventy years old, the penitentiary was still in operation and housing hundreds of inmates. After his appeals for a new trial had all been turned down, and twenty-six months after his conviction, Charles Galbreath had driven John Randolph Clarke to the front door of his new home. Clarke stepped out of the car, shook hands with his lawyer, and then, carrying a duffel bag, walked through the gates where he would spend the next nine years of his life enjoying the Tennessee State Prison near downtown Nashville. The accommodations were sparse, a ten-foot private cell, a toilet, mattress, and sink.

It was clear from the documents that the prison system had been thorough with Inmate #62250. Every facet of Clarke had been analyzed: his social history, employment record, marital record, education, military experience, religion, IQ, and arrest record. The sources for the information were noted as well: prison interview, FBI report, family questionnaire, prison physician's findings, chaplain's interview, and a non-verbal IQ test known as a Beta Test, as well as direct observation:

> This is a forty-one-year-old white male, standing 5′11″ tall and weighing 199 pounds. He has been married for 17 years, but has no children. Subject served in the US Navy from 1943 until 1945 when he received a medical discharge. Family letter indicates subject has blackout spells and a back injury but this is unverified. He has two years of college. No criminal record for other members of the family.
>
> - October 1942 charge of forgery.
> - Unauthorized use of automobile, 1946 in Washington, DC
> - Disorderly conduct arrest in Nashville.
> - First-degree murder conviction—Nashville.
>
> Subject's attitude during the interview was friendly and responsive. Subject stated it was hard to describe his feelings about being here. It was different than what he expected it to be. Very intelligent person.

The penultimate item was Clarke's birth date—February 21, 1925. As I read the date, I wondered what Clarke had been doing on his thirty-ninth birthday, the night before Paula Herring had been murdered. The bigger surprise, however, was on the last page of the report, which was a copy of Certificate Number 21746, issued by the Tennessee Board of Pardons and Paroles. After serving less than nine years of a thirty-year sentence, the governor had reduced Clarke's conviction from thirty years to twenty-five years, which in parole board math meant Clarke had already served enough time to be eligible for an early release. And indeed, according to the record, John Randolph Clarke had been released from prison on October 3, 1975. I was astonished at the short term.

The additional language on the certificate indicated that the chairman and director of the Board of Pardons and Paroles were of the opinion that Clarke's release "was not incompatible with the welfare of society" and that the "Board is satisfied he will be suitably employed in self-sustaining employment or that he will not become a public charge on release."[4]

After a week of library work and another week visiting various Metro government offices, I discovered that John Randolph Clarke and his wife had purchased a home on Thunderbird Drive in West Nashville for $36,000 following his release from prison. The home was close to what would later become a shopping area known as Nashville West.

Upon inspection, the actual house was on a sloping lot, with a small garage and basement. It was also completely surrounded by a chain-link fence and had gates across the concrete driveway. It had the odd appearance of a home sitting inside a prison yard. A For Sale sign was posted, and the house looked empty.

I rang the doorbell of a neighbor's home, and a sixtyish woman with gray hair and thick glasses answered the door.[5] I offered my best version of good morning, quickly followed by, "I'm sorry to bother you. I'm wondering if you could tell me about the house for sale next door?"

"Well it's been for sale for a few weeks now. You can call the realtor listed on the sign."

As she said this, her demeanor took on a hardened edge.

"Yes, ma'am, I'm actually looking for a former owner of that property. Clarke was his name. John Clarke; John Randolph Clarke, and I think his wife's name was Callie Clarke. Maybe you would remember them living there?"

After I said the name "Clarke," she stepped out of the doorway and began moving toward me with fire in her eyes and her jaw firmly set. I took a subtle step backward.

"He's dead. Yes, sir, he dropped dead right there in his garage after mowing his yard."

Her words took the wind out of me, as I instantly ran through the good news, bad news impact of her information. The bad news meant that I would not be posing any questions directly to John Randolph Clarke, which would be a major setback in my quest to answer the two major questions in my research project. The good news was that I probably was avoiding a potentially awkward, even dangerous, attempt at interviewing a convicted murderer.

"I wasn't aware of that," I said. I cast a wistful, long glance at Clarke's former home. "About how long ago did he die?"

"I think it was 1985 or maybe 1986. I know his wife died about six or seven years later. I'm pretty sure they're both buried somewhere around Smithville, Tennessee. Why do you want to know?"

"Well, I don't know how to explain this, but I'll try. I'm doing some research on the teenage girl that John Clarke was convicted of murdering in 1964."

"I know that story," she replied. "He was a bad man. My husband and I kept a close eye on him, because we had a teenage daughter in the house the whole time he lived right there."

"That must have been stressful," I replied.

"He got out of prison early, did you know that?"

"Yes, ma'am. I just stumbled across that information not long ago. He was sentenced to thirty years for first-degree murder, but he served less than ten."

"That's because he paid $10,000 to get out early. He paid that crook of a governor we had, Ray Blanton, for a pardon."[6]

"I hadn't heard that part," I offered, remembering the former governor of Tennessee and his reign of corruption, highlighted by the selling of pardons and liquor licenses, and eventually his own prison sentence for the crimes.

"Did he have a job or do any work while they lived next door?" I inquired.

"Work? I guess you didn't know he was a preacher, did you?"

"No, ma'am. Are you sure about that?" I asked.

"Oh, I'm sure. Some preacher though. He was arrested with a prostitute at one of those seedy motels out on Dickerson Road. It was in the newspaper, but I don't guess that got back to his congregation."[7]

"Why not?" I asked.

"Because his church was one of those giant RV parks down in Florida, and he was the so-called chaplain. Every winter, he and his wife would pack up their things and go down there. He was cutting his grass and getting ready to leave for Florida when he had the heart attack."

Thinking that the neighbor might have been only too happy to spread a rumor about the deceased felon, I attempted to verify her story. And I quickly found that her version was completely accurate. In the summer of 1982, then fifty-seven-year-old Reverend John Randolph Clarke had been arrested after picking up a twenty-two-year-old prostitute at the corner of Dickerson Road and Trinity Lane and then proceeding to a nearby motel room. Clarke was charged with aiding and abetting prostitution and posted a $62.50 bond for his release. He had no comment for newspaper reporters, other than to direct questions to an attorney he hadn't spoken with in fifteen years, Charles Galbreath. When Galbreath was asked by reporters about his former client, he quickly informed them that he would bet his house on the fact that Clarke hadn't killed Paula Herring.[8]

CHAPTER TEN

SOMETHING'S FISHY

It was at the intersection of curiosity and geography that I found myself a few days later, taking a drive near Gallatin, Tennessee, in search of Crestview Memorial Gardens. I had written down the name of the cemetery from the *Nashville Tennessean*'s coverage of Paula's graveside service.

For a memorial garden that was essentially located out in the countryside, I was surprised to find an on-site business office: a small wooden building the size of a tiny apartment. And it appeared that I was in luck, given that a pickup truck was parked near the open front door as I eased my car into the driveway.

Stepping onto the front porch, I could see that the one-room office was complete with desk, filing cabinets, and a couple of worn chairs for guests. A mountain of loose papers and time sheets was stacked next to an ancient computer on the work desk.

Inside the office, I was greeted by a thirty-something employee pulling files from an old metal filing cabinet. He introduced himself as part of the management company for the cemetery.[1] He was tall and wiry, dressed in work boots, blue jeans, and a sweat-soaked shirt. After a brief exchange, I explained that I was trying to locate Paula Herring's resting place.

After punching a few keystrokes into what must have been one of the first personal computers ever built, the young man surprised me by saying, "Nope, she's not buried here."

"I'm fairly certain she's here," I replied.

"Oh, wait a minute, when did she die?"

"February 1964."

"That's the problem. We computerized all of our records back in the eighties, but for the old ones we still have to look through the card files."

With that, he moved to a different file cabinet, and quickly produced a small, yellow index card with information about Paula Herring.

Minutes later, I was carrying a photocopied map of the cemetery plots and walking carefully through a grassy area of gravesites located several hundred feet from the office building. Even using the map for reference, and cross-checking it against markers that the office manager had noted for me as being near Paula Herring's gravesite, I still couldn't find it. At least it seemed that way, until I tripped over a rock. But it wasn't a rock. Instead of a headstone noting Paula's final resting spot, I had tripped over a footstone, a small metal plate engraved with the words:

Paula Jenoise Herring
August 21, 1945–February 22, 1964

I stepped back and froze. *What happened to the monument?* I turned completely around, afraid that I was standing in the middle of her grave and looking in the wrong direction. But it wasn't a mistake. The foot-marker was the only indicator of Paula Herring's presence.

Puzzled, I returned to my car and negotiated the gravel driveway back to the tiny office to inquire about this discovery. Luckily, the front door was still open, and the workman was still shuffling paperwork at his desk. Before I could pose my question, he looked up to ask one of me.[2]

"Hey, I was just about to come find you. I was wondering if you have a current address on Mrs. Herring?"

"No, I'm sorry I don't," I replied.

"Well, it looks like it's been a while since we had correspondence with her. I've got her on Timberhill Drive in Nashville. I wanted to see if she'd be interested in selling that other plot?"

"I'm not following you," I said.

"I looked at the information we have on file for Paula Herring, and I can see a Mrs. Jo Herring bought two cemetery plots back in February 1964."

"Two?"

"Yep, she bought them both in February of 1964."

My head was spinning at this unexpected news, but not so much that I was speechless.

"So if Paula Herring is buried in one of the plots, who's buried in the other one?"

"Nobody. It's empty."

"It was never used?" I asked.

"That's right. She bought them both at the same time, side by side. According to our records, she paid cash, ninety dollars for each. And I'd be interested in buying one back from her, but like I said, the only address I have on the family is Timberhill Drive, in Nashville."

At this point the office manager stopped studying the paper records and looked up at me. I knew what was coming next.

"Aren't you family?"

"No, but I know the Herrings lived on Timberhill Drive back then. I'm just doing some research on Paula Herring." Then I remembered my original reason for returning to the office.

"There's no headstone on Paula Herring's grave."

As I spoke, the manager stood and returned the index card to the open file cabinet before answering. "Oh, that happens sometimes. Most people buy a headstone, but in a few cases they never do, and when it happens, we mark the gravesite with a footstone, that plate you saw. At least that way we can keep up with where they're buried."

The Beaman Library, on the campus of David Lipscomb University (which would drop the first part of its name in 2005), was a perfect location to work on my new research project.[3] In each corner of the upper floor of the library, study rooms could be found, roughly ten feet by ten feet, each furnished with a large work table, wooden chairs, and a dry-erase whiteboard covering most of one wall, and a window with a view of the campus.

After the unusual experience with the cemetery visit, I took the time to sequester myself in the Beaman Library and again review the list of forty stories and descriptions. After a half hour of reading through the list, I could see that the project would be overwhelming due to the amount of time needed to explore each one. More than that, the moral dilemma of replaying some of the worst moments in the lives of Nashville's citizen's seemed highly questionable. Unless there was some new update to share or a hidden truth that needed to come to light, what was the point of reliving these tragic episodes?

It was with this ethical dilemma in mind that I took a hard second look at the babysitter murder. It had certainly grabbed me in a way that the other stories had not. Perhaps it was the unique aspect of a little boy sleeping through his sister's murder that held my mind captive. And my initial research had certainly uncovered some additional questions that I wanted to answer.

With an empty dry-erase board in front of me and a stack of papers and notes littering my work table, I stood and began writing out my questions on the board:

killer spares the little boy why?
missing suicide note?
the mother buys two graves, but only one body?
defense lawyer would bet his house on this client

After taking a seat at the work table and studying the board, I made a decision to spend no more than thirty days attempting to answer the first two questions on the list. To my way of thinking, this would allow enough time to fairly explore the Paula Herring story. If nothing new surfaced after thirty days of research then I would walk away with the knowledge that I had given it a fair effort.

CHAPTER ELEVEN

POLICE ARCHIVES

Visiting the Metro Nashville Police Archives wasn't in my original plan. In fact, it wasn't in my plan at all until I had been shut out at every other government office involved in the handling of paperwork for the Paula Herring murder case. The Nashville District Attorney's Office told me that their records had burned in an office fire sometime around 1966, about the time that Harry Nichol had retired and been replaced by the new district attorney general, Thomas Shriver.

The Davidson County Criminal Court was also at a loss for records and suggested that anything they might have had related to the biggest homicide in Metro's young history would have moved right along in the chain of evidence with the prosecution of John Randolph Clarke. Multiple calls to the Metropolitan Police Department were more frustrating than baffling. As long as I had the precise case number to request, they could search for records related to the Paula Herring homicide. But it was a perfect catch twenty-two, as I didn't have a case number until I had a record to review, and they would not search for a record until I provided the exact case number. This maddening process went on for months.

I was unwilling to antagonize the police department with a letter referring to the Tennessee Public Records Act, so after several back and forth exchanges I decided to take a different approach and simply asked to visit the Metropolitan Police Archives. The result? Request granted. Amazing.

It would be many weeks after this session before I realized that the two detectives who had interviewed me were following all of the standard protocols to read my body language, eye movements, and microexpressions, all the while analyzing my verbal responses for deception and assessing whether the Davidson County resident before them was offering honest responses or had something more devious in mind.

After showing identification, signing in at a bulletproof window with the clerk, and completing a lengthy preadmittance document, I was led down a narrow hallway to a small office shared by a couple of detectives. Both men were in their forties, by my guess, and both were wearing white shirts and ties, sans jackets, one thin, the other thickly built, and both armed with large-caliber pistols on their hips. Like any professional who relies on gathering information, they had a natural gift for quickly putting a subject at ease, while asking questions in order to observe the answers.

Mostly, they seemed to be intrigued that an amateur researcher had taken the initiative to show interest in their crime closet. During the visit, I learned that their case files, reports, and evidence, were stored in the Police Archives. As I had accidentally learned in August of 1997, decades later those same records would eventually make their way to the Metro Government Archives for storage.

The interview itself was informal. The heavy detective sat behind the desk, and the thin one balanced half on the desk corner with one foot on the floor, as I sat in a wooden chair facing both men. When the time came to identify which specific case held my interest, I decided to avoid asking about the Paula Herring murder and instead dropped the bombshell that there could be as many as forty. Laughter filled the room until I quickly reeled off the names of a half-dozen cases from past decades, starting with the 1934 unsolved kidnapping and murder of six-year-old Dorothy Distelhurst, whose eyes had been burned out with acid and body buried in a shallow grave on the grounds of a nearby tuberculosis hospital.

The two detectives quickly switched from skepticism to encouragement, offering their perspective and even a few gems of insider information that could be useful down the road.

The whole interview lasted less than thirty minutes, and near the end it was obvious that I had passed the initial test to gain admittance to their historic crime vault.

A few days later, I dialed a number for the Metro Police Archives and spoke to an officer about the pre-access meeting with the two detectives, and she let me know that she had gotten word that a visit to the vault had been approved. She also suggested, strongly, that the visit take place the following day.

The following morning, I made my way downtown to a small paved parking lot surrounded by a tall fence topped with razor wire and a building located in back of the new Justice Center. It seemed to be hidden in plain view among a cluster of bail bond store fronts and law offices. After a couple of deep breaths, I entered the front door of the Metro Police Archives.

The lobby area just inside the doorway was barely large enough for a couple of chairs and a long narrow desk almost chest high. Behind the desk, on a facing wall, was a doorway marked Secure Area. A tall female officer, early fifties I speculated, with gray hair and almost no makeup, greeted me as if they were used to having a steady stream of people walking in off of the street, asking for directions or a cup of free coffee.

After I signed in and offered a photo ID, she motioned for me to follow her through the secure doorway behind the desk. Just before I took a step toward her, she said that I would have to leave any pens, papers, cameras, or phones with her while I was inside. For once, I had guessed correctly and had left all such collateral in my car.

Having visited libraries and museums all of my life, I had a few mental images of what I might expect to find inside a police archives facility, but I could not have been more mistaken in the scene waiting for me just beyond the door. It was an island of misfit toys. File cabinets of every color, shape, and size filled an enormous warehouse, nearly as far as the eye could see. It was as if every file cabinet no longer needed by a local high school or government agency had been shipped to the Police Archives for their use.

I had no idea how anyone could know where to look for a specific year of files, let alone a specific case file. The giant warehouse was arranged with rows and rows of file cabinets of all types. Most were four drawers, some were three, and some were five. In the back of the warehouse, the file cabinets were stacked two high, and a ladder was needed to explore the contents of the upper cabinets.

But with my specific request came a specific fulfillment. I was led to the south side of the giant warehouse and was directed to a single file cabinet halfway down a long wall of cabinets. The guidance provided was that I could explore only the top two drawers in the assigned cabinet and nothing more. My compliance with this request was not left to chance or voluntary acquiescence. A large uniformed police officer showed up moments after my arrival and took up residence in a folding chair positioned within ten feet of my work space. He brought a morning newspaper to read and a cup of coffee to sip while making sure I did not stray from my work area. I did not fail to notice the large-caliber pistol at his side.

My specific file cabinet was labeled as a 1960s storage unit for closed homicide cases that included the letters H through P. This meant I could review the file for William "Big Bill" Powell, a former Vanderbilt football star and Capitol Chevrolet executive, accused of murdering the seventy-two-year-old owner of the dealership during a midday car ride in May 1968. Fellow dealership executives contributed fifty-thousand dollars for Powell's defense fund. Ironically, the shooting had taken place a few blocks from the Metro Archives building where I had first discovered the Paula Herring file. With master attorney Jack Norman Sr. on his team, forty-one-year-old Powell walked free in 1969, and with his freedom came the ownership of the lucrative Capitol Chevrolet franchise.

Within the first hour of exploration, I also found an empty folder labeled "Herring," and I wondered if perhaps the missing file in the Police Archives was the very file that I had stumbled upon one rainy afternoon in the Metro Archives building.

The state of Tennessee is well known for its Grand Divisions, described as East, West, and Middle. Perhaps less well known to many of its citizens is that the highest court in the state, the Tennessee Supreme Court, is also divided into the same three divisions, with locations in Jackson, Knoxville, and Nashville. In the search for trial evidence, especially documentation of criminal proceedings, I was guided by more than one helpful clerk toward the notion that, as John Randolph Clarke's case had been appealed by his attorney, his court records might have traveled along with any formal motion by counsel. Thus, armed with this bit of knowledge, I started my trial transcript search in Music City.

After making a midday trek to the 7th Avenue North location of the Tennessee Supreme Court, I stepped into the most solidly built marble structure I had ever entered and immediately adopted the somber tone I perceived to be seeping from the walls. It felt like Fort Knox and the Vatican had opened a law practice together. It was also a reminder that my simple plan of research was now entering a world of real consequence. I decided to tread carefully within these historic and hallowed walls.

The initial version of my plan, at least as it related to answering the questions haunting me, had been to find John Randolph Clarke alive and well. However, the conversation with Clarke's former next-door neighbor confirmed that I had struck out with that plan, so my next option was to find the criminal trial transcript from the Paula Herring case in hopes of uncovering the answer as to why Clarke hadn't also killed Alan Herring on the night of Paula's murder. In combination with the trial transcript search, I thought perhaps a conversation with the lead attorneys from both the prosecution and the defense teams might also be revealing.

After locating the administrative office of the court, I was greeted by a young woman dressed in a blue suit who offered assistance with a smile. I proffered the "I hope you can help me" introduction, quickly followed by the story of a little boy who had slept through his sister's murder as part of the request for the *State v. John Randolph Clarke* criminal trial transcript. I was confident that the clerk had not heard this kind of request before, mostly because of the growing height of her eyebrows as I reeled out my brief narrative.

Her response was most positive, though she warned me that records from a decades-old criminal case might take several days to locate. I assured her that I could wait.

It was with much anticipation a few days later that I found myself almost jogging back to the Tennessee Supreme Court building to discover why the helpful clerk had requested a subsequent meeting with me. After entering the massive doors to the building and crossing the lobby into the clerk's office, the young woman who had previously helped me flashed a knowing smile in my direction as I approached the counter.

"I was able to find the transcript for your case."

"What do I owe you? Do you need a new car, a vacation perhaps?"

She laughed and said that she was happy to find the case, and, as she spoke, she began pulling thick legal-sized documents from under the counter and stacking them in front of me. Decades earlier, someone had sorted the eventual 1,200 pages of court reporter output into sections of two-hundred pages each, then had bound the legal-sized pages with a brown wrapper, now crumbling with age at the edges. As the stack began rising, I stared open-mouthed at the sheer volume of transcript.

"You can review these here in my presence but I would suggest that you take them one at a time into the little hallway behind you to review. The documents can't leave the building, unless you want us to copy them for you, and that runs one dollar per page. We would need a certified check to get started, and it would be a few days before we'd have them ready for pickup." It seemed like minutes had passed before I finally remembered to mumble, "Thank you," and, "This is amazing."

Seconds later, I stood in a hallway where lawyers and paralegals and reporters would stop by to inspect a wooden tray holding copies of recent rulings, filings, and motions from the various judges. For the next ten minutes, I thought of every option imaginable to walk out the door with more than a thousand pages of criminal trial transcript. Being comfortable with personal computers and the technology that accompanied them, I thought about using a scanner hooked to a laptop computer to scan every page, but the technology was too unwieldy for this option, not to mention cost prohibitive for managing and indexing a thousand pages of legal-sized images. I wondered if hiring a court reporter to read and reenter the trial text into a fresh version of transcript might be doable, but the dollars for this exercise would eclipse the dollar-per-page option.

I stepped back into the clerk's office and meekly inquired whether or not I could checkout the transcript as I might do with a library book. But I was quickly told, in no uncertain terms, that I could not walk away with a criminal trial transcript as if the highest court in Tennessee offered some sort of interlibrary loan program. But she quickly followed with a surprising solution: "You can submit a motion to one of the justices on behalf of the surviving family member, to review the documents outside of our offices for a short period of time, and you might get lucky."

Over the next few minutes, this legal angel explained that the judges would not waste their time writing a response to my request to access the documents, but I could submit a formal motion to the court, and at some point, the motion would be reviewed and acted upon, either with agreement or rejection.

I restrained my enthusiasm long enough to thank her for the guidance and also to acknowledge that I had zero experience in writing the formal motion, short of hiring a lawyer to write it for me. The young clerk graciously offered a couple of samples that I could use to model my request.

Hours later I sent a note to Alan Herring, letting him know that there was a possibility of obtaining a copy of the transcript from the 1964 criminal trial, and with his approval I would submit the motion as his "reporter" in the request. Alan agreed to the plan and over the weekend, I wrote the motion, created an affidavit to be notarized, and also created a formal order for the eventual judge to sign if he agreed to the motion. By Monday morning I had gotten the affidavit notarized, and then dropped the documents off with the clerk where it was dutifully stamped into formal receipt, though there was no estimate as to how long it might take for a judge to respond to my motion.

True to her word, a few months after dropping off the motion, I received another call from the helpful clerk. Justice Alan E. Highers of the Western Division of the Tennessee Court of Appeals, had agreed to my motion to remove the transcript documents from the court's offices for a period of three business days.[1] I was ecstatic at the news, notwithstanding the fact that I would have to pay to make two copies of more than one thousand legal-sized pages of trial transcripts.

Alan Highers was a familiar name to me, primarily because I knew that among Churches of Christ, Judge Alan Highers was a regular speaker, debater, and also the editor of a publication out of Memphis, known as *The Spiritual Sword*.[2] Given Wilmer Herring's family background and their prominence among the Churches of Christ in the hill country of Texas, it seemed a bit ironic to me that Justice Highers was the one agreeing to the motion.

After picking up the documents on a Friday afternoon, I descended upon a print shop in Green Hills in Nashville and began to homestead a couple of the machines for several hours, making copies, rebinding pages, and attempting to speedread my way through hundreds of pages of trial transcripts as the machines did their work. The following morning, I returned the original transcript to the clerk of the court and then buried myself in my new reading assignment.

CHAPTER TWELVE

SIX GIRLS

After a careful study of the 1963–1964 yearbook from the University of Tennessee, I started calling girls who had lived in New West Dormitory, where Paula Herring had been elected president of her floor. Surely, there would be students who remembered Paula. Not only was my assumption correct, I discovered that a number of these former coeds deeply cared about their lost classmate.[1]

I began to compile my notes from various telephone calls and even a few in-person meetings with those in close proximity of the Knoxville campus, and I learned that in 1964 Paula Herring was having the time of her life while attending the University of Tennessee. She clearly viewed college life as an escape from the sadness of her father's death and her mother's alcoholism and lifestyle choices. And it seems that she viewed her new life as the best way to help her younger brother back home in Nashville.

In her first term in Knoxville, Paula was selected to room with a studious girl from Johnson City, Tennessee. But the girl was a poor match for Paula, who went out a lot and liked to date and party. By the time Winter Quarter began in January, 1964, Paula had found a new roommate named Julia "JuJu" Nicholson, and they were a much better match. According to one of Paula's other dorm mates, Paula and her friends would make frequent trips to nearby Cumberland Avenue to drink chocolate sodas and sit and gossip.[2] According to one of her friends, Paula didn't rush a sorority in the fall of 1963, but after Christmas, they learned that a girl who had previously pledged Alpha Omicron Pi sorority had not been initiated, and Paula Herring gladly rushed when the Winter Quarter began.[3] The sorority assigned her to Big Sister Dottie Whelan in February 1964. The plan was to formally initiate Paula into the sorority in April or May.

But Paula, who had pledged her loyalty and devotion to Alpha Omicron Pi, flew home for the weekend in late February and never returned.

When I asked the woman, whom I will call Virginia, if she and others from UT had attended Paula's funeral, I was told that several girls from the dorm had made the trip, and that they had stayed overnight in Nashville. According to Virginia, the funeral had been open casket, and the funeral home personnel had covered up Paula's facial wounds. She did remember that Paula's little brother was noticeably absent, and the girls could only guess the reason. Was he traumatized? Or was he being hidden from people? No one knew the answer.

When I asked why she had such clear memories of Paula Herring, Virginia said that she and Paula discovered that they had been classmates in elementary school in Gallatin, Tennessee, in grades three and four.[4] They hadn't realized it until they both moved into the same dorm on the same floor in Knoxville. At the end of our meeting, Virginia graciously offered photographs of Paula, taken inside the New West Dormitory during her brief time in school.

The photos included one of Paula sitting on her bed in the dorm with a stuffed kitten in her lap, dated February 1964. It was possibly the last photograph ever taken of Paula Herring while she was still alive. In the background you can see other photos on the wall:

- A prom party photograph from an AOPi function
- The AOPi class with her Big Sister, Dottie Whelan
- A Sadie Hawkins party with an unknown date in a straw hat
- A photo of little brother, Alan Herring, on her corner table

A few days after our meeting, I received a note from Virginia:

> Dear Michael,
>
> I also had another impression about Paula and that was that she and her mother did not get along well. I also remember Paula using her money to buy clothes for ski equipment and not having enough for food for the rest of the quarter, not uncommon for a lot of students, but very uncommon for someone who had just pledged a sorority.
>
> Sincerely,
> Virginia[5]

On a summer afternoon decades after Paula Herring was murdered, I stumbled upon a small article in the archived files of the University of Tennessee student newspaper, at the time known as the *Orange and White.* The note, published on page ten of their February 21, 1964, edition included a headline that read "Six Panhellenic Representatives to Attend Ole Miss Meeting." The article noted that a group of girls from the school were traveling from Knoxville to Oxford, Mississippi, to attend the annual Southeastern Panhellenic Conference. The reporter had been kind enough to include the names of the girls attending the sorority conference, as well as the ironic news that the girls were traveling on the exact same Friday afternoon that Paula Herring would have been flying from Knoxville to Nashville—February 21, 1964.

After reviewing the article, I realized that one of the last names in the group was also a match for a name in the Ski Club photo that had included Paula Herring. The girl, named Susan, was also noted as the Panhellenic Rush Chairman.

It took a few weeks of careful research, but eventually I discovered that the skiing sorority member had also lived in New West Dorm. Not many days before she was murdered, Paula Herring had announced to her mother that she was changing her major to pre-law, from the biology major that she had initially chosen, and that she was also going to increase the focus on her undergraduate studies to ensure that she would eventually be accepted into law school.[6] My assumption was that someone, perhaps a professor who had observed her keen mind in class, a mentor of some type, had influenced Paula to change paths. It was a long shot, but I called the University of Tennessee Alumni Association Office and posed a simple question: did a former student, the skiing sorority member, have a degree or focus of pre-law while enrolled at the University of Tennessee. The answer was yes. A few weeks later, I found her.

"Hi Susan. I'm a graduate of the University of Tennessee, doing some research, and I spoke with your mother in East Tennessee. She gave me your number if you've got a moment to chat?"[7]

"Yes, are you fundraising for the school?"

"No, this is a research project on a tragic story from 1964. I'm sorry to start the conversation with such an unpleasant topic. The story involves a former UT student named Paula Herring."

"It sends shivers up my back to even hear her mentioned again."

"That's certainly a consistent theme among those I've spoken with from New West Dorm. I'm thinking you lived at New West in the 1963–1964 school year?"

"Yes, I was a counselor in the dorm," she said.

"What we used to call a resident advisor, that sort of role?" I asked.

"Yes."

"What sends the shivers upon recalling the name?" I inquired.

"Before I get too far into this, tell me again who you are?"

"My apologies, I attended the University of Tennessee in the early eighties. I can provide references if that is helpful, and we can chat at some future time when it feels appropriate to you? Or not; it's completely at your discretion," I said.

"And what's your link to this?" she asked.

After explaining my acquired interest in the topic, the woman on the other end of the conversation chose to go forward with the discussion. I explained that, after reading the newspaper accounts, I found the Paula Herring story to be perplexing. So much so that I had begun researching the story in earnest, almost to the jeopardy of my regular employment.

"What happened to Paula's mother?" she asked.

"Good question. She died in the mid-seventies in Texas."

"I always suspected that her mother was an alcoholic."

"Your impression was correct. Apparently alcohol abuse was at the center of her demise," I noted.

"And what about Paula's father?" she asked.

"Records indicate that he committed suicide at a Nashville hotel in 1960, a couple of weeks after Paula's fifteenth birthday."

"I didn't know that. In fact I think Paula may have indicated that he died in a car accident or something like that."

"I can confirm that the cause of death listed was ingestion of poison, a suicide."

"There was a little boy in the house, her brother, right?" she asked softly.

"Yes. And the man convicted in Paula's wrongful death spent nine years in prison, was paroled in 1975, and died in 1986. His wife died about seven years later. They had no children."

"So what makes this an unusual story to you, short of the obvious?" she asked.

"The district attorney general from 1964, the chief of police, the mayor of Nashville, have all passed away in the past decade or so. People on one side of the aisle, legally speaking, kept saying, 'Yes, we got the right person for the crime.' On the other side of the aisle, the answer was, 'No, you absolutely got the wrong person,'" I said.

"Well, I'll never forget it. Paula was on my hall in the dormitory. And we were good friends. I was haunted by the story. And I think about it from time to time. Every now and then something triggers my recollection," she noted.

"Do you remember the plane ride you took the weekend Paula was killed?" I asked.

"It seems like Paula and I left Knoxville on the same flight."

"Were you coming to spend the weekend with her in Nashville?" I asked.

"No, but I don't remember where I was going."

"If I said Oxford, Mississippi, would that help?"

"Oh, yes, there was a group of us going to a sorority conference," she said.

"But Paula didn't fly all the way to the conference?" I asked.

"No, I distinctly remember that we sat together on the flight, and she got off the plane in Nashville to visit her family for the weekend. I assume you're calling to ask me what I remember."

"Yes, I was simply calling to find someone willing to talk about their remembrances of Paula. I'll confess that's been difficult," I said.

"Well, I was questioned by one of the investigators. I remember that happened maybe on Monday or Tuesday after the weekend."

"Really?"

"Yes, and I remember that the plane stopped in Nashville on the way back to Knoxville on Sunday afternoon. And Paula didn't get back on the plane. She had a seat next to me coming and going, and she didn't get back on the plane."

"I'm sorry," I said softly.

"I remember being surprised and then thinking, well maybe she caught a car ride back to campus. Then I heard the news that night when I got back to the dorm."

"I can only imagine the shock," I said.

"It still troubles me when I think about her."

"So I was thinking, you might have majored in pre-law?" I asked.

"Yes, why does that matter?"

"Because for some reason, Paula Herring had settled on a plan to go to law school, and I made the assumption that someone she knew, perhaps a mentor, had influenced her to do so. Susan, would you happen to know why Paula wanted to change majors?"

"I'm sorry, I don't. Though I think she would have been successful in that field. She was very bright."

"Any chance that a male student from the University of Tennessee might have had an agenda with Paula and was perhaps involved in her, uh, demise?" I inquired.

"No, never. To me it always seemed something wasn't right with the story, but I didn't have access to all the details."

In the summer of 1999, I made a significant discovery after researching and contacting the members of the University of Tennessee's first snow skiing club, formed in the winter of 1964. A man named Paul Pharr, who had been elected as the first president of the UT Ski Club, confessed that he had been dating Paula Herring in the days and weeks prior to her tragic death. When I asked how long they had been dating, the man indicated "every weekend for three weeks prior to Paula's murder." Paul Pharr remembered that Paula enjoyed dancing and movies and that she was going home that fateful weekend in February. He said he was shocked when he had heard the news of Paula's murder. "I thought she was a nice person and couldn't understand why someone would kill her," he said.[8]

Shortly after the exchange with Paul Pharr, I was able to verify Paula Herring's class schedule for the Winter Term of 1964. She was enrolled in English 112, Elementary Spanish, General Zoology, Physical Education, Deductive Logic, and Background of Modern Civilization.

One of her dorm mates, a girl I'll call Claire, had the exact same classes except for Deductive Logic. I couldn't resist tracking down Claire and inquiring about her former friend:

Me: You might've been Paula's roommate, winter of 1964?
Claire: No.
Me: You might have loaned her a book?
Claire: Yes, I remember the title.
Me: *All the King's Men*?
Claire: Yes.
Me: Can you describe Paula or tell me about her?
Claire: She was athletic, not pretentious, not the cheerleader type, didn't date much, but was known throughout the dorm.
Me: Did you know Paula before Knoxville?
Claire: No.
Me: Did you live in the same dorm?
Claire: I don't remember.
Me: Did you come to Paula's funeral?
Claire: I don't remember.
Me: Did you come home that weekend in February?
Claire: I don't think so.
Me: Did the police come to see you in Knoxville?
Claire: I gave a statement I think or maybe I went to court.
Me: Where?
Claire: I don't remember. It was all very spooky, scary.
Me: On the surface, this story looks like they caught the right guy, but the more I research it, the more I'm intrigued, because my intuition says something's wrong.[9]

Two days later, I called back:

Me: Hello? Mike Bishop calling from Nashville, Tennessee.
Claire: I'm not interested. Please don't call me again.

Not long after my conversation with "Claire," I found Paula Herring's first roommate, the studious girl from Johnson City, Tennessee. This girl, I'll call Kay Masterson, and now married with children of her own, was quickly spooked by my research into her former roommate. After a few unsuccessful attempts at reaching her by phone, I penned a letter to her:

> Dear Ms. Masterson,
>
> I hope you can help me with a current writing/research project based out of Nashville. I'm a graduate of the University of Tennessee and for the past months I've been working on a book project.
>
> The focus has been to cover some of the more newsworthy moments in Nashville's history. One of the more sensational yet tragic moments took place on February 22, 1964, the death of babysitter Paula Herring.
>
> I would like to speak with you briefly regarding your remembrances of your 1963 Fall Quarter dorm mate, Paula Herring, and the atmosphere of college life in '63–'64. Thank you for your time and consideration.
>
> Sincerely, Michael Bishop

Approximately three weeks later, I received a response:

> Dear Mr. Bishop,
>
> I'm sorry that you've had trouble reaching me. My house-sitter tells me that you've made several calls. I have been in Canada for quite a while on assignment.
>
> I'm enclosing some materials for you that I thought might be of some help for your research. This is all I have, items that were tucked away in an old scrapbook. I personally do not have any memories of that time, tried very hard to block them out and ultimately succeeded!
>
> *Please do not call me again.* I will be leaving for another extended trip abroad soon. Good luck with your continued research.
>
> Sincerely, Kay Masterson[10]

The helpful, but not helpful, note led me to the unsavory world of true detective magazines.[11] When Kay returned my attempted communication with the "don't call me" letter, she also included a copy of *True Detective* magazine from July 1964. I wondered how painful it must have been for Paula's friends and family to read the magazine article's characterization of Paula's murder, along with news and notes about Alan, Jo, and even Wilmer Herring. The photographs in the magazine article showed no mercy, as they were brutally graphic, even more so than the local newspapers that had covered the girl's slaying. After the Kay Masterson exchange, my list of former Paula Herring classmates to contact moved from Knoxville back to Nashville, where Paula had attended high school. And thus began my long search for a girl named Carmen Lee.

One of the more noteworthy deals with the devil, at least musically speaking, was the one Robert Johnson made in 1937 in a delta town in northwest Mississippi.[12] As historians tell it, no one ever before or since has played a blues guitar with the sweet sound of Robert Leroy Johnson. He was so good, in fact, because, according to Johnson, he made a deal personally with Satan himself at the intersection of a two-lane blacktop known as Highway 61 and Highway 49 in Clarksdale, Mississippi.

The monument to Robert Johnson's deal is still standing, one of the loftier visuals in a town mostly filled with poor folk trying to make a living surrounded by thousands of acres of delta cotton and soybeans. Farther south, you can find where most of the devil's dealers end up, in Parchman, Mississippi, a prison of considerable bad karma, where many of its residents finish this life with a thousand volts of electricity burning up their anatomy.[13] It would be in the town of Clarksdale, Mississippi, near Johnson's Memorial, that I, too, would make a deal that would begin to unravel the case against John Randolph Clarke.

Based on a brief conversation with one of the basketball players on Paula's team, I learned that one of Paula's best friends at John Overton High School was a girl who was one class behind Paula. Thus, in the winter of 1964, this girl was a senior basketball player on the Overton High School girls' team.[14]

So it seemed plausible to me that if there were one and only one person Paula Herring might visit while she was home during the weekend of February 22 it would be her best friend, Carmen Lee. Their homes were in the same neighborhood, and they easily could visit with each other that weekend.

But there was a problem. There was nothing in the court record that suggested Paula and her best friend, Carmen, had spent any time together that weekend. In fact, Jo Herring was the only one to briefly mention Paula's last day on earth. And Jo's timeline of that Saturday was simply that Paula had awoken, had breakfast with her mother and her little brother, made a trip to get the car serviced, picked up some contact lenses, and then had settled in for a long afternoon and evening of report writing for her class at the University of Tennessee—and, of course, according to Jo, making the generous offer to stay home and babysit Alan while her mother went to dinner with friends. No mention of Carmen Lee, not even so much as a phone call.

So decades later, to say the trail of Carmen Lee had grown cold was a vast understatement. Off and on for years, I had been hunting for Carmen and had still not found her. I could find remnants of her family scattered throughout the southeastern United States, but no Carmen. When I thought I had found her living in Wisconsin, I flew to Chicago, drove to a little lakeside community where it appeared she owned some real estate, at least according to the county clerk's office, only to find an empty house. It was supremely frustrating. It was as if Carmen's instincts were warning her that someone was on her trail, and she would escape just before I could get to her.

The most recent attempt at tracking her down indicated that she might be living near the famous crossroads of Robert Johnson's monument in the little delta town of Clarksdale, Mississippi. With nothing more than an address and some time to waste, I made my way past cotton fields and the famous intersection at Highways 61 and 49, and slowly drove past older Craftsman-style homes on quiet streets with Native American names, such as Chickasaw and Cheyenne. The extra-wide streets were lined with giant oak trees that appeared to be a century old or more. In fact, the streets were so wide that they could have been restriped as four-lane highways, though there appeared to be little need for such an enhancement, as the amount of traffic I encountered was hardly worth the trouble.

It was a warm Saturday morning in September 2009, when I located the most recent address that had Carmen's name attached to it. After chasing her across the country, I was beginning to wonder if Carmen had parlayed some wealth into real estate speculation or rental properties, because although her name or someone with the same name was attached to ownership records, I never seemed to find her living at the address I was checking.

With the sun rising higher in a cloudless morning sky and the humidity reaching an uncomfortable level, I parked my car on the street, parallel in front of a well-kept, 1950s brick bungalow. I had just rolled down the car windows in hopes of a cooling breeze when a late-model sedan, driven by a woman I guessed could be the age of Carmen Lee, passed me and then turned into the driveway of the home I had come to visit. *I must be living right,* I thought to myself.

The woman exited the car and was now walking up the sidewalk to the front door. She was tall and athletic looking, with brown hair styled in a short, attractive haircut and an outfit that made me think she might be a club tennis player or perhaps a golf professional. At least those were my initial intuitions. In one hand, she held a chain of car keys, and in the other a white plastic bag with a couple of items inside. So, on the spur of the moment, I stepped out of my car and called out to her. "Carmen? Carmen Lee?"

My words were effective, and the woman halted in her tracks, but I didn't detect any smile or warmth being reflected back to me. Instead, I was seeing the woman's eyes narrow, and she took a defensive posture as I approached.

"Good morning, I thought you might be Carmen Lee."

"No, who are you?"

"Are you related to her?" I asked, as I blocked her path to the doorway in hopes of at least getting some insight before she retreated inside and I was left out of options for yet another search.

"No, why are you looking for Carmen?"

"I'm sorry, I didn't introduce myself. My name is Michael Bishop. I'm from Nashville, Tennessee, where Carmen graduated high school back in the 1960s. I'm trying to find her. In fact, I've been trying to find Carmen for several years, and the reason is, well, I'll just tell you straight up, the reason I need to find her is about her best friend's murder when Carmen was a senior in high school in 1964. But I'm guessing you're not Carmen?"

"No, I'm not."

With this last comment, I assumed she was going to ask me to step off her property, but, to my surprise, she didn't move away, nor did she appear to want to get away from me.

"Are you a detective?" she asked.

"No, ma'am, I'm just researching the 1964 murder case. There's been some new information discovered recently that makes me think the person convicted of the crime was not the person who should have been convicted." I was hoping this last bit of confession might strike a chord with this woman. Her reply was delivered flatly and without any emotion. "I don't know where she is, and I can't help you."

"But she's been here, in this town, maybe in the last year?"

"Maybe, but I can't help you. I'm sorry," she said.

"No, I completely understand, I'm only interested in asking her a few questions."

As I said this, I was hoping for any shift in body language or facial expression that would indicate that I might be able to sway her toward helping me. I was hoping that the negative attitude was not toward me and was instead toward whatever business or personal dealings she had had with Paula Herring's former best friend. As I waited, a small dog scampered down the middle of the quiet street.

"Are you staying here in Clarksdale?" she asked.

"No, I literally just got here in the past half-hour. I had barely parked my car when you pulled into the driveway. Maybe it's fate, both of us here at the same time?"

I could see she was thinking about helping me, so I gave her a moment to consider my "fate" remark, before adding, "Anything, and I mean anything that you could do to point me in the right direction would be appreciated far more than you know. It seems I've been all over the country trying to find her, and I thought you might have been Carmen when I saw you step out of the car."

She looked away and took a very deep breath, then turned back to face me. "I might have an old phone number you can try, but I'm not confident it's still in service. Would you want that?"

"Yes, definitely. I'm at zero right now; anything you have is helpful."

"Okay, I'm going to go inside and get the number for you, and after I give it to you, you are never to come back here, ever. It sounds like a really tragic story, and maybe you can find her and get what you need. Is that a deal?"

"It's a rock solid deal. I owe you, thank you."

A few moments later, I copied down a cell phone number, and within five minutes I was halfway out of town when a disturbing thought crossed my mind. I nearly ran over the curb as I pulled into the parking lot of an old grocery market to stop the car and analyze the situation. I was talking to myself out loud:

Did I just get played by Paula Herring's very clever friend? Is it possible that the woman I just met was in fact Carmen Lee? She looks athletic enough; she's the right age, certainly looks like someone who could be a 1964 Overton graduate. Why would she try to dupe me?

I reached into my pocket for the scrap of paper, thought about dialing the number right then, but decided I would let twenty-four hours pass before I dialed. What I couldn't foresee was that it would be almost a year before I would speak to Carmen Lee.

CHAPTER THIRTEEN

TRIAL OF THE BLOODY MAN

During the criminal trial in Jackson, Tennessee, neither the prosecution nor the defense had made any attempt at putting Alan Prewitt Jr. on the witness stand to validate Jo Herring's story of the night she had met John Randolph Clarke in Ruth's Diner.[1] After tracking down Mr. Prewitt's particulars, I quickly realized that he either had had nothing to add to the trial or perhaps had used his family connection to avoid testifying, given that he was the son of the recently retired chief justice of the Tennessee Supreme Court.[2]

This meant that Jo Herring had met the son of an East Tennessee judge, John Clarke, on the same night that she was having dinner with the son of the former chief justice of the highest court in Tennessee. Perhaps the younger Prewitt's access to power was of interest to the registered nurse?

Another curious aspect of the trial record was the realization that the night manager of the Krystal hamburger restaurant, the woman brought in to view a 1:00 a.m. lineup that included John Randolph Clarke, had not testified at the criminal trial in Jackson. Clarke's attorney made a point of confirming this lack of evidence in a later exchange with one of the investigators from the DA's office.

> Galbreath: Did you consider it strong evidence in this case, that an eyewitness had seen the defendant in a bloody condition a few miles from the murder scene?
>
> George Currey: Yes.
>
> Galbreath: Yet she wasn't called as a witness in this trial by the state?
>
> Currey: I don't believe she was. We didn't use her as a witness.

Galbreath: As a matter of fact, you rejected her statement.
Currey: I didn't. I didn't.
Galbreath: Well do you believe, was it your position that she had indeed seen John Clarke?
Currey: I don't know.
Galbreath: You don't know.
Currey: No.[3]

As I mulled over these inconsistencies and questions, I was surprised to receive a late afternoon phone call on a Friday from the clerk of the Supreme Court. The helpful administrator called to apologize for not realizing that an additional trial transcript had been omitted in her review for me, and the other transcript, a civil case, also involved John Randolph Clarke. When I politely disagreed, she confirmed that she only had provided the criminal trial transcript while failing to realize that a civil trial transcript also was available.

Before I could ask her to expand on the details of the civil case, she mentioned the 1965 date of the trial and suggested that it would have been covered in newspapers from across Tennessee if I wanted to review any articles before picking up the transcript on Monday morning.

It didn't take me long to track down the bombshell article, published in the *Knoxville News Sentinel.* The story, by Dana Ford Thomas, was printed on May 18, 1965, and recounted how a noisy car that might have been involved in the slaying of Paula Herring had been given to a professional wrestler and his wife on February 23, 1964, one day after the girl's murder. The couple, who at the time of the article were living in Kingsport, Tennessee, were perplexed by the generous gift from a man they barely knew, one Sam Carlton of Nashville. The wife further noted that Carlton's face had been scratched when he arrived at their home.[4]

Davidson County district attorney general Harry Nichol was noted as being willing to question the couple but was not reopening the case.

The discovery of this news was not just a bombshell to the case against John Randolph Clarke, it was also a major dilemma for me, almost thirty-five years after Clarke's conviction. What if Sam Carlton had murdered Paula Herring and gotten away with the slaying, while Clarke went to prison? Would Alan Herring try to do something about it? What if Carlton was completely innocent but looked guilty? And where was Sam Carlton now, dead or alive? It seemed that the wisest course of action was to run down the answers to these questions.

A few weeks after Clarke's conviction, the city of Boston finally caught their elusive killer.[5] And the story ended with a twist, as the Strangler, Albert DeSalvo, turned out to be a man of many disguises, his most recent being that of a police detective.

In mid-October of 1964, Charles Galbreath and his client caught a break. A woman who had testified as a character witness for John Randolph Clarke, Ruthmary Cobb, was visited late one night by Dr. Murray Cook, one of the 1963 Christmas Eve participants who had teased John Randolph Clarke into firing his pistol into a snowy sidewalk on 18th Avenue South. Cook had met the Cobb woman a party a few weeks prior, and he chose the odd timing of his visit to discuss the facts of the Clarke case and told Mrs. Cobb that he knew Clarke was innocent and that a close friend of his, one Al Baker, was guilty and offered to prove it.[6]

The visit so upset the woman that she filed a notarized deposition with Charles Galbreath in hopes that it might help her redheaded friend, John Randolph Clarke. The woman stated that Cook, in her presence on the night of his visit, then telephoned Harry Nichol, the district attorney general, and also a newspaper reporter for the *Nashville Banner*, and told both parties the same thing—that Baker was guilty and Clarke was innocent.

A few days later, Charles Galbreath received a phone call from another member of the Nashville Bar Association. The attorney on the other end of the line greeted Galbreath with the news that Charlie owed him $250. The attorney, W. B. Hogan, said he had a witness who not only could identify the bloody man at the Krystal hamburger restaurant, but that his client, a railroad worker, had known the bloody man for several years. There was no doubt that the reward would have to be paid.

Within hours of the call, the two attorneys met to formulate a game plan, and quite naturally the plan included litigation. The two lawyers decided that Galbreath would refuse to pay the reward, thus forcing Hogan to sue him in open court on behalf of his client. It was a perfect setup. At some point, the civil suit would end up on the docket of some unsuspecting judge, with the goal of overturning Clarke's conviction and winning a new trial or, better yet, uncovering the identity of Paula Herring's real killer.

Six months later, in April 1965, the civil suit came up on the docket of a local circuit judge. After Galbreath and Hogan explained the particulars of the case, the judge allowed the case to proceed.

W. B. Hogan's star witness, and also the man laying claim to the reward, was a fellow named Henry King.[7] Henry and his brother both worked for the L & N Railroad.

According to Henry, on the night of Saturday, February 22, 1964, he had been at the Parkview Hospital in Nashville, where his wife was recovering from surgery. When visiting hours were over, Henry left the hospital and decided to stop by and see his sister and brother-in-law, who lived just off Franklin Road in South Nashville.

When Henry King got to his sister's home and discovered that no one was there, he drove around the corner to get a cup of coffee at the Krystal hamburger restaurant on Franklin Road. King parked his car in front of the store and, just as he was about to enter the front door, a man came out who Henry recognized immediately as Sam Carlton.

Henry said that he had gotten to know Sam and his brother years earlier, when the two brothers had been operating a restaurant on Clarksville Highway. Henry said that, when he realized Sam was bleeding from his head and that he had blood on his arm and pants, he asked him what had happened. Carlton's response was that he'd been knocked in the head by two men and that he was going home to get his gun and kill them.

On Sunday morning, when King returned to Parkview Hospital, his wife was reading a Sunday newspaper and commented upon the tragic news regarding the babysitter who had been murdered in Crieve Hall the night before. The news stunned Henry, and he told his wife of the encounter with a bloody Sam Carlton. But Henry didn't mention the story again, and it was forgotten.

When Galbreath took his turn at cross-examination, his obvious question to King was "Why?" Why had Henry not come forward fourteen months earlier, when the event had taken place? Henry's answer was that he didn't want to get involved and that he had read in the newspaper that a suspect had been taken into custody for the murder and he had seen the Mayor's announcement on television the week of the murder. Galbreath asked why, then, when he knew that a man had been convicted of murder in the Paula Herring case, in part due to the testimony of a restaurant manager who saw a bloody man at the Krystal restaurant, why had he not come forward to exonerate Galbreath's poor client. Again, King said that he did not want to get involved in the case, but when he saw Galbreath's October reward offered in the afternoon newspaper, he felt he should contact someone, and the someone turned out to be attorney W. B. Hogan.

Next up on the witness stand was Sam Carlton.[8] Carlton was an imposing figure, dressed in boots and heavy denim work clothes, sensible attire for a man who worked at a truck stop. In the days before interstate travel, when almost every eighteen wheeler made its way through the intersection of 1st Avenue and Broadway in downtown Nashville, Carlton's truck stop was one of the highest volume fuel retailers in the South.

From the start, Carlton made it clear that he wasn't happy to be in court. Upon being seated in the witness box, he didn't wait to be asked any questions; he had a few of his own. He wanted to know who was going to pay him for his time away from work, and whether he should have brought his own attorney with him.

Galbreath ignored the first question, and, with a straight face, suggested that no attorney was needed since Carlton was merely appearing as a witness in a small civil suit.

Big Sam wasn't buying any of it. He knew exactly why he'd been subpoenaed, and he had a very simple explanation for his appearance at the Krystal hamburger restaurant in a bloody condition: Henry King was just confused about the date. Carlton didn't argue with the fact that he'd been at the restaurant in a bloody condition, or even that it had been on a Saturday night, but Carlton put the date as November 3, 1963.

W. B. Hogan had been ready for such a story, and he offered two depositions to the judge. One was a sworn statement from Henry King's wife, who indicated that her husband had visited her on Sunday morning, February 23, while she was in the hospital in Nashville, and had mentioned having run into Sam Carlton the night before. Hogan also included a bill from the hospital, reflecting that, indeed, Mrs. King had been a patient at Parkview Hospital during the February timeline in question.

When Galbreath quizzed Carlton about why he had such a clear recollection of the date being three months earlier, the truck stop manager said that he and his wife had been to a birthday party for a friend who owned a shoe shop directly across from the Krystal restaurant on Franklin Road. The party had been held in the basement of the store. Sometime around 10:00 p.m. that night, a fight had broken out among two partygoers, and when Sam tried to break it up, someone tagged him on the head with a soft drink bottle.

Carlton said that he'd been dazed and was bleeding from his head when he staggered over to the Krystal and attempted to use the phone to call a cab. With this opening, and the star witness testifying in open court, Galbreath changed gears and caught the big man off guard with his next question:

Galbreath: Mr. Carlton, I'd like to know about your mode of transportation that night. How did you arrive at this alleged party? Did you take a cab over there?

Carlton: Of course not, I drove my own car and my wife took it back home.

Galbreath asked about the car, the make, model, and whether or not it had any mechanical problems or made any noise of any kind.

Carlton: I sold it.

Galbreath: Excuse me?

Carlton: I sold the car to a professional wrestler who needed some transportation.

Galbreath: Where's the car now?

Carlton: It was wrecked and towed somewhere up in East Tennessee. I don't know what they did with it.
Galbreath: What kind of car was it, Mr. Carlton?
Carlton: 1956 Chrysler Imperial.
Galbreath: I see, and when did you sell it?
Carlton: First week of March.
Galbreath: This year?
Carlton: Last year.
Galbreath: Oh, you mean you sold it the first week of March 1964. Let's see, that would have been within days of the murder of that poor little girl in Crieve Hall. What was her name? Herring. Yes, Paula Herring. Did you know the Herring family, Mr. Carlton?
Carlton: No.
Galbreath: You weren't acquainted with the dead girl's mother or her little brother?
Carlton: No.
Galbreath: I see. Well, when you sold your car to this wrestler, did you get a bill of sale? I'd like to see it if you did.
Carlton: I sold it on terms.
Galbreath: Terms, what does that mean exactly?
Carlton: I gave the man the car, and he was supposed to pay me when he could.
Galbreath: Let me get this straight. Within days of the murder of one Paula Herring, you gave away the only car you owned with the understanding that the buyer would pay you whenever he could get around to it? Is that what you're telling me, Mr. Carlton?
Carlton: That's what I'm telling you.
Galbreath: You are one fine citizen.[9]

A moment later, Galbreath asked Carlton where he had been living in February of 1964. Carlton offered up a street name, which Galbreath noted just happened to cross Timberhill Drive a short distance from where the Herring family lived.

A few weeks after the civil trial, John Randolph Clarke became the recipient of bad news. The civil suit that Galbreath and Hogan had taken to court turned out to be a loser. According to the judge in the case, Henry King had not proven that the bloody man he saw on the night of February 22 was Sam Carlton. And King was not due the reward, thus effectively eliminating the foundation that Galbreath wanted to use in building a case for a new trial for John Clarke.

But a few months later, the bad news was quickly reversed when appellate judge Thomas Shriver saw it the way King said the events had happened. The bloody man at the Krystal hamburger restaurant on the night of Paula Herring's murder was indeed the truck stop manager Sam Carlton. Thus, Galbreath and his client eventually paid the reward money to W. B. Hogan's client. But the verdict from Judge Shriver was too little and too late, and eventually had no bearing on Clarke's criminal trial verdict, even though Charles Galbreath had been working furiously to sway the Tennessee Supreme Court to find that his client had been convicted in error.

Buried within one of the pleadings by Galbreath was commentary by a police detective named R. B. Owen that he had witnessed one of his fellow officers physically handling Clarke's clothing and that of Paula Herring. According to Owen, he had given orders that under no circumstances was anyone to handle the evidence, except himself. Owen stated that he had observed another officer with the forbidden items of clothing with fibers on some paper in one hand and a strand of fibers in another. In Galbreath's view, this was grounds for a new trial given that the fibers from Paula Herring's sweater had found a new home on John Randolph Clarke's coat just prior to those articles of clothing being hand delivered to the FBI.[10]

And the language in the appeal regarding the bullet discovered on 18th Avenue South was also illuminating:

> Assuming that the defendant or one of his drunken friends shot his pistol at the ground on 18th Avenue, South, and it is likely this happened, can any reasonable person believe the bullet found on the second search by the police was the bullet fired that night? Consider. The bullet found was some two-thirds of its length into the ground with its nose resting against a concrete paving stone. Obvious question? Was it fired there or placed there by someone who did not know the concrete block was just beneath the surface. . . . This bullet which

> a mine detector failed to locate the day before during a search of hours; this bullet was found with the naked eye the next day sticking out of the ground; this bullet was not damaged by the concrete. And the concrete was not damaged by the bullet. The only logical conclusion is that this bullet was fired somewhere else, removed, and then placed manually where the police found it.[11]

But these bits of remarkable news fell on deaf ears. Primarily because every appeal that Charles Galbreath filed on Clarke's behalf was turned down, including the appeal to the United States Supreme Court.

CHAPTER FOURTEEN

RED ACE

He answered the phone on the second ring, with a high-pitched voice and a pistol-quick delivery style. My reason for calling was that I was interested in writing a story that included some of the older companies from the 1960s era of Nashville and that I had been told that the man on the other end of the telephone line might have worked at a Red Ace gasoline station during those years.[1]

"Yeah, that was a long time ago. Not many of those still around anymore."

What I didn't say was that I also had spent the prior months running down every resident of 18th Avenue in Nashville during 1963 and 1964, in an attempt to find the final Christmas Eve quartet member, Jesse Henderson. After dozens of phone calls, I finally stumbled upon an elderly woman, a former resident of 18th Avenue, who remembered a man in his thirties who lived next door to her during the timeline in question. More importantly, she thought the man had worked for a Red Ace gasoline station near Elliston Place in Nashville at about that same time.

After the Red Ace moniker, I offered the Krystal hamburger name, and simply commented that the Krystal was still making burgers. I didn't mention that the Krystal had started in Chattanooga, Tennessee, not Music City.[2]

In 1964, Red Ace was a chain of locally owned service stations, which included the truck stop where Sam Carlton worked at 1st Avenue and Broadway in Nashville. My Red Ace attendant didn't work at the truck stop downtown, but rather at a small station at Elliston Place near Vanderbilt University.

Elliston Place is a short street with a long history. Elliston Place cuts diagonally from the end of Church Street and Baptist Hospital (now known as Saint Thomas Mid-Town Hospital), through a five-point intersection, and then ends up at a side entrance to Centennial Park, near West End and 25th Avenue. For many years, the street boasted popular restaurants on either end, with an array of specialty stores, coffee houses, gasoline service stations, and even Father Ryan High School.

Father Ryan eventually departed Elliston Place for the suburbs, but on the east end of the street diners still frequent the Elliston Place Soda Shop, at one time owned by attorney Charles Galbreath, and on the west end Rotier's Restaurant still serves one of Nashville's best cheeseburgers.[3]

In 1964, the Red Ace gasoline station was located across the street from the present day Rotier's Restaurant and next door to Sonny's Car Wash. Many people stopped on the way in and out of downtown to refuel at Red Ace and have their car washed at Sonny's.

Ruth's Diner, the location so key to the tragic Saturday night in February 1964, was across the street from the Hippodrome and on the same side of the street as Centennial Park. The Hippodrome was the place to go for professional wrestling matches held a couple of nights each week.

The home John Randolph Clarke shared with his wife, Callie, was on Dudley Avenue. Today, that property is made up of parking lots directly across the street from the Vanderbilt University track and field complex. Back in the day, Red Clarke could take a five-minute stroll from his home on Dudley Avenue to Ruth's Diner, a quick stroll down West End Avenue to the Hippodrome, another five-minute walk to the Red Ace gasoline station at Elliston Place, and then complete the circuit with a ten-minute walk back to his home.

It was at the Red Ace location on Elliston Place that my new phone acquaintance, Jesse Henderson, had pumped gasoline, washed windshields, and checked oil levels for customers in that ancient ritual of yesteryear. Jesse, in his mid-thirties at the time, lived with his mother, a registered nurse, in a house near Music Row, on 18th Avenue. And the Henderson apartment address just happened to be the exact location where the third and matching bullet in the John Randolph Clarke matter was found near the sidewalk, five days after Paula Herring was slain.

With this background, it was a short conversation to move from the possible connection of the bloody man and his employment at the Red Ace truck stop in downtown Nashville to another Red Ace worker who just happened to live where the most critical evidence against John Randolph Clarke had been found. While on the phone with Mr. Red Ace, who was by this time in his early seventies, I wondered about the chance that he knew the bloody man, and perhaps much more?

"When would be good time to interview you?" I inquired. "I could stop by for lunch or bring a pizza or sandwiches, if you eat that kind of food?"

"Oh, I don't eat much and I'm mostly in bed. I can't help you."

"Oh, I'm sorry to hear that. I hope you get to feeling better soon, Mr. Henderson."[4]

After several weeks had passed, I dialed the same number, and the same high-pitched voice answered again:

Me: How are you today, Mr. Henderson?

Henderson: Alright, I reckon. What'cha calling about?

Me: The Paula Herring murder in 1964.

Henderson: Who?

Me: Herring. Paula Herring. You're the Jesse Henderson that worked at the Red Ace service station on Elliston Place back in February 1964, aren't you?

Henderson: Don't know her, never heard of her. What did you say her name was?

Me: Paula Herring.

Henderson: Oh, yeah, I didn't know that was her name. Yeah, that son-of-a-gun what was his name, shot her.

Me: Clarke?

Henderson: Yeah, he shot her. We used to go to the same barber over on Charlotte. I was there at the party where he fired that gun in the ground. That policemen said it was a wonder he hadn't shot me.

Me: When would be a good time to come by and see you? It looks like you live on White Bridge Road and I'm just around the corner.

Henderson: I'm in bad health.

Me: How about lunchtime next week? Thursday work for you?

Henderson: Call me first when you're coming and don't bring a bunch of women up here. I'm mostly in my pajamas.[5]

I laughed at this last comment, and made a mental note that Mr. Red Ace himself, Jesse Henderson, had moved to the top of the leader board for interviews.

The following Thursday, I drove to an apartment complex on White Bridge Road near the Lions Head shopping complex, parked my car, and approached the entrance, where I discovered that the large front doors were locked and secure. There was no way to enter the building without a key. And there was no speaker or buzzer to press to request entrance. My first thought was that Mr. Red Ace had known exactly what was going to happen when I arrived, and if he didn't want to see me, he didn't have to see me.

As I turned to walk back to my car, a little woman with a bag of groceries in her lap was maneuvering her wheelchair toward the entrance. As she waved her card at the security system, the lock clicked, and like a gentleman I opened the door for her. She flashed a smile at me and asked if I could help wheel her into the building. "My pleasure," I replied.

As we approached the elevator, she asked who I was visiting, and when I replied with the name "Jesse Henderson," she said, "Oh, he lives on my floor, just ride the elevator with me and I'll show you which apartment."

A few doors down the hall from the elevator, I knocked lightly on the door of apartment 803. With no sound of footsteps or movement from inside, I knocked again a few moments later, and, from within the unit, I heard a distinctive high-pitched voice saying, "It's open, come on in."

For all of the modern exterior and well-kept interiors of the apartment complex, stepping into unit 803 was like stepping into a haunted house. I stepped inside but immediately came to a halt to let my eyes adjust to the dim light. The two-room apartment was dark, save for a flickering light in a room on my left and a bit of sunshine as a backdrop for a dingy curtain in the small living room directly in front of me.

On my right, the kitchen counter was covered in dust, candy wrappers, and stacks of unopened Pepsi Cola cans. It appeared that a real meal hadn't been prepared in the unit in years. The small living room had a worn-out recliner and a few boxes of books scattered around the floor and stacked on a small table. There was nothing on the walls, no photos or art work, just a coat of beige paint. It looked as if someone had moved in decades earlier and simply had never bothered to unpack their meager belongings.

"I'm in here."

The tinny voice startled me, and I took a step toward the darkened doorway on my left. Another step closer and I stood just outside the room, while my eyes adjusted to the lighting to see an old man lying under a white sheet on a twin-sized bed. His medium-length gray hair looked as if it had been styled with a comb full of firecrackers, with no rhyme or reason as to where any particular section was pointing. He was wearing a pair of discolored, large-framed eye glasses that looked like they had been prescribed in the 1960s. His shirt was a simple t-shirt, which may have been white when new but was now a dingy gray.

"Mr. Henderson?"

"Yeah, they let you in downstairs?"

"I guess you could say that. I was helping one of your neighbors, and she said I could find you here."

"Oh, yeah, that's Miss Busybody. She's always trying to leave me some food or checking on me."

As I quickly surveyed the small bedroom, I could see the hand of the same decorator who had designed the kitchen and living room. The room contained a twin bed, a few boxes adorned with stacks of hardback and paperback books. The source of the flickering light turned out to be a 1970s-style television on a rolling cart at the end of the bed. A tiny table with a small wooden chair was at the end of the bed as well. The strong odor of stale cigar smoke was unmistakable.

Henderson appeared to be perhaps five foot eight, very thin, and probably hadn't been out of the building in months. He was sporting a patchy growth of gray and white whiskers that hadn't been cut in perhaps the past ten days. If the kitchen were any indication, his diet was junk food, colas, and cigars—not the picture of health.

"Thanks for seeing me today," I cheerily offered with a smile.[6]

"Yeah, what's up? You researching that Clarke fella?"

"I suppose."

"You a writer?"

"No, just an amateur researcher, I'll put it that way."

"We used to get our hair cut at the same barber."

"Yes, I remember you mentioning that on the phone. I was actually more curious about your participation on the night of the Christmas Eve party with John Randolph Clarke in 1963."

As I made this statement, I was closely observing the old man. He was propped up on his right side, two pillows under his head. He seemed to be ignoring my question, as he reached down by the bedside and grabbed a can of soda with his left hand, then took a long sip.

"Mind if I sit down?" Before he had a chance to answer, I made a quick move to the end of the bed, reached over the television cart, and picked up the small wooden chair with one hand, swinging it up and over Jesse Henderson's prone body so I could place it at the head of the bed and sit perpendicular to him. For a split second, I got the impression that Henderson had flinched and perhaps was thinking that I would attack him with the chair. It was a fleeting thought.

"I read where you were living in the Music Row area when they searched for the bullet that Clarke fired into the ground in your front yard. You and your wife lived there?"

"No, my mother."

"No wife?"

"Oh, yeah, I was married. I think she's in Georgia. I wasn't married when that girl got killed, but I've got a daughter I haven't seen in a while."

"Mr. Henderson, how did you come to be in the car on Christmas Eve with John Randolph Clarke?"

"Me and Murray and BlueSky had been to a party where Clarke and that Al Baker had been, and we caught a ride with them."

"BlueSky?" I asked.

"Ah, just some guy I drank with back then."

"And Murray Cook?"

"Yeah, he was a doctor, a smart son of a gun too, had an IQ of 160. He was the chess champion of Georgia at one time."

As Henderson ran though the details about his friend, I remembered that I had already attempted to meet with Al Baker, but he had quickly declined, and soon thereafter I had discovered that Murray Cook was dead. So I was down to one Christmas Eve participant.

Murray Cook had been brought to Jackson, Tennessee, to testify in the criminal trial in 1964. On the witness stand, Cook explained his credentials, which included Doctor of Psychology, and then described the snowy Christmas Eve with the gun fired by Red Clarke. When one of the defense attorneys for Clarke asked Dr. Cook if he were employed at the time of the Christmas Eve event, the answer was a simple "No," and that he had been mostly under a physician's care.

"So were you working at Red Ace at the time of the Christmas Eve car ride?" I asked Henderson.

"Oh no, they let us out that weekend."

"They, who's they?"

"The VA."

"The VA Hospital?"

"Yeah, if you had a place to go, they'd furlough you out on the weekends. Me and Murray were psych patients at the VA."

"You and the doctor were both psych patients," I replied, my eyes rolling at this news.

"Yeah, he was a manic depressive, tried to kill himself with lithium. Not sure where he is nowadays."

"I can answer that for you. Murray Cook died in 1969 in New York City."

"I guess he finally did himself in."

"I don't know anything about the cause of death, just that he is in fact deceased. By the way, did Red Clarke work with you at the Red Ace service station?"

"Ha, he didn't do much work. He mostly bummed money off of his wife so he could go drinking. She was a schoolteacher. You know that lawyer of his should have gone for the insanity plea."

"Insanity plea for Clarke, why's that?" I asked.

"He was all the time picking up the phone and telling no one that he was Agent XY14 checking in for messages."

Thinking at any moment I might be asked to leave, I decided to push the Red Clarke button a bit more firmly and observe the response. "Well, he may have been crazy, but I don't think he shot that Herring girl."

"Somebody better go out to the cemetery and wake him up and tell him! That jury sure thought he did it. He went to prison for it. I know he drove that old black Cadillac that made a lot of noise and the neighbors heard it that night."

"No, Clarke didn't drive a Cadillac," I said.

"Oh, I thought he did."

"What if they convicted the wrong man?"

This comment was not well received. Henderson's thin body became tense, and his face reddened up by two shades of crimson. He was shaking a long finger in the direction of his feet as he spit out a reply: "I believe Booth shot Lincoln, Oswald shot Kennedy, and Red Clarke killed that girl."

This statement became the opening I had wanted from the start, so I continued my interrogation with a trick question to see how Henderson would respond: "What about that other man? The one you worked with at Red Ace, Sam Carlton?"

Henderson flung his soda can back to the floor, cursing at me as he did. "I don't know Sam Carlton. Why don't you get out of here?"

I replied with a soft, "Sorry to bother you, I'm leaving."

And without attempting to replace the chair in its original position, I stood up and backed my way out of the room, turning toward the front door. As I reached for the doorknob, Henderson's calm voice surprised me:

"You think she lived a while?"

I pulled my hand back from the doorknob in slow motion, and turned to the bedroom door, taking two slow steps as I thought about what seemed to be an important answer.

"Yeah, I do. I think she lived a while. What do you think?"

"Me, too."

"So, Jesse, how much time are you thinking?"

"I don't know, maybe a half-hour, maybe longer."

Two minutes later I was out of the apartment building and safely back in my car. My heart was racing and when I glanced in the rearview mirror my eyes looked like I had just exited a haunted house. I knew that I needed to make notes of the encounter with Jesse Henderson, so I grabbed a small notebook from the glove compartment and began writing down Jesse's comments, as well as the questions I was quickly formulating in my brain.

Notes from Jesse Henderson Interview:

- This old man seems to be serving out some kind of self-imposed prison sentence.
- Might have mental health issues, paranoid, schizophrenic, or ?
- Knows the details of the slaying as if he read the trial transcript this morning.
- Knows when Clarke got out of prison, how long he served, and that Clarke is dead.
- Could Jesse Henderson have killed Paula Herring?
- Could Jesse have been with Red Clarke when Paula Herring was killed?
- Who is BlueSky?

CHAPTER FIFTEEN

LAWYERS

The first big murder case in Metro Nashville's young life was, by all accounts, the babysitter murder involving eighteen-year-old Paula Herring. It was also one of the biggest cases handled by then thirty-one-year-old John Hollins, a blond assistant district attorney, whose good looks and stylish wardrobe made him the focus of much of the trial coverage from Jackson.

Known as "Big-un" by friends and family, the tall, large-framed Hollins wore designer sunglasses and smoked expensive cigars when walking the paparazzi-filled route between the Madison County Courthouse and the New Southern Hotel during Clarke's criminal trial. When the attorney general for Nashville, Harry Nichol, chose not to lead the case against John Randolph Clarke, "Big-un" was given the lead trial lawyer's role in Jackson. Hollins had been up to the task, obtaining a first-degree murder conviction against Clarke in five sensational days.[1]

Hollins certainly had earned his role in prosecuting the babysitter case, having graduated in the famous "Class of 1957" from Vanderbilt University Law School with Jim Neal. Neal went on to fame as the prosecutor of labor kingpin Jimmy Hoffa, and also of various Nixon officials in the Watergate scandal. Hollins worked as a Nashville prosecutor in 1961, followed by a stint as assistant district attorney when the new Metro government was formed, a position he held until 1969.[2]

Parlaying the babysitter murder conviction into even more success, Hollins already had switched to the other side of the aisle when he was retained to defend a local teenager named Jeffrey Womack, who had been formally and informally pursued for decades as the teenage killer of nine-year-old Marsha Trimble. Trimble had disappeared in late February 1975 while delivering Girl Scout cookies in an upper class neighborhood in Nashville. Though volunteers, psychics, and bloodhounds had searched in vain for the girl over a thirty-three day period, she was found on Easter Sunday morning in a garage 150 feet from her home, and was deemed to have been strangled to death weeks earlier.

John Hollins and his teenage client got the last word, however, when more than three decades later a convicted sex offender's DNA was perfectly matched to the samples retained from the Girl Scout's 1975 autopsy.[3] The real suspect in the Trimble murder was either ignored or unknown to authorities at the time, though he was discovered to have raped several women in the area in the months leading up to Marsha Trimble's slaying.

A few years later, in 2012, Hollins and Womack released a book describing the nightmarish experience of being suspect number one, while knowing he was innocent of killing his young neighbor. Even the former editor and publisher of the *Tennessean,* John Seigenthaler, took time to write a scathing foreword for the book, describing the shameful conduct of Metro authorities in pursuing the wrong suspect from the start.[4]

It wasn't long after this victory that I met with Hollins in his office high in the SunTrust Bank Building in downtown Nashville, where his personal career had morphed into a successful stint as a divorce attorney and matrimonial lawyer to the stars.[5]

When we met, the big man was impeccably dressed and more than eager to review one of the highlight cases of his career. We met in his private office, overlooking the city landscape, a power room filled with leather and wood and walls covered with letters of commendation and photographs of Hollins posing with some of America's famous citizens and politicians.

After shaking hands, but before I could sit down, the esteemed attorney surprised me with his opening statement: "You know, some people thought the mother did it!"

I nearly spilled my portfolio at this surprising comment but managed to position myself in a leather chair across from the attorney, as he sat down at his massive desk.

"I hadn't heard that," I replied.

Hollins didn't bother to respond but instead chose to begin speaking about his career while slowly turning the pages of a giant album filled with newspaper articles, headlines, and the journalistic record of his achievements. I began taking notes as he spoke and only interrupted with a few questions so as not to impede his free-flowing style.

He began the session by recounting his scholastic achievements at Vanderbilt University, talking about Phi Beta Kappa and mentioning his famous law school classmates by name, as well as regaling me with stories of his older brother's football prowess as an All-American quarterback for the Vanderbilt University Commodores. But moments later, he switched to the 1964 criminal trial:

"You've got to understand the ambience of the time. There was a great interest in the trial from the local people in and around Jackson, Tennessee. Lawyers and judges from all over the area were attending the courtroom sessions, even some appellate judges. And everyone was staying at the New Southern Hotel that week. It was the talk of the south. All of the witnesses, the lawyers, even the jurors were all in the same location. I remember Judge Taylor only had five days on his calendar where he could preside over the trial, and that's exactly how long it took us, five days."[6]

I initially interrupted the flow of information to ask how Hollins, and not Harry Nichol, the attorney general, had come to lead the prosecution's charge.

"I guess you could say I was his fair-haired boy. And the press noticed that I didn't lose any cases. We had a strong team with Howard Butler; Al Gore's uncle Whit LaFon from Jackson; and the attorney general from Jackson, David Murray. Judge Taylor ran the trial from nine in the morning until nine o'clock at night, and then, after hours, we interviewed witnesses. You have to understand that everyone in the hotel was involved in the trial."

"All work and no play?" I quizzed.

Hollins laughed a throaty chuckle. "Well, there was one of Jo Herring's friends, Evelyn Johnson, who tried to put the move on one of our investigators."

"How so?" I asked.

"As I remember it, someone had put her up to sneaking into the hotel room of George Currey, and then she got into his bed and wasn't wearing much except a negligee when he opened the door. He was definitely surprised and not very happy about it."

As he spoke, Hollins turned to a photograph in his album of a Tennessee Bureau of Investigation expert, and he chuckled as he remembered that it was the TBI guru who had brought a microscope to the courtroom to show the jurors the perfect match between the bullets pulled out of the den floor on Timberhill Drive and the Christmas Eve bullet dug out of the ground on 18th Avenue.[7]

"Judge Taylor didn't give Charlie Galbreath much room to present his theatrical skills. Charlie was a skilled actor and he did his best, but he didn't have very credible witnesses."

"It sure seemed like you had the strongest witnesses in the courtroom," I offered, while silently noting to myself that attempting to bring up the alternate theory that Paula Herring had been killed by an angry truck stop manager was probably a waste of time in the hallowed halls of this famous former prosecutor.

"Yes, we did. I remember A. J. Meadows Jr. was one of the witnesses. I attended Montgomery Bell Academy as a young boy, and I had gotten to know that jokester when he and I were teenagers and he was at Isaac Litton High School in East Nashville," he stated.

"No doubt that Clarke was guilty?" I questioned.

"That's right. When it was all said and done, this case was about a group of people who drank beer, and they moved around from tavern to tavern. They'd go from Ruth's Diner and then on to places like Brown's Diner and others. It was a drinking group; it wasn't about sex. They just liked to drink, and this Clarke fellow was one of them and he went out to see the girl's mother, and found the girl home instead."

"How about Jo Herring? What can you remember about her?" I asked.

"She wasn't unattractive, and she was likable. I think she got laid a lot, and she was certainly a part of the group that liked to drink. I suspect she also may have been an alcoholic." Hollins stopped turning pages, looked up at me, and then added, "I remember a rumor that the girl had bitten off her attacker's penis."

"Wherever did you hear that?" I inquired.

"I think I heard it from the grand jury foreman."

As Hollins continued his storytelling, I couldn't help but wonder how such a rumor could have started? Especially given that the only two people in the house immediately after the murder would have been the deceased victim and her sleepy brother. How would anyone know about a bitten penis? Was it left on the floor? Part of it? Did someone make a late night visit to an emergency room for assistance with what had to be an unusual wound? If the rumor were true, it would seem to create an easy verification process of "did he do it or did he not?"

A few moments later, as I was leaving Hollins's office, the big lawyer suggested that he would like to review the manuscript that might result from my research, prior to publication. It was a request that I politely declined, though I was certainly intrigued at his interest.

Approximately three-and-a-half years after John Randolph Clarke entered the state prison system in Nashville, he became eligible for transfer to the romantic but secluded town of Petros, Tennessee, near Frozen Head State Park and a few miles northwest of Oak Ridge, Tennessee. But Petros was not at all romantic for Clarke, as the little community was also home to a group of buildings referred to by locals as "Brushy."[8]

Brushy Mountain State Penitentiary was a notorious maximum security prison that would eventually become the home of James Earl Ray, who was convicted of slaying Martin Luther King Jr.[9] Brushy housed the worst of the worst, inmates whose sentences were often described in centuries rather than decades or years. It was not uncommon for a Brushy inmate to carry a prison sentence of two or three hundred years for their heinous crimes.

Clarke earned his transfer to Brushy while teaching in the Nashville prison's adult education program. While away from his cell, guards found that Clarke had hidden twenty-seven "pep pills" and a syringe in his locker. For this sin, he earned ten days in Brushy Mountain's solitary confinement and lost six months of honor time as well.

After ten days in a cell without light or heat, and nothing but a mattress on the floor and two buckets, one for water and one for bathroom needs, Clarke apparently became a changed man, and he was returned to his former cell in Nashville.

In February 1964, after his indictment by the grand jury for murder and rape, John Randolph Clarke needed money to retain legal counsel. His brother-in-law pledged personal property as collateral for Clarke's bail, but it didn't begin to cover the kind of funds needed to hire a top-notch defense attorney. Within forty-eight hours of being questioned all night by the police, Clarke met with one of the top attorneys in town, Jack Norman Sr., a legend in the Nashville legal community. But having no steady employment, nor the kind of assets needed to pay the best of the best, Clarke had to look for other options.

A review of Nashville's top lawyers in 1964 also would have included John J. Hooker Sr. Hooker and Norman were revered far and wide for holding juries and audiences spellbound with their courtroom oration. If Clarke could have retained either of these legal heavyweights, he might have won his freedom before ever stepping foot inside a courtroom, especially when the evidence against him appeared to be circumstantial. Jack Norman and John Hooker were just that good.

Not many hours after meeting with Jack Norman, Clarke retained Metro government's public defender, Charles Galbreath, as his criminal defense attorney.[10] But in March of 1964, Galbreath had other plans, and he gave up his public defender's role in order to represent Clarke as his private attorney for the princely sum of $10,000.[11] It was a fee roughly equivalent to two years' worth of salary for the average worker in 1964, and Clarke's family provided the funds.

What Clarke may not have realized was that, because of the sensational aspect of the trial, Charles Galbreath was going to make out like a king. Galbreath not only would be paid $10,000 from his client, but he also would be on the receiving end of more newspaper and television coverage than he could purchase in a lifetime. There would be no end to the number of reporters and journalists writing stories and seeking comment from the attorney representing such a cold-blooded killer as John Randolph Clarke. And for Galbreath, the press coverage would be completely free, though possibly at the expense of his client's reputation.

What Charles Galbreath may have lacked in oratory skills, at least in comparison to Jack Norman or John J. Hooker, he made up for in sheer flamboyance. As a trained actor who participated in local theater productions, Galbreath was a shrewd self-promoter; at times he more resembled a carnival barker and street corner huckster than a criminal defense attorney. Still, he was an effective counselor for his clients.

Galbreath, born and raised in Nashville during the Great Depression, graduated from East High School, served in the United States Marine Corps, and then attended Cumberland School of Law in Lebanon, Tennessee.

Through the decades, he had been a member of the Tennessee legislature, the first Metro public defender, an appellate judge, and host of numerous radio programs where callers could pose questions on the air related to matters of business and law. He also had seen more than one contempt of court citation, along with an arrest and jailing for arguing too vigorously with a local judge.

At one point during his tenure as a criminal court appeals judge, Galbreath had used his official State of Tennessee letterhead to send a much publicized and very risqué letter to *Hustler Magazine*'s Larry Flynt, applauding the publisher's work and offering his admiration for the magazine's content.[12] Not surprisingly, Larry Flynt published Galbreath's letter, and the conservative residents of Music City were less than impressed with Galbreath's antics. But Charles Galbreath was not concerned in the least. His letter writing was just another way to get free publicity and keep his name in the public eye.

In the summer of 1998, after the session with Hollins, I telephoned Charles Galbreath with a request to meet and discuss his former client, John Randolph Clarke. Galbreath agreed to the meeting and as follow up sent me a letter in reply. Using the formal stationery of his Capitol Hill office on Polk Avenue in Nashville and also his still-active law practice in the Stahlman Building downtown, the letter simply stated that the retired judge would attempt to find his files related to John Randolph Clarke. It was Galbreath's opinion that the research into the babysitter story was important work, and he would gladly hand over the files in an attempt to exonerate his deceased client.

The final paragraph of the letter mentioned that it was Galbreath's belief that the bloody man had taken refuge at the York Motel after the crime, and that appellate judge Thomas Shriver's opinion in the civil trial detailed "clear evidence establishing beyond a preponderance, that the truck stop manager was the bloody-faced man seen at the Krystal restaurant soon after the murder."[13]

Approximately two weeks later, I met Charles Galbreath at his ninth-floor office in the Stahlman Building in downtown Nashville. Until the Life and Casualty Tower was erected in 1957, the Stahlman Building held the record as Nashville's tallest skyscraper for almost fifty years. Skyscraper is a relative term, as the Stahlman had just twelve floors of office space on Union Street. The current towers dotting the landscape in downtown Nashville are more than triple its height.

During our session, Galbreath, with a full head of gray hair and a feisty demeanor, recounted his career as the first public defender in Metro Nashville history and how his office, which had consisted of a single attorney—himself—had been a former restroom in the Stahlman Building. When I inquired as to how he had been relegated to a restroom, his response was enlightening: "Mayor Briley hated me. He never wanted the office of public defender created in the first place," he said.[14]

When I inquired about his career in the Tennessee legislature, Galbreath described having seen the play *Inherit the Wind* in New York City. The play, a loose take on the Scopes Monkey Trial of the 1920s, had so moved Charles Galbreath that he worked to overturn the Tennessee law that had been used as a test case in the little town of Dayton. The actual case was *State of Tennessee v. John Thomas Scopes.* Scopes was a teacher and had offered to be arrested for promoting evolution instead of creation in the classroom in order to bring the issue to trial. The event was of such importance that it was the first trial in a United States courtroom to be broadcast over radio.

"I couldn't believe those stupid people and their belief in literal creation. When Scopes came to lecture at Vanderbilt in the late

1960s, I took him a framed copy of the bill that I had successfully sponsored to overturn the statute that had been used to convict him in 1925," Galbreath said.

On the topic of his former client John Clarke, Galbreath said that he had gotten to know Clarke through his work in local theater productions and that he had felt compelled to aid with John's defense. After Clarke's conviction in the criminal trial, Galbreath worked tirelessly—and some would also say profitably—to overturn the conviction.

"I only had two clients that were convicted that I knew were absolutely innocent of their charges. And I mean 'innocent,' as in they didn't do the crime. One was John Randolph Clarke and the other was a pharmacist here in Nashville," Galbreath recounted.

"I told everybody who would listen to me that I'd serve Clarke's time if he killed again, and I meant it, too. I never thought John hurt that girl. Never. He didn't have any scratches on him. I know that for a fact," he said.

"Mr. Galbreath, there was a rumor going around that the killer had been bitten by Paula Herring. And it was enough of a bite to leave a significant wound to his genitals. Did you hear that as well?" I asked.

"Oh, yes. W. B. Hogan and I had John drop his drawers down at the old Maxwell House Hotel, in the restroom, just to see if he was still intact. And he was. He didn't kill that Herring girl. I'd bet my house on that."

On a hot day in June 1998, I met for lunch at a Captain D's restaurant in West Nashville with attorney W. B. Hogan, and was surprised to learn how helpful and energetic a retired seventy-six-year-old could be on the topic of law and order during the early days of Metro Nashville. Hogan, a former Marine and a World War II veteran, had served his military time in the South Pacific for six years. He was balding, with only a little white hair. He wore wire-rimmed glasses, was tall and physically fit, and offered a strong handshake as we sat down to lunch. After offering the reason for my interest in the babysitter case, I quickly moved to the question of Sam Carlton's potential involvement in the Paula Herring murder. Hogan didn't hesitate to put things in perspective for me:

"I think his own wife may have thought he was guilty. Just my opinion of it. During the trial over the reward money, Carlton's wife sat in the back of the courtroom with another woman, and then later during a recess, there was a commotion out in the hallway and she was reading him the riot act. I was there. I remember it happening."[15]

With this startling bit of news being delivered before I could even take my first bite of food, I felt the painful realization that, once again, another insider was completely convinced that someone other than John Randolph Clarke had killed Paula Herring. W. B. Hogan had my attention. When asked how Henry King's involvement had come into play for the reward money, Hogan said that Henry had called him up and said that he saw Sam Carlton at the restaurant on the night of Paula Herring's murder. He thought Henry was going to come forward anyway, no matter the reward incentive.

"So you interviewed Sam Carlton before you ever put him on the witness stand?" I asked.

"Oh, yes. Charlie Galbreath and I went down to First Avenue, to the Red Ace truck stop where Sam worked, and interviewed him in the back of the shop, in a storage room. Me and Charlie were both former Marines, but Carlton was a big sucker. He had these big, rough hands, and he sat there on a crate and rubbed them together a lot while we interviewed him. I knew there was something wrong with him, but we couldn't get the district attorney to move on it at all. They didn't want to hear about it. In their minds, since the jury said Clarke was guilty, they didn't want to hear about anyone else."

"So you thought he did it? Killed the girl?" I asked.

"My opinion has always been that Carlton either did it or he knew something about it. I always thought he knew the girl's mother. She was a nurse. Is she still living? And where's Sam Carlton today?" Hogan inquired.

"No, Paula's mother died about a dozen years after the murder. And Carlton died in 1987 of a heart attack," I said.

Hogan was undeterred at this news. "Sam had that old automobile that made a noise and people heard him drive away that night. He gave it to that professional wrestler, the Belkas fellow," he noted.

As the lunch traffic picked up, customers started sitting at the tables nearby, and I began to wonder if our topic of conversation might ruin the appetite of the diners closest to us.

"Charlie Galbreath and I went up to Kingsport, Tennessee, and took a deposition from that wrestler, Belkas. Charlie was a notary, so the paperwork was good. And both the wrestler and his wife thought Sam had something to do with the girl's murder. Sam hung around wrestlers a lot," Hogan said.

At this point, I mentioned my theory of identifying Paula Herring's killer by verifying the rumor that was being spread after the slaying.

Hogan took a long sip of iced tea, and then said, "Oh, the one where the dead girl was supposed to have bitten off a penis?"

"Yes, that's the one," I replied.

"At the time, they said she bit it totally off. So how would you go about confirming that rumor?"

"I was thinking about just asking Sam Carlton's widow if Sam maybe had an injury to his uh, 'member' after that Saturday night. But I haven't had the courage to do that yet."

Hogan didn't hesitate. "Why not? I'll talk to her. She'd probably tell you all about him. Remember, surprise is your best offense. Just knock on the door. 'Are you Sam Carlton's widow? I'd like to talk to you,' simple as that. We can go see her today if you want to. I'd be happy to help you. I don't have a lot to do these days, and it would be good for me to help out on something like this."

I responded that the offer was a gracious one, but I hadn't thought about hiring an attorney to help with the research. Hogan noted that he would help out with the conversation with Sam Carlton's widow for no other reason than to know, once and for all, if Sam Carlton had killed the Herring girl. Moments later, W. B. Hogan and I made a quick plan to meet up again the following week and go knock on the widow's door. Two days before the planned visit, the old lawyer was mentioned in the morning newspaper. Unfortunately, he was mentioned in the obituary list. W. B. Hogan was dead.

✧✧✧

If only to honor W. B. Hogan's planned visit with Sam Carlton's wife, it was with much trepidation that I found myself waiting for the bloody man's widow at a restaurant a short distance from the Herring home on Timberhill Drive. I had not suggested my preferred meeting location, a certain Krystal hamburger restaurant on nearby Franklin Road.

The bloody man's widow had volunteered to meet me for a cup of coffee at 10:00 a.m., and I decided that she must have had at least some level of suspicion about my interest, only because there was no sane explanation as to why an elderly woman would want to meet a complete stranger at a local restaurant to discuss her deceased husband's truck stop career.

Sitting at a table positioned near the entrance of the restaurant, I was surprised to see not one, but two women entering the establishment with a look on their faces that said they weren't interested in seeing a menu. The older woman, in her early seventies I surmised, was of medium build and wearing a comfortable one-piece dress with short sleeves. Her hair was gray and mostly pushed behind her ears and away from her face. In her right hand, carried loosely at her side, appeared to be a large picture frame. Our eyes met as I stood to greet her. The widow then introduced me to the younger woman, who turned out to be her oldest daughter, Deborah. I guessed mid-forties for her age. Deborah was tall, curvaceous, and yet powerfully built. She had shoulder-length blond hair and was wearing a polo shirt and blue jeans.

"Thank you for taking the time to meet with me," I offered, in my most soothing "I come here in peace" voice. "Please have a seat. How about some coffee, or something cold to drink?" As I inquired about the coffee, a friendly waitress wearing a white apron and carrying an order pad appeared at our table and offered assistance. One glass of ice water, and two glasses of iced-tea were selected. Both women were seated opposite me, with the older woman directly across from me and Deborah sitting to her mother's left, next to the restaurant's front window.

"Now tell me again why you wanted to meet me? I was trying to explain it to Deborah, and she was curious about you."[16]

As my gaze met Deborah's, I decided it would be a very good time to calculate the number of steps from my chair to the front door and whether I was still fast enough to sprint to my car and drive away before being chased down by my dining companions.

"Ah, yes, ma'am. The reason for my call was that I'm interested in the Red Ace gasoline company. I'm working on some stories from Nashville that took place back in the 1960s, and a couple of former Red Ace employees mentioned Mr. Sam Carlton to me."

As soon as I spoke, Mrs. Carlton reached for the framed photo and presented it to me. The photograph turned out to be a framed certificate of appreciation from the Red Ace gasoline company to the big bloody man himself, Sam Carlton.

"Clearly, he played a major role in the Red Ace gasoline business through the sixties, maybe longer," I offered. "And if I understand the history correctly, back in the pre-interstate days just about every truck traveling through Nashville had to come through First Avenue right past the place where your husband was working. Does that sound about right?"

This early conversational tactic appeared to be successful. I could see a bit of relaxation in their jawlines, and the shift in body language was in my favor. *There's no way you're going to be asking the "bitten" question,* I told myself, *absolutely no way.*

For the next few minutes, we talked of the fuel company, the owner's family, and his affection for "Big Sam." And according to the widow, Sam Carlton had practically mentored the young business owner on the more practical aspects of the fuel distribution business. After a few more minutes passed, I decided to venture toward the dark side.

"Well, I don't know how to bring up this next topic, so let me just say that I will share with you how I stumbled upon it, and I can share an update with you that may be of interest."

As my words filled the air, both women shifted their position as if this were the bad mojo they had been expecting. Deborah took a long sip of her drink and gazed out the window. Her mother looked down at her own glass, avoiding direct eye contact with me.

So I began by explaining how I had found the Paula Herring documents, and then mustering a bit of courage, I offered that it appeared to me that Sam Carlton possibly had been setup in an initial attempt to make him the patsy in the murder of an eighteen-year-old. Deborah was the first to speak, and she surprised me when she said that she remembered the night of the Herring girl's murder.

"How is it that you remember so clearly?"

"I was babysitting my younger brothers," she said.[17]

"Really? Another babysitter," I muttered.

And then she looked at her mother and said, "And because I remember that you and daddy went out to dinner that night and then came home early, a lot earlier than I was expecting, and he got a phone call from some woman and had to go right back out after ya'll got home."

I looked at Mrs. Carlton for a response, and her facial expression was troubling. Her nostrils flared for a brief moment, but then she regained her composure long enough to utter words that I hadn't expected to hear:

"I know where he went that night, and that's all that matters."

The widow's eyes narrowed to a laser focus, and, as her words filled the air, she slowly moved her right arm across the table top and clamped a hand firmly on Deborah's forearm. The message was crystal clear, and Deborah didn't offer another sound, but the widow wasn't finished.

"Is that what you're going to write? You're going to put my husband in the middle of this story just like they did back then? Is that what you're going to do?"

For the next several minutes, I attempted to describe a ream of information pointing to what I believed to be an accurate assessment of Sam's appearance at the Krystal hamburger restaurant on the night of the slaying. But the widow was not to be persuaded, and after a few more uncomfortable moments she and her daughter left the restaurant.

CHAPTER SIXTEEN

AUTOPSY REPORT

Among the list of character witnesses in the trial of John Randolph Clarke, I found his personal physician, Dr. Ed Tarpley. It didn't take me long to locate the aged physician and I invited him to lunch at a restaurant near his home, a location across from Saint Thomas Hospital on Harding Road.

At noon, I found myself seated at a small table mid-restaurant, opposite an older gentlemen dressed in a plaid sports jacket, white shirt, and wire-rimmed glasses. Before he sat down, I guessed the height of his slight frame at five-foot-six, and he didn't look like much of an eater. Given his thin frame, I thought he might sip a cup of coffee or, at most, indulge in a bowl of soup. After the introduction, Dr. Tarpley made a quick glance at the menu, placed an order with the waitress, and, over the next hour, downed a salad that would have fed two hungry people, along with a large sandwich and an ample portion of fries.[1]

"So, Dr. Tarpley, you're retired?"

"Oh, heavens, no. I still do physicals for the local military inductees."

Tarpley was curious as to my interest in his friend John Randolph Clarke. The aged doctor proffered that Callie Clarke was a delightful person who simply loved John as he was. "She didn't try to remake him or anything like that. I think if she were here, she'd tell you that John was a teenager in a forty-year-old man's body."

According to the elderly physician, Callie Clarke had a graduate degree in education and was working toward a doctorate at the time of her husband's unfortunate arrest.

"You spent time socially with John and Callie Clarke?" I asked.

"Yes, from time to time we played bridge with them and also with another physician friend and his wife."

Wanting to bear down on the main topic I had in mind, I asked whether or not John Clarke had been bitten during the melee on Timberhill Drive, especially given that Clarke had admitted to seeing his physician within hours of the murder, and that multiple trial attorneys had offered up the "he was bitten" story.

If John Clarke had been bitten, or worse, I was hoping that Dr. Tarpley would be willing to share that information with me. Could Tarpley have some exculpatory information available? Maybe there was an internal need to release some long-held evidence against his friend? Perhaps he had held Clarke's wife, Callie, in such high regard that he hadn't wanted to embarrass her in 1964, and he instead had used the doctor-patient privilege to hold onto some less than flattering information regarding his infamous client? Perhaps the good doctor was simply doing the math in his head to ensure that whatever he might have said in 1964 wasn't putting him in jeopardy of a perjury charge decades later?

"Dr. Tarpley, there's a rumor that I recently heard related to the Paula Herring case, and that was that the killer had been bitten by the victim."

"Bitten? How so?"

"Well, as the story goes, Paula Herring had bitten her assailant and inflicted such damage that she may have bitten off his member."

"I never heard that."

"So part of the reason I wanted to meet you is to ask about John Clarke's visit with you, just hours after Paula Herring's murder, on the Monday after the weekend slaying. Monday, February 24, 1964. I know that was a long time ago."

"Oh, no. I remember it. John had a bad heart. So did Callie. Both were under my care. He came to me after that weekend, when the Herring girl was killed, very agitated as I remember it," the doctor noted.

"Was he injured? Did he complain of anything related to a potential bite or other injury, perhaps?" I asked.

"No, not at all. He wasn't injured in any way. He was just agitated, and his blood pressure and heart were the only problems."

"I read somewhere that he had blackout spells?"

"That was an occasional symptom, yes. When I saw him on that Monday, I had prescribed some sedatives to calm him down. He was emotionally upset, with a rapid heartbeat."

"And the blackout spells, perhaps a war-related injury?" I asked.

"No, cardiac related."

"You testified that you saw him again the morning after his all-night interrogation?"

"Yes, and he was very agitated and fatigued."

"Just curious—was the Monday morning visit to you already scheduled or something that John Clarke requested on the fly?"

"He called me. It wasn't a regular checkup. Seems like it was Tuesday after his all-night trip to the police station I put him in Parkview Hospital for a few days. After word leaked out in the newspaper that he was the primary suspect in the Herring girl's death, the head of staff at the hospital called me and said, 'This man is wanted for murder, get him out of the hospital.' And I said, 'Well, he's my patient.' Then the chief of police and one of the newsmen wanted to know if I would release John from the hospital. They wanted him. I said, 'You've certainly got enough police to take him, why don't you just go right on in and do that?' But they backed off. They had those large searchlights parked right in front of the hospital, I remember that."

"And the newspapers reported that John Clarke soon left Parkview and then was transferred to the old Nashville General Hospital, does that sound correct?" I asked.

"Yes, and from there he went over to Vanderbilt for some brain tests to see if we could uncover the reason for the seizures."

"I know he went back to General Hospital after the testing at Vanderbilt because that's where the police served him with the warrant for murder and attempted rape. How did the hospitalization turn out for your patient?"

"I told him he was going to need a pacemaker and, sadly, I was correct. He ultimately died of a coronary while mowing the yard."

"And his wife?" I inquired.

"Callie took John a basket of food every week to the prison. She never believed he killed that girl, nor did any of his family believe it either."

"I saw that you may have testified at the trial in Jackson, Tennessee? At least you were subpoenaed, right?"

"Yes. I said I had no knowledge of this affair. I remember the lawyer for John demanded $10,000 in advance. They had to mortgage their house and borrow from family to pay the fee."

"You don't see John Clarke as having committed this murder?"

"Oh, definitely not," the physician replied.

"The victim's mother was a nurse. Did you know Jo Herring?" I asked.

"No. John was stupid. He brought a lot of this on himself."

"You mean seeing other women while married to Callie?"

"Yes, and playing around with the mother and daughter."

Time stood still and all restaurant conversation came to a screeching halt, at least in my mind.

"Excuse me?"

"He was seeing the mother *and* the daughter."

"I hadn't heard that story. That would be unusual, don't you think? You mean John Clarke was having sex with both mother and daughter. That's hard for me to believe," I responded.

"That was the story I heard at the time."

"Do you remember how you came to hear that information, perhaps directly through John Clarke or his wife?"

"No. It wasn't through either of them. But it was what I heard, perhaps through one of the defense attorneys. That, I don't remember."

"Mother and daughter, that's amazing," I responded.

I kept wondering about the early newspaper reporting of three gunshot wounds at the time of Paula's murder and then only two gunshot wounds being noted on the witness stand in September of 1964. The photographs that Hubert Kemp had retained were in agreement with the three-shot theory. Those photographs were taken with a purpose in mind, to show, in tragic black and white, that Paula Herring had been shot exactly three times. The investigating officers in the photograph were each pointing at the wounds on Paula's body and flashing a "three" sign with their fingers. It made me wonder what was so important to them that they needed to show solidarity regarding their theory of the crime. And it appeared that they wanted photographic evidence for backup.

But when the Nashville medical examiner, old Dr. Core, was on the witness stand, he only spoke of the two gunshot wounds in Paula's back. The front collarbone wound never came up for discussion, though it had clearly been mentioned in the initial newspaper stories. Perhaps Dr. Core had focused on the two gunshots in the back that had ended Paula's life and simply chose not to dwell on the other one.

More disturbing to me was a conversation I had had with a former police lieutenant, who informed me that no autopsy had been needed for Paula Herring because they knew that two gunshots through the heart had killed her.[2]

On the topic of what an autopsy might have revealed, I knew that Paula Herring would have been weighed, measured, and inspected for scars and wounds. Hair and nail samples would have been taken from her, and evidence of any gun powder residue could have been noted, if, for example, Paula had fired a gun while defending herself during the attack.

All of her organs would have been removed, weighed, and then examined. Tissue samples would have been taken and notes made about the contents of her stomach, as well as body fluids tested to determine if any drugs or infection were present.

The deliberate skipping of Paula's autopsy made me wonder if someone was concerned that it might reveal a surprise. Not having a handy rolodex of forensic experts on hand, I felt emboldened enough to call the man described by many as the world's leading forensic expert, the legendary Dr. Henry C. Lee.

When Henry Lee wasn't being retained for high-profile criminal cases, such as the O. J. Simpson trial in Los Angeles, the Martha Moxley murder case in Greenwich, Connecticut, or the JonBenét Ramsey case in Boulder, Colorado, he was busy at the Henry C. Lee Institute of Forensic Science at the University of New Haven, Connecticut. The new institute had been in business only a handful of years when I attempted to contact the famous forensic expert.

After an email and a couple of phone calls to Connecticut, I was routed to Dr. Al Harper, the executive director of the institute. After expressing my desire to reach the famous physician, Dr. Harper explained to me that Henry Lee had earned a PhD in Biochemistry from New York University and was not a medical doctor, and that Lee's schedule of work, other than a few events per year at the institute, found him all over the globe.[3]

With this news, and as concisely as I could manage, I attempted to describe my situation, noting the fact that I had copies of photographs from a crime scene, as well as photographs of the victim, and that I did not understand what I was seeing. I made it clear that I wasn't attempting to exonerate the defendant, John Randolph Clarke, but instead I was completely focused on unraveling the truth, and I believed that the crime-scene photographs could point me in that direction.

I don't know if it was the helplessness in my voice or simply the heartbreaking aspect of a six-year-old boy sleeping through his sister's murder that caused Dr. Harper to offer assistance. Perhaps it was my mention that J. Edgar Hoover had been involved in the case and that the case was tied to the birth of Metro Nashville in the 1960s that elicited Harper's response. To his great credit, he said he would review in confidence anything I sent to the Henry Lee Institute.

Not wanting to send my only copies of the photographs, I made another trek to the print shop in Green Hills. I spent the first few moments of my visit getting instructions on using a high-resolution scanner to capture and copy the extremely graphic crime-scene photographs onto a CD that I could mail to Dr. Harper. I got more than a few wide-eyed looks from the technician who assisted me, and I had to offer a detailed explanation of the images and ask that they be erased from any hard drive when I finished my scanning work. I got no argument on this latter point.

Many months passed before I would learn of the results from Dr. Harper's review. One of his graduate students had initially made a first pass at the photographs in the summer of 2004, but then the student had taken a job at another university and the files were ultimately determined to have been lost in the move. So I repeated the process of creating a CD and resent it to Dr. Harper. In late October of 2005, I was scheduled to attend a meeting at Yale University in New Haven, which by car was less than ten minutes from the University of New Haven, and Dr. Harper graciously invited me to visit with him about the Herring case.

Harper, with doctoral degrees in forensic anthropology as well as law, was a most gracious host when I arrived at Dodds Hall and found his office on the fourth floor of the red-brick building. The big man, with his salt-and-pepper beard, receding hairline, and wire-rimmed glasses, was eager to discuss the particulars of his initial review, and, after I took a seat opposite him, he got right to the point.

"I can't speak to the sequence of the gunshot wounds, but I can confirm that there is one entry wound in the upper shoulder near the victim's collarbone area, and two gunshot entry wounds in her back."[4]

"No question about those?"

"None; they are all classic gunshot entry wounds. Do you have a theory as to why they didn't mention all three gunshots at the criminal trial?"

"I'm not sure, unless someone thought that maybe two different guns were involved in the girl's murder and they wanted to hide the trail to the owner of one of them. It's just a random theory on my part and most likely a wrong one."

A smile crossed Harper's face as he asked his next question: "Do you know where any of the bullets are being kept at this point in time? I see two exit wounds on the front of the girl's chest, but no exit wound on her back where the front collarbone shot might have ended up."

"Yes, I do. The two bullets fired into her back are stored in evidence with the exhibits from the criminal trial in Tennessee. Why do you ask?"

"We can easily discover if two different guns were involved in the shooting. We'd need a funeral home, and a ballistics expert at some point, and either a family member to approve the exhumation or a court order to let us proceed."

"Proceed?"

"We'd dig her up. I'd fly to Tennessee with the current chief medical examiner for Connecticut. He's a friend of mine and a colleague. We could fly in on a Friday, exhume the body, conduct the autopsy on Saturday, and fly out on Sunday. We would likely find a third bullet near the victim's spine, or perhaps in the bottom of the casket."

"I certainly hadn't thought of that option."

"You understand there would still be significant expense. You'd have to pay for an exhumation, and pay the funeral home for a place to do the work, and then pay for the reburial. The ballistics analysis would likely run a few hundred dollars as well. If you can get us there, and provide the hotel rooms, and maybe some good bourbon, it would be fun to try to unravel the mystery."

"It's a lot to think about, and a very gracious offer. While I'm thinking, may I pose another question to you?"

"Please do."

"If the victim were shot in the collarbone area first, how long could she live until the two shots in the back were fired into her?"

Harper gazed at the doorway a moment and then turned his eyes toward me. "Young people can exhibit an unusual ability to hang on. Not knowing for certain the trajectory of the bullet, this girl could have survived a half hour, perhaps much longer. It all depends."

"Thank you, Dr. Harper."

PART III

TRUE DETECTIVE

Just find who did this.

—Jo Herring

CHAPTER SEVENTEEN

GIRL NEXT DOOR

In November 2005, a few weeks after the visit with Dr. Al Harper, my wife and I went out to dinner with some friends who lived across town from us. We decided to meet in the Cool Springs area south of Nashville, at one of the easy-to-find restaurants convenient for both couples. My wife and I had not seen Steve or Becky Brewer in a long time, and there was a history between Steve and myself that went back to 1986. Steve had been a company officer at a large corporation when he walked into the computer business where I worked to explore using a personal computers as part of their network. My role in the project was to coordinate our technical resources to prove the concept and deliver the computers needed through our distribution channel. It was during this informal business partnership that I had eventually gotten to know Steve's wife, Becky, who worked as an officer for a small regional bank.

I was looking forward to reconnecting with Steve and Becky, in part, because for some time I had been attempting to avoid the obvious fact that the Paula Herring research project was near the end. With W. B. Hogan's death, and the puzzling comments of Dr. Ed Tarpley, combined with the potential cost of an exhumation that might be fruitless, it felt like there was nothing else to be gained from continuing down the same path. It was a painful reminder that I was on the verge of failing in my quest. Thus, the promise of seeing old friends felt like an excellent alternative to a decision I had been avoiding for weeks.

After the requisite hugs and greetings, we settled into our table at a large log cabin–style restaurant, built to mimic a Rocky Mountain hunting lodge with all of the typical adornments—moose and elk heads, giant trout, salmon, and walleye mounted throughout the restaurant. We hadn't gotten too far on the theme of "What's new with you?" when my wife offered the news that I had been working on a research project for a rather long time. I attempted to downplay it, saying it was an old story from early Nashville Metro history. When quizzed about the subject matter, I muttered a few words about it being a murder that had taken place in Nashville back in the sixties, a babysitter who had been killed in the Crieve Hall area on a Saturday night in February 1964. My wife offered up the victim's name, and the next words I heard came from the mouth of Becky.:

"She was my next door neighbor."[1]

"Huh?" I astutely replied.

"Paula Herring. She was my next-door neighbor. We were good friends. She and her little brother practically grew up with us. She went to Overton High School, and we lived next to each other."

I was silent for a moment, but then quickly decided it was all a clever trick. So I turned to my wife and said, "Nice setup, very funny. You guys are good, but that's not possible."

Becky leaned in with a somber, sober expression and slowly said again, "Paula Herring was our neighbor on Timberhill Drive. Our houses were literally next door to each other."

My head felt like it was being overwhelmed with images, sound clips, bits of legal transcript flying by, while I silently made a mad attempt at making order out of chaos and correlating the history and facts that I knew. I didn't say anything for a full minute, as I sat blank faced.

"You're not old enough," was my first response. I wasn't attempting to flatter her, but I didn't see how Becky could make the cut, age wise. She looked far too young for that to be possible.

"Yes, I am," came the soft reply.

I looked at Steve. "You're in on this? A group prank, right?"

"Oh, no. I grew up in East Tennessee. Don't look at me, I don't know this story."

I turned back to Becky with what must have been an incredulous look on my face. "You were Paula's next-door neighbor? Did you go to the funeral?"

"Yes, it was awful."

Becky's expression appeared to be genuine. There wasn't any duping delight in evidence.

I said, "I've known you both for dozen years, and now this news?"

I took a long sip of iced tea and then shifted into interview mode. "At the murder trial, Paula's mother said that Paula's cab fare was paid by a neighbor when she came home from Knoxville the Friday night before she was murdered. Was she talking about your mother?"

"Yes. Paula was always out of money."

"Okay, no offense, I don't believe you but I think I might believe you." At this point, my wife offered up that I had been seriously invested in the project for some time.

Becky offered the next obvious question: "Why are you doing this? Why are you researching Paula's murder?"

I settled in for a long meal and began to unwind the story thread. After a couple of hours, and the eventual goodbyes, I promised to call Becky later in the week to finish our discussion.

As my wife and I drove home after dinner, she posed a simple question to me: "How much longer?"

"I don't understand the question."

"How much longer until you're finished with Paula Herring? You've been doing this almost as long as we've been married, did you realize that?"

I was silent for a few moments, and then offered the most honest answer I could muster: "I don't know. I don't think I will let it go until I get to the truth, and based on the dinner conversation you just witnessed, I don't think I'm there yet."

Not surprisingly, the rest of the trip home was a silent one.

The next morning, I made a phone call to Becky Brewer, and we picked up where we'd left off the previous evening:[2]

Becky: I haven't had anyone to talk to about this.

Me: Why is that?

Becky: I wasn't home the weekend that Paula was killed. I flew to Daytona to watch the race.

Me: A race in February; you mean the Daytona 500?

Becky: Yes. My dad was involved with the Nashville racetrack back then, and he loved racing. I left on Friday afternoon to go to Daytona, not realizing that Paula was coming home that same afternoon.

Me: At the trial, Jo Herring said that Paula went next door to visit with you that Friday night?

Becky: That's not true. I wasn't at home. In fact, I always felt it was my fault for not being home, because earlier in the week I told Paula that I would be. I heard the news on the radio late at night, on Sunday night, while riding in a car back to Nashville. I couldn't believe it.

Me: You knew Paula pretty well?

Becky: Sure. We'd sit in Alan's inflatable pool in the backyard and hang out when it was hot. That's when we worked on Paula's hair, during that summer before she was killed.

Me: I don't understand.

Becky: I was into makeup. My mother had done some modeling work, and Paula didn't have much interest in the makeup routine. She was really into basketball and sports, but we made Paula's hair lighter and blonder. My mom thought it looked great, and she egged it on.

Me: Did your mom have anything to say about the murder?

Becky: My mother helped babysit Alan the night of the murder and that Paula might have been hit with a bowling trophy.

Me: I know there were some trophies in the house; I suppose it was possible. So you were doing a lot of dating, and Paula not so much?

Becky: Yes. In fact, you remember Gregg Allman? Carol Blake and I were dating him when he was in town. He went to Castle Heights Military School as a kid, the school in Lebanon, Tennessee.[3]

Me: Gregg Allman, as in the Allman Brothers Band? The guy who was once upon a time married to Cher? That Gregg Allman?

Becky: Yes, he and his brother Duane were born here, and after they moved to Daytona Beach they'd come home during the summers to stay with their uncle. In fact, one of the uncles was a Metro cop. They used to play some of the dances around town back then, when they were teenagers and known as the Allman Joys.[4]

Me: America's biggest small town. I can just see me asking Gregg Allman and his uncle about the Paula Herring murder. On a different topic, any chance the Herrings had more than one car? Maybe Paula had a car in Knoxville at school?

Becky: No. They just had one car, the Ford.

Me: Any chance your mom was not home at the actual time of the murder?

Becky: She was not. I was returning from the Daytona stock car race with my dad, and my mother was in Waverly, Tennessee, visiting family until late Saturday night.

Me: What do you remember about Paula, personality-wise?

Becky: Paula had a temper. She did not like her mother's friends and could have or would have mouthed off to them. Paula was mostly embarrassed about her mother, especially the drinking.

Me: Did your family keep up with Jo Herring after Paula's murder?

Becky: No, after Paula's death, we moved out of the area pretty quickly.

CHAPTER EIGHTEEN

VANDY KIDS

Remembering my troubling correspondence with two of Paula Herring's dorm mates, I realized I had made a pivotal mistake while researching the babysitter story. In rereading the criminal trial testimony, I found where one of the detectives had stated that his team followed the time-honored tradition of starting with the victim, then investigating the victim's family, then family friends, etc., essentially working the circle outward from the victim. And I had spent countless hours unaware of this process and looking at random suspects instead.

When I reviewed my notes, I found that one of the Nashville television stations had reported that Metro police arrested a couple of Vanderbilt University students on suspicion of murdering Paula Herring and that they also had retrieved a gun and processed it for comparison to the slugs found at the scene. But, curiously, they released the Vanderbilt students a few hours later. After going back through the trial testimony, I found mention of a student named Jerome Shepherd as being one of those who had been arrested and released. Perhaps there was more to discover on this topic.

My research into the Vandy students led me to some illustrious fraternity brethren, a prestigious group known as the "Dekes."[1] In 1962, the president of the fraternity was Andrew Lamar Alexander, who would later serve as governor and senator of Tennessee, United States secretary of education, and president of the University of Tennessee. Secretary of the fraternity was future bestselling author and comic Roy Blount Jr. Blount was senior editor of the Vanderbilt student newspaper, *The Hustler*. It was an impressive group, and Jerome was one of their own.

A brief conversation with the registrar's office took my breath away when they confirmed that Shepherd had been enrolled at Vanderbilt University from the fall of 1961 through the fall of 1963 but then had dropped out of school on February 29, 1964, one week after the murder. Based on the knowledge that several of the fraternity members had eventually gone to law school, I called the Tennessee Bar Association to see if Jerome might have followed the law as a profession after his arrest in February 1964.[2]

The man who answered the phone delivered the news that Jerome Shepherd had received his law degree from Emory University. The helpful clerk also said that I should be able to find Shepherd practicing law in a sleepy little town within an hour's drive of Knoxville.

A few days later, I was returning from East Tennessee and made a lunchtime stop in a small town southwest of Knoxville and north of the Georgia state line. The setting was idyllic and supremely Southern. Two blocks from a small private university, I found the address of Jerome Shepherd's law practice. It was a 1950s-style bungalow home with established shrubs, a small front yard, and giant oak trees.

The side yard had been turned into a parking lot, and I could see one sedan parked under a tree. Given that it was lunchtime, I thought it possible that the office was closed and no one was at home. But I was wrong.

I grabbed my leather portfolio and made my way up the steps to the front door. Out of habit, I knocked, and I heard a young woman's voice telling me to come in.

To my surprise, a thirty-something receptionist was working with a stack of papers at her desk. She appeared to be a paralegal. Inside the house, the front room had been turned into a waiting area, and the bedrooms in the back appeared to be the law offices for Jerome and anyone else he might have working for him.

"Hi, how can we help you? Do you have an appointment?"

"Oh, no, ma'am, actually I'm just dropping by to meet Mr. Shepherd. I wasn't sure if this was the law office of the Jerome Shepherd that might have attended Vanderbilt University back in the sixties?"

"Yes, that's him. He should be back any minute now. He went to grab a sandwich. How do you two know each other?"

I smiled and chuckled at her question as I stood in the middle of the waiting room.

"Well, this will sound a little odd, but maybe not so much given that this is a law office. I want to ask him about an event that took place back in February 1964 when he was a student at Vanderbilt University."

The paralegal dropped her paperwork and looked directly at me. "He won't stop talking about it. I bet I've heard that story a dozen times since I started working here."

My mouth must have been open down to my knees, but I was able to squeak out a few words: "Are you talking about him being arrested on a Saturday night in Nashville?"

"That's the story! I'm not kidding; I've heard it at least a dozen times right here in this office."

As her words echoed in my ears, out of the corner of my eye I saw movement on the front lawn, and I turned to see a well-dressed man making his way up the front steps, carrying a sandwich bag in one hand and a bottle of water in the other.

"There he is. He can tell you all about it."

I smiled at the man entering the front door of the Craftsman home. Shepherd was wearing a white starched shirt with loosened tie and gray suit slacks. His frame was medium build, just under six feet tall, and he had wire-rimmed glasses and thinning, gray hair. He offered a friendly "Hey, how are you?" upon opening the door, and raised both hands to announce, "Lunch." I laughed and had an immediate good vibe. Jerome's receptionist did the introductions and then spilled the beans. "Mr. Bishop is from Nashville, and he wants to hear you tell that Vanderbilt story about the night you were arrested in Nashville in the 1960s."

Shepherd looked at me and smiled a puzzled smile. "Is that right? Do we know each other?"[3]

I laughed. "She's right. I did drop by just to hear about that night. But there's more that I should add about my motivation. I'm, uh, how shall I say this? I'm researching an old murder case that took place on a Saturday night in Nashville, Tennessee. It was on the very weekend that you were arrested, February 22, 1964."

Jerome looked at his paralegal.

"Do I have any appointments this afternoon?"

"Not a one. You've got a clean slate until your dinner meeting," she replied.

At this news, the lawyer waved me toward an adjoining room. "This should be the most interesting meeting I've had in a long time."

"I wouldn't argue with that," I replied.

As he sat down at his desk and further loosened his tie, I took a seat opposite him and settled in for what I hoped would be an enlightening conversation.

"You want something to drink or perhaps part of this wonderful fast food lunch?"

"Oh, thank you, no, I ate earlier."

As he took a long sip of his drink, he pulled a sandwich from the paper sack. "So, I take it you're a private investigator working for a family member perhaps?"

"That would be an obvious guess, and a good one as well, but no, I'm actually a private citizen living in Nashville, who stumbled upon some information in a file that makes me think the babysitter murder case may have ended in a wrongful conviction. I'm not certain, but I'm leaning that way."

"So, you're a lawyer?"

"Maybe I should have been, but, no, I'm just a salesman, as they say. I work in the technology and healthcare sector." What I didn't offer was that my interviewing skills, thanks to the Paula Herring project, were beginning to improve, a definite side benefit to my sales career when meeting with strangers, prospects, and clients. It allowed me to quickly read body language, watch for microexpressions that might indicate deception, and analyze any words coming my way as if I were reading them off of a teletype machine. But I kept these new skills close and never let on the amount of analysis taking place behind the pleasant smile and calm facial expression that I was transmitting to the person on the other side of the desk.

After taking the next few minutes to walk through the background of how I had happened to find my way into a law office in East Tennessee on this day, Jerome released a long, low whistle.

"You know, not many people do what you're doing."

"I know."

"Well, let me tell you about that Saturday night, and then we'll see how this compares with what you know; does that work for you?"

"Certainly."

About to take another bite of his sandwich, he paused. "Oh, wait a minute. Are you here because you're looking at me as a suspect in the murder?"

"No, no, I'm sorry I didn't make that clear up front," I said.

He laughed and said, "Well, that's a relief. Don't take this the wrong way, but should I be?"

"Not that I know of," I said with a smile, and as I settled back to take notes, Jerome Shepherd began telling his story.

"We were Dekes, Delta Kappa Epsilon fraternity. Fairly prestigious, and just so you know, more United States Presidents have been Dekes than any other fraternity. Even Dan Quayle was a Deke."

"Impressive."

"On that Saturday night, we'd had a party out on Davidson Road at a log house we called 'on the rocks.' Lots of pledges, students, even some Danish Airmen were there that night. I have no idea who brought them. And my friend John Wilkes is driving a turbo-charged Corvair back into town, early Sunday morning, down West End Avenue, and I'm in the car with him. Wilkes had to go into town because he was the pledge trainer, and the pledges had to clean up the fraternity house that morning."

"What time of day was this?"

"Sunday morning, very early, like daybreak Sunday morning. So we're riding down West End, and we're almost back to Vanderbilt when I decide it would be a great time to fire a few rounds from the pistol I had bought from a pawnshop in Nashville. So I rolled down the car window, and fired three shots."

"And then what happened?" I asked.

"Neither one of us realized that there was a cop car right behind us, about to pull us over for speeding. My firing the gun made the cops think I was shooting at them."

"Um, bad move, right?"

"Yeah, they encapsulated us. They pulled us over, two cops with guns drawn. They made us get out of the car and made me reach back into the car to retrieve the gun I had fired. They held a gun to

Wilkes head to ensure I complied with their request. I did exactly as told, all in slow motion, I remember that."

"You were arrested, I take it?"

"Yes, we were taken in a paddy wagon to jail. Wilkes got out later in the day on that Sunday. The school head of security came and bonded him out."

"What about you?"

"The security guy said he was authorized to get only one of us out of jail, and it wasn't me, so I stayed for three days before getting out late on Tuesday. I had already had some run-ins with the Vanderbilt administration, and the arrest was just icing on the cake. My dad told the cops to just keep me there for a few days. He wouldn't bond me out. So after I did get out, school officials immediately told me I could withdraw from school or they would withdraw me."

"You finished undergrad and law school elsewhere?"

"Correct."

"And Wilkes, what happened to him?"

"I took the heat and saved Wilkes, because I knew my Vanderbilt career was over. He finished undergrad at Vanderbilt and then law school. John Burwell Wilkes was a big deal. He was the first night court judge in Nashville, and before that he clerked for Charles Galbreath and eventually built a career as an airline executive."

"No kidding," I replied. "So I forgot to ask, the gun you had was a .32-caliber pistol?"

"Yes."

"Beretta?"

"No, I only wanted a gun made in the USA, nothing foreign. I believe it was a Remington."

"Did you realize that the cops were possibly looking at you and Wilkes as suspects in the babysitter's murder?"

"Yes. I remember on the way to jail in the paddy wagon, the driver was saying that the cops were looking for kids, that some students had murdered a girl out in Crieve Hall."

"Are you sure about that?" I asked.

"I'm sure, yes. And that would have been a big, big stink if Vanderbilt students had murdered a University of Tennessee coed. That would have started a war. You get the picture?"

CHAPTER NINETEEN

BRIDGE CLUB

One of the comments I noted during my dinner with Paula Herring's friend and next-door neighbor was about Jo Herring being a bridge player. It was this card-playing proclivity that spurred me to track down her bridge group for any insider information she might have shared with the players.

I had the name of a woman who had lived around the corner from the Herrings in 1964 and appeared to still reside at the same address on Briarwood Drive. Much to my surprise, even though she was almost eighty, she was in good health and more than willing to meet with me to discuss her former neighbors.

The house was yet another red-brick, ranch-style home with windows trimmed in white paint and dark shutters. The neat yard, tidy landscaping, and sloping front lawn reminded me of the house on Timberhill Drive.

I soon found myself seated in the front living room on an ancient couch, accepting a glass of iced tea from a charming and impeccably dressed woman with gray-white hair, wire-framed glasses, and a warm smile.

After explaining my research regarding the strange and tragic events of 1964, she began to offer responses in a voice hinting of a Boston background, delivered at a pace just a half step slower than typical.

It didn't take me long to appreciate the clear diction and professorial style. We hit it off immediately.

In a room surrounded by family photographs, I began slowly easing into the topics I wanted to cover by asking the general state of the neighborhood at the time of Paula's death, carefully avoiding words that might be deemed as insensitive.

"Miss Hattie, I heard that the neighborhood was like an armed camp around the time of Paula's tragedy. Is that how you remember it?"

"Yes. You couldn't go to the door. And you thought that there was a deranged killer at large. And when you did look outside you'd see the police dressed in those dark uniforms, looking like black penguins searching all the ditches after Paula's murder. It was a shock to all of us."[1]

"And Paula's mother?"

"I knew the mother was alcoholic, but I didn't know she was entertaining men. It wasn't something she ever mentioned. She called me early that Sunday morning. She wanted me to come down to her house."

"Really? About what time was that do you think?" I inquired.

"Oh, just at daybreak. So I got dressed and walked around the corner to her house. It was a short walk to their house."

"She needed your help?" I asked.

"She just needed me to be a little bit of comfort to her; then I came home and a little later the police came by and asked me what I knew. And did I know Paula was coming home that weekend. I didn't know she was here until after I heard that she had been killed."

"Very interesting; so you get the call at daybreak, you spend a few hours at Jo Herring's, come back home, and, shortly after, the detectives knock on your door and want to know what you may have heard or seen at Jo Herring's house?" I asked.

"That's right. Jo had asked me a few weeks earlier to ride with her to Knoxville to see Paula, but I refused, because the weather was bad and Jo was alcoholic."

"How did you get to know Jo Herring?" I inquired.

"Jo and I, well, we used to sit out in the sun together and played bridge together. But I was married with a family, and what went on in the evenings other than the bridge I didn't know. I felt so sorry for her. I really did. It was awful."

I was taking notes as we talked, and at the mention of bridge I needed to confirm the few details I knew about the game.

"I never played bridge, but I'm thinking this is the card game played by foursomes, where two players partner up against the other two players, right?"

"That's right. We played a lot of bridge in those days."

"So you got to know Jo, Paula, and Alan after they moved into Crieve Hall?"

"Yes, but I never knew Jo's husband before he died."

I shook my head as I noted that it was one tragedy after another for the Herring family. "First the dad, then the daughter found dead."

"Well she made the remark to me that it was all her fault. Both her husband's death and Paula's," she said.

As I heard these words, I stopped making notes and looked directly at my hostess.

She continued. "That's right. I don't know what she meant by that. I just assumed she meant her drinking problems had created all of this drama."

"Did you play bridge with other friends who may be living today?" I asked.

"Well, yes, there was a nurse friend also who played. She was Jo's close friend who lived on Battery Lane. I went over there with Jo to play bridge many times."

"Do you remember a name?"

"I think her name was Amanda. She was much younger, and she had been a nursing student at Vanderbilt. That's when she got to know Jo Herring."

"I would love to find her," I responded.

"You should try. Amanda was Jo's really close friend, who was with her when they discovered Wilmer Herring's body at the Noel Hotel."

My heart was pounding at this news, and it must have shown on my face.

"Jo Herring was the person who first discovered her husband dead at the Noel Hotel?"

"Yes."

"And she had a nursing student, this Amanda person, with her at the time?"

"That's right."

I wanted to believe this nugget of new information, though it just didn't sound right to me, so I continued with a few additional questions.

"So, when it came to Paula's murder?" I asked.

"Well, it was so publicized. It was horrible, and it was all over the news, all the time. It rocked the town. We weren't used to that sort of thing in a suburban neighborhood; it was such a shock."

"I understand that Jo Herring moved away from Nashville some months after Paula was killed?"

"Yes, at my urging. You see, she would go 'dry out' every once in a while. And in one of those drying out periods, I said 'Jo you need to go where family can help you. You've got to go back to Texas.' The situation here was really awful, and I didn't want to sit by and watch it."

At this point, Miss Hattie noticed my empty tea glass and exited the living room to replenish my drink. Moments later, she was back and continued the story.

"Jo told me her trauma had really affected her, and she went to work for an allergist after she left Vanderbilt. I know the allergist took a chance on her."

"I would think so. Did you hear that Jo Herring was released by Vanderbilt University Hospital after Paula was killed? I mean that they fired her?" I asked.

"No, I didn't know that. I know it wasn't long after she left here, or so it seemed to me, that I didn't get Christmas cards anymore. So I suspected she had died."

"Yes, sometime around 1976 in Texas as I understand it."[2]

"It was a sad, sad story."

The chance that I could find a woman named Amanda based on a decades-old remembrance was, in my opinion, simply ridiculous. There was little to go on except a first name, and even that was questionable, since it was based on Miss Hattie's aging memory. I might as well have been asking people to help me track down a dog that had crossed a Nashville street corner on a Saturday afternoon in September 1960. As I pondered this dilemma, I remembered that I had at least one solid fact. Amanda had been a nursing school student at Vanderbilt and had a connection to Jo Herring as an instructor at some point prior to 1960. I could guess a range of age and perhaps correlate it with Vanderbilt Nursing students in the 1950s.

After a couple of weeks of challenging research at more than one Vanderbilt University Library, along with cross-referencing Tennessee death records, the field eventually narrowed to a woman named Amanda from Savannah, Tennessee. Amanda had been a nursing school student in the 1950s, an attractive young woman with brunette hair and a winning smile. I parlayed this information into Amanda's current address and phone number, some fifty years after she had graduated from nursing school.

Two days later, after a couple of rings, a woman with a youthful sounding voice answered the telephone. My introduction was the standard one I had used successfully in dozens of calls: "Hello, I'm calling about an event that took place forty years ago that involved you."

After the initial stunned silence, followed by my expanded explanation, the woman on the phone volleyed a couple of questions at me:

"Why? How did you find me?"[3]

After going into detail on how she had been found after so many decades, I said, "Well, I've been doing some research into the Paula Herring story. It was the first big homicide case in Metro Nashville history, in part because it was so tragic, and in part because the whole community was in an uproar over the perceived lack of police protection in the suburbs. But I'm primarily interested in the death of Paula's father at the Noel Hotel in Nashville, around September 1960," I said.[4]

"Why is that important now? Don't you accept the police report?"

"There wasn't one," I replied.

"How in the world could there not be?"

"Part of the reason I'm calling is to see what light you can shed on this. There are no records anywhere—none," I said.

"How can that be? They knew I was there at the Noel Hotel with Jo."

I gulped hard at this response, given that it appeared to confirm Hattie's remark about Amanda having gone with Jo to find Wilmer's body at the hotel.

"Alan?" she questioned.

"Pardon me?"

"Are you really Alan Herring? And this is your way of getting information from me?"

"No, no. I can assure you that I'm not Alan Herring. I'm happy to meet you in person if that helps to allay any of your concerns."

"What I know won't help anybody. It was sordid."

"I'm not surprised," I said.

"I was good friends with Jo Herring. She was older. She worked as a public health nurse in Sumner County, the 1950s in Gallatin, Tennessee. You know the area?"

"Yes, ma'am, north of Nashville," I replied.

"Vanderbilt Nursing students did their rotation with Jo in her duties as a county nurse. Jo did some work with the American Red Cross, doing blood drives and similar and then started working at Vanderbilt Hospital later on. I worked as a public health nurse in that same area and then at Vanderbilt Hospital."

"Can you tell me about finding Wilmer Herring?" I asked.

"Jo asked me to come with her to the Nöel Hotel. I remember thinking that it was odd that Jo knew where he was."

"What happened when you got to the Noel?"

"Jo talked the front desk clerk into giving her a key to the room."

"She must've been persuasive."

"Oh, she was. And we walked in and found him. He was on the bed, and dead. He'd been there a while I think."

"Was there anything else in the room with Mr. Herring?"

"A liquor bottle and a bottle of rat poison."

"Was he dressed or undressed when you found him?"

"Just lying on the bed, but dressed."

"By the way, can you describe Wilmer Herring's physical appearance for me? Not when you last saw him at the Noel Hotel, I mean just regular appearance. I've never seen a photo of him and have no idea if he was tall, short, thin, heavyset, red-headed, suit and tie, or just anything about him would be helpful."

"He was about five-foot ten, and thin. He had very dark hair, black hair."

"What about the suicide letter, or suicide note?" I asked.

"There wasn't one."

"Are you sure?"

"There was no note, nothing like that," she said softly.

"Then what happened?" I asked.

"Jo used the telephone in the room to call the police. We waited for them to arrive."

"Was this daytime or at night?"

"It was daytime when we found him," she said.

"Did the police question you?" I asked.

"No."

"What about Jo Herring? Did they take her anywhere for questioning?"

"No, they just went about their business," she said.

"The event at the Noel Hotel was upsetting for you?"

"Of course it was!"

I could hear the righteous tone of indignation in her voice. "Well, to me it appears that Jo knew exactly where to find Wilmer. Did that concern you?" I asked.

"I thought he committed suicide. I was naive, but I initially thought he did."

An interesting change of view, I thought.

"You and Jo parted company after this event?"

"Yes, seems like I was busy doing one thing and she was doing something else."

"Any thoughts on why Wilmer committed suicide, assuming he did?" I quizzed.

"There was a lot of drinking involved, a lot of drinking. And she never told me if she was running around on Wilmer. She never mentioned anybody serious. What she did, she never told me. I know she was out in bars and such, but I didn't know where she was."

"Anyone ever contact you about this in all these years?"

"No. Never, not one person. It was troublesome that it all happened."

"I'm sure it was. You knew Paula, right?" I asked.

"Yes, from an early age. She grew into a bright, delightful young woman. When she was killed, all I had heard was that someone came back to the house that Paula knew and she let them into the house. Jo told me that it was someone Paula knew."

"Were you still running around with Jo in 1964?"

As the words "running around" crossed my lips, I instantly realized my mistake and wasn't surprised at the tone of indignation on the other end of the line.

"Oh, I was not worldly wise at the time, Mr. Bishop."

"Right, of course not."

"I just wasn't involved with Jo when Paula died."

But you were part of the bridge group, so this must be your attempt at distancing yourself, I thought. "Yes, ma'am. So did anyone question you about Paula's murder?"

She cut me off before I could finish my sentence.

"No, no one questioned me about Paula's death. I may have gone to the funeral, I can't remember. And I have to run some errands right now. Perhaps you could call me back tomorrow?" she asked.

"Certainly," I replied.

The following day, I attempted to contact Amanda again by telephone. After hearing my voice, she hung up on me. Seconds later, a second attempt, same response. I waited a few minutes then tried again, and, on my third attempt, she apparently had a change of heart and decided to take my call. But her phone demeanor was now markedly different. Now she was nervous. Two minutes into the call she found those precious three words that all interviewers loathe:

"I don't remember."[5]

And just as quickly, she introduced two new words into the conversation—foul play—and skillfully wove them into her new firewall: "I don't remember any foul play." She said this at least four times in a span of three minutes. Interestingly, I hadn't asked her if there had been any foul play.

The only additional insight that Amanda would offer was that Jo and Wilmer Herring were in bad financial straits at the time of Wilmer's death, and that they drank a lot. She remembered that Jo Herring had blamed Wilmer's employer for his suicide.

"It's not like I've thought about this for forty years."

"No, ma'am, I'm sure you haven't."

On a return trip to visit with Miss Hattie, I implored her to try and remember the other bridge players in Jo Herring's group, especially any nurses who may or may not have been working at Vanderbilt University Hospital at the time of Paula's murder. After a few days,

Miss Hattie offered the first and last name of a nurse who might have played bridge once or twice as a substitute partner.

After a tortuous period of research into the substitute's whereabouts for the previous decades, I found that she appeared to still be living in Middle Tennessee. When I spoke with the woman by phone and described my topic of interest, rather than being alarmed, she welcomed the chance to talk about the 1964 tragedy and invited me to her home for the discussion.

On a scalding hot day in early May, I navigated through an upscale residential area just outside the city limits of Franklin, Tennessee, to a well-kept home on a large lot. After I rang the doorbell, the door was answered by a tall, fit, seventy-ish-year-old woman with dark hair, dressed comfortably in warm-up pants and a nylon jacket. She invited me in to spend a few moments chatting about her old friend Jo Herring.

The woman, named Evelyn, was quite comfortable allowing a stranger, me, into her home. If she had any concerns about my visit, I soon learned that she had a large group of family members—her siblings and her now-grown children—living nearby. And for the next hour, the phone rang as if on a regular schedule, though she declined to take calls and instead simply reviewed her call identifier and then told me the name of each person calling and their likely reason for dialing her number. The reasons ranged from a gambling trip to a casino in a nearby state, a visit to Birmingham, Alabama, to see a cousin, shopping trips, and more. Based on my brief interaction, I assumed she had the energy for all of it.

"Tell me Mike, how in the world did you get onto this? That was such a long time ago."[6]

As she proffered this ice-breaker, we were sitting in her den. I was on a comfortable but worn couch, and she was in a leather recliner surrounded by the comforts of a senior-citizen lifestyle: a side table littered with a remote control for her television, telephone handset, reading glasses, cough drops, a couple of medicine bottles, magazines, morning newspaper, and a cold cup of coffee.

After I explained the background of my research, Evelyn launched into a narrative that had me raising my eyebrows numerous times and scribbling notes as quickly as possible along the way.

"Paula was very smart. But her mother, she was really smart."

"You worked with Paula's mother at the hospital?" I asked.

"Yes, Jo was a floor nurse, but she knew more than the doctors, let me tell you."

Wanting to refresh her recollection, I circled back to the week of the murder: "Do you remember the time period when Paula was killed?"

"Yes, I do. I had just returned from a day trip to Chattanooga when Jo called me."

"You mean she called you to go out to dinner with her on that Saturday night?" I asked.

"No, she called me screaming about Paula and wanting me to come to her house."

My eyes dilated to their full capacity. "I bet that was not the phone call you were expecting?"

"Not in the least. She called me around 9:00 p.m., and I stopped to buy gas over on Murfreesboro Road on the way to her house. When I got to Timberhill, Jo was standing on the front porch as if waiting for me to pull in the driveway. I thought it a bit strange."

"You and Jo had worked together that Saturday?" I asked.

"No, I saw Jo the night before at the Wedgewood Diner."

"So, you think she called you around 9:00 p.m.? I was thinking she called the police, or someone called the police to report the murder just after 11:00 p.m." I inquired.

"No, it was around 9:00 p.m. when she called me, and it was almost 9:30 p.m. when I got there."

"Anyone else at the house?"

"No, it was just Jo and Alan and the body. I nearly beat the police there. They were getting there about the same time as I did."

"So, Miss Evelyn, what kind of car did the Herrings have?"

"Jo was a Ford person."

"Where was the car on that night?" I asked.

"It was there. It wasn't in the garage, because they never used the garage to house the car. But I remember having to step over a busted light or some kind of car part that was just lying in the driveway when I got out of my car. But the Ford was parked where it always was outside."

With this update, I knew I had to ask about the strange circumstances regarding Jo's dinner dates.

"You say it was just you, Jo, and Alan at first, but what about Billy Vanderpool and A. J. Meadows, the two guys Jo had been to dinner with that night?"

"They weren't there."

"I don't understand. Multiple people testified in open court that Vanderpool and Meadows were with Jo Herring when she found Paula lying in the den." I said.

"I can't help what anybody said in court, they weren't with Jo that night. I know a couple of the detectives were right there about the same time I drove up. They wouldn't let me in the den, and they made me and Jo wait in the front of the house while they talked to Alan in the bedroom."

"It sounds like an awful experience," I said.

Uh-oh. This changes everything, I was thinking. *If it's true, then somebody is hiding something. Evelyn arrives almost ninety minutes before the police dispatcher is called and now says the men who claimed to be with Jo Herring weren't with her at all?*

"It was really bad. At first the detectives thought I had been there all along, but I explained to them that I had stopped at a gas station on my way over. I think they checked that out just to make sure I was telling the truth. When I found out that Jo knew that Randolph Clarke fellow, it was a surprise to me. But I guess our schedules were so different at times, I didn't know all of the people she was running with."

"Hmm, maybe she had been out with the Clarke fellow that night?" I asked.

"I don't know for certain; it was all very strange to me. I remember a day or so later I was with Jo in Gallatin at the funeral home and somebody called her on the phone and it was one of the detectives asking about Randolph Clarke. And, boy, she was mad. She said, 'Yes, I dated him. He was a nice guy. Why would he want to kill Paula?'"

"What do you think happened to Paula? Any guesses?"

"I just don't believe that Randolph Clarke did anything to her. I don't believe he had anything to do with it. My feelings about Jo coming home and finding Paula, and then the story about those two guys with her, and them leaving as soon as they had hardly walked in the door? It never made sense to me. I know Vanderpool and Meadows weren't with her. And I thought, well, Jo, who *was* with you? Why didn't they stay with you? I just couldn't believe anybody would walk off and leave her like that. But she wouldn't say. In fact, at first I thought she called me to give somebody a ride."

When I walked out of the session with Nurse Evelyn, my head was still spinning at the small bombshell she had just dropped into my research project. Jo Herring and her two male friends all claimed to have arrived at the Timberhill Drive home at 11:00 p.m. Yet here was Nurse Evelyn telling me that the men weren't with Jo and that Jo Herring could have arrived home as much as two hours earlier?

CHAPTER TWENTY

TRUE DETECTIVE

With a handful of murder suspects to consider, I made a return trip to Lipscomb University to review them, again to one of the study rooms on the second floor of the Beaman Library. After a quick dump of my books and backpack, I began creating a simple spreadsheet on the white board using a dry-erase marker. Down the left-hand side of the board I placed the names of Clarke, Bloody Man, Al Baker, Jesse Henderson, and the Crieve Hall Prowler. Beside each name I began to list the pros and cons of why they might or might not have murdered Paula Herring, in hopes that this exercise would provide some much needed clarity to my muddled thinking.

Clarke's entry included nothing I hadn't already considered, though it was helpful to me to see it in writing. If he did kill Paula Herring, he certainly had offered a reasonable motive to Al Baker while at Ruth's Diner on that Saturday night. But on the side of his innocence, he had no scratches, no bloodstained clothes, and no bite marks on his person. The prosecution team did attempt to tie him to fibers from the victim's clothing, but Charles Galbreath noted that he had been contacted by a detective who stated that those fibers might have been tampered with in the chain of evidence. More than that, when Clarke's garments were retrieved from the laundry, it seemed reasonable to assume that a laundry or dry cleaner would have had millions of fibers on their premises.

And if Clarke had done the deed, how could he have left Alan Herring alive, knowing that if Alan had seen him on the night of Paula's murder, the little boy would remember Clarke as the man who had given him a horsey-back ride to bed approximately ten days earlier, on the same night that Clarke had a one-night stand with Jo

Herring. The bloody man as a murder suspect was a more compelling option to me. By all appearances, he had been engaged in a fight or struggle just prior to arriving at a fast food establishment scant minutes from the Herring home. What were the chances that this event was completely unrelated to the slaying of the eighteen-year-old babysitter? Charles Galbreath and W. B. Hogan both thought that the bloody man, Sam Carlton, either did the deed or had knowledge of who did. So why should I dismiss the opinion of two savvy attorneys? I tended to agree with Hogan when he said, "Carlton either did it or he knew something about it."

Next to Al Baker's name I jotted a couple of notes related to his own less than detailed alibi on the night of the slaying, as well as his unusual interaction with a newspaper reporter at the criminal trial, when he had identified himself as the person who fired the gunshot into a snowbank near Music Row. How much did Baker know but wasn't telling? Had Dr. Murray Cook been correct when he pointed the finger at Baker as the killer?

Moving down my list, if Jesse Henderson wasn't involved in Paula Herring's murder, he certainly knew a lot about it. Did he obtain his inside information from his old friend BlueSky? Or was he perhaps just a collector of theories and enjoyed doling out cryptic clues to me? Or could the quartet of Clarke, Baker, Henderson, and Cook simply have repeated their Christmas Eve joyride and then entered the home on Timberhill Drive on that fateful Saturday night while looking for Jo Herring, but found Paula home instead, and the evening turned into an unexpected and horrific slaying?

As I sat down to mull over the entries on the board, I was thinking that the Crieve Hall Prowler was not the culprit. Paula hadn't been raped, as had been confirmed by the medical examiner, Dr. Core. And prowling events in the same neighborhood continued immediately after the murder. It was as if the prowler hadn't read the newspapers of the day and was unaware of how many citizens and resources were lined up to catch him.

But my new entry on the suspect board was a person I had not previously considered until my last conversation with Nurse Evelyn, and that was Eva Jo Herring. As unfathomable as it was to think that a mother could be involved in taking the life of her only daughter, there was still a nagging question in my mind that would not go away. How could Jo Herring be the first person to discover her dead husband in a hotel room in September of 1960, and then three and a half years later be the first person to discover her dead daughter? I couldn't calculate the odds of such unfortunate luck. Yet, as far as I knew, the investigators and detectives hadn't so much as pointed a finger at Jo Herring as a possible culprit on the night of Paula's slaying. John Clarke's defense attorney, Charles Galbreath, did attempt to tie Wilmer Herring's life insurance proceeds to his suspicious death at the Noel Hotel, but the trial judge had nipped that attempt in the bud. In the end, could Jo Herring be considered a reasonable suspect in Paula's murder, even if Nashville law enforcement officials didn't view her in that light?

And then it occurred to me that I had overlooked an obvious murder suspect, though a nameless one. Not once during the criminal trial of John Clarke did Charles Galbreath attempt to point suspicion toward a young man of Paula Herring's acquaintance. The subject of a potential boyfriend or a Saturday night date on the night of the murder never bubbled up during testimony. If Clarke's defense team had been looking for an alternative suspect, what better direction to point jurors toward than a young man visiting Paula while her mother was out of the house? It was tailor-made for a "reasonable doubt" defense.

More than that, why would a girl staying home to write a book report, curled up on a couch in the den, be dressed up in a new outfit and new penny loafers? Wouldn't she have been in pajamas or some warm and comfortable clothing more suitable for a long study session?

But if the actual plan had been to encourage her mother to go out to dinner, put her little brother to bed, and then await a young man who would arrive after Paula was "alone" at home, then the outfit she wore would have been exactly as expected. If things had gone terribly wrong between the young man and Paula while they were in the den, the assailant could have left the premises just before Jo Herring arrived and without being seen by Paula's little brother. If the young man had parked his car at the Crieve Hall Church of Christ on Trousdale Drive, the street to the west of Timberhill, and walked directly to the Herring home through a couple of yards, he also might have escaped notice by the neighbors. It was a troubling thought.

When Kay Masterson, one of Paula Herring's dorm mates at the University of Tennessee, had sent me a copy of a 1964 true detective–styled magazine, it was my first look at one of the most popular publications of the 1940s, 1950s, and 1960s.[1] What I might initially have described as a disturbing and morbid genre turned out to have been enormously popular with the public, to the tune of a couple of million subscribers per month during its heyday. But with the advent of competing pulp fiction paperbacks, such as the ones John Randolph Clarke read, the detective magazine genre began taking a nosedive in popularity and eventually ceased publication by the mid-1990s.[2]

The photographs inside the magazines were so graphic that multiple psychiatrists and forensic psychologists had determined that a high percentage of the perpetrators of sexual crimes comprised the main readership of such magazines. It was not a comforting thought. To put it simply, the detective magazine genre had been used as a type of sadistic pornography, but, with the advent of the Internet, the World Wide Web effectively replaced the magazine delivery model and ultimately provided a different source of even more graphic material for some of its disturbed readers.[3]

Unfortunately, I now had a need to discover what had been written in the genre about the Paula Herring murder case. After an extended search, I stumbled upon a source of archived detective magazines from the 1950s and 1960s, from a company known as Patterson Smith. I phoned the company, based in New Jersey, and explained that I needed to supplement my research into a 1964 murder case with any magazines that might have covered the crime in the same timeline. When asked about key words for indexing the search, I offered up a short list of names to use for cross-reference: Paula Herring, Jo Herring, John Randolph Clarke, and Red Clarke.

The Patterson Smith contact softened my view of the genre by noting that, in many cases, the old magazines had provided clues and comfort to family members researching past tragedies or themselves exploring cold murder cases. Two weeks later, the Patterson Smith representative let me know that they had found multiple sources of coverage of the Paula Herring slaying, and, for a reasonable fee, I could receive a handful of the original magazines in my mailbox. I didn't hesitate to place an order.

Three days later, I received the publications, each individually wrapped in plastic to protect pages that were now almost four decades old and yellowing. The magazines ran sixty-five to seventy-five pages each. Their dimensions were the size of any modern-day magazine, and when initially circulated ranged in price from twenty-five to thirty-five cents, published by companies based in New York, New Jersey, and Chicago. I noted that a three-year subscription could be had for the tidy sum of $11.00 for most of the publications.

Inside every magazine, the nostalgic advertisements of yesteryear were splashed from front to back. In 1964, one could become a fingerprint expert or detective simply by training at home via correspondence course; or one could study law in their spare time while earning a degree from a correspondence institution located in Chicago. Rupture relief for men and the shrinking of hemorrhoids also appeared to be recurring themes throughout the periodicals. Or one could learn electric appliance repair, and earn five to six dollars per hour with this new skillset.

Every magazine front cover was produced in full color, but the interior pages and photographs were in simple black and white. The editors appeared to know their readership, as each issue showed an attractive woman in some pose of intrigue or distress on the front cover.

The cover of one magazine revealed a young, blond woman in a low-cut black dress, holding a lever-action rifle while investigating a strange bump in the night. Another showed an attractive redhead lying in a small wooden boat, with a rope and anchor tied around her neck. Yet another magazine had a photo of a sleeping blond woman with perfect hair and red lipstick, being approached by a Danny Kaye–lookalike, who was dressed in a gray trench coat and holding a bottle of what must have been chloroform in one hand and a handkerchief in the other.

Upon closer inspection, almost every magazine carried the story of Paula Herring on its front cover, perhaps knowing that the slaying of a pretty college coed would increase sales of the publication. It would be a few weeks before I would learn that newspaper reporters, especially those working the police beat, were the ones who usually leveraged their police insider contacts to write stories for the magazines, often under fictitious names. In the economy of the 1940s and 1950s, the "penny a word" articles were a source of extra income for reporters and their alter-egos.

CHAPTER TWENTY-ONE

RETURN OF JIM SQUIRES

In August of 2002, when I first heard that Jim Squires was coming back to Nashville, I panicked. Not so much because I was in awe of the former Nashvillian—which I was—but mostly because I was afraid that my work schedule would prevent me from meeting Squires while he was in town, which in turn would prevent me from interviewing the famous author about the night of Paula Herring's murder.

In the ensuing span of almost forty years since Squires had penned his first story on Paula Herring's murder, he had gone from working for John Seigenthaler Sr., who himself would later become founding editorial director of *USA Today*, to overseeing his own Pulitzer Prize–winning staff as editor of the *Chicago Tribune*. After that, he had served as Ross Perot's first presidential campaign spokesman, then settled into a life of breeding Kentucky race horses and writing books of literary merit and critical acclaim.

The reason for Squires's most recent return to Music City was to promote his book about breeding the 2001 Kentucky Derby winner, a spectacular stallion named Monarchos, a horse who had turned in the second fastest time in Derby history, second only to Secretariat himself.[1]

By the time Saturday arrived, it already had been a long, hot, and busy week for the celebrated journalist. He had taped an interview with John Seigenthaler Sr. for the local public television affiliate, then a stint on one of the morning talk-radio programs, followed by a midweek autograph party at a swanky book retailer, and ending with an appearance slated for BookManBookWoman, a city favorite for used books, located near Vanderbilt University. My plan to meet Squires hinged on both of us arriving early at this last event, hopefully allowing me a few uninterrupted moments to discuss the Paula Herring story with him before the autograph seekers descended.

I made it to BookManBookWoman just before noon, as I had hoped. And Squires had unwittingly contributed to my plan as well, having arrived early for his own event. From inside my car's vantage point, parked along the street in front of the aging red-brick building, the fifty-nine-year-old Squires looked almost regal as he sat at a writing table inside the store's front window. With a full head of more-white-than-silver hair and wire-rimmed glasses resting atop his nose, Squires appeared to be thoughtfully inspecting each of the dozen or so newly minted books stacked before him, awaiting the first of his many fans and well-wishers.

The entry bell gave a modest ring as I entered the popular bookstore and quickly recognized my greeter as one of the store's owners. When she asked if I needed assistance, I introduced myself and replied that I wanted to meet the famous author. She didn't seem to notice the manila folder that I was carrying at my side as I made the request.

The owner escorted me past rows of bookshelves and up two steps into an adjoining room, where Squires was waiting for his guests on an elevated section of the floor next to the front window. There, in ceremonial fashion, she made the introduction before returning to her sentry post:

"Mr. Squires, I'd like you to meet Michael Bishop."

As Squires stood and extended his hand, I offered not only a compliment but a truth that I was sure would please him:

"Mr. Squires, I've already read *Horse of a Different Color*, and I must tell you that I loved your call of the Derby. It was just like being there, only better." Squires responded with a genuine smile, offered a polite thank you, and made a sweeping motion for me to take a seat across from him at the writing table.

Up close, I decided that Squires indeed looked more like the horseman whom he had become rather than the journalist and author whom he had been for most of his working life. And from my close proximity the transition seemed to suit him well, as evidenced by the tailored white shirt and stylish leather boots that he wore. Assuming that I was there for an autograph, Squires spoke first:

"Do you have a copy of my book with you? I'd be happy to sign it for you if you do. Or you can purchase one, of course."[2]

"No, actually I don't," I responded, "but I do have something you might be interested in seeing."

Without another word, I brought the manila folder into view, retrieved a copy of a photograph from it, and placed the large print carefully on the table in front of me. Slowly, I pushed the photograph across the table toward Squires with my fingertips.

"Do you remember this?" I asked.

Squires didn't answer immediately. His gaze never left the sobering image of the blond girl lying facedown on the floor in a pool of blood, in what appeared to be a family den, circa 1960s.

"I sure do. That's that poor little girl—Paula?"

Before Squires could conjure up the victim's last name, I rescued him.

"Herring. Paula Herring."

"I sat right there on the edge of the sofa next to the victim, trampled all over the crime scene, too. Unfortunately, we did that in those days. In fact, I nearly threw up there in the den, and would have, but I'd had exposure to these kinds of cases before."

As he spoke, Squires held the photocopy in both hands, as if attempting to extract additional memories from the print.

"That was my first big murder case."

"I know," I replied. "February 1964; a long time ago."

"Did he ever confess?" Squires inquired.

"You mean John Randolph Clarke?"

"Yes."

"No, he never did," I said.

With the instincts of a good journalist, but still studying the photograph, Squires ventured his next question.

"Anything unusual come up since then?"

"Yes, quite a lot, actually," I said.

Not unexpectedly, after a few moments of additional conversation we were interrupted by a group of men and women who were determined to meet Jim Squires, an American success story. The leader of the pack, a woman dressed in skin-tight country-western clothing, almost fell into the author's lap, ignoring the fact that he was already in mid-conversation with me. Her mouth ran nonstop with questions about Kentucky bloodlines and famous broodmares.

As Squires looked up to see who was interrupting our conversation, I retrieved the crime-scene photo from him and returned it to the folder before prying eyes could grasp the subject matter. I quickly said that I would try to find him later, waved goodbye and, a few moments later, left the bookstore.

CHAPTER TWENTY-TWO

GOT ANY VETERANS?

JESSE HENDERSON: PHONE CALL

Jesse: (answers phone) Yeah?[1]
Me: How've you been?
Jesse: Who is this?
Me: Your new friend, the guy who stopped by to visit with you.
Jesse: Oh yeah, the cheap detective.
Me: What did you call me? A cheap detective?
Jesse: Yeah, you know that old movie with Peter Falk.
Me: Yeah, well, I guess I am a cheap detective of sorts. Hey, I've got a few things for you. Thought I'd drop them by; a few books and some candy bars.
Jesse: You don't have to do that. You still looking for those killers?
Me: Did you say killers?
Jesse: You're that little boy, aren't you?
Me: I'm sorry, I'm not following you. Little boy? You think I'm the Herring girl's little brother now grown up and coming back to town looking for answers?
Jesse: Yeah, that's what you're doing.
Me: No, no. But what if that were true? I'm not saying it is, I'm just asking if you can help me?
Jesse: You still think I was involved in all that?
Me: I'm not sure. I could believe about anything. There's probably some statute of limitations that has run out by now, don't you think?
Jesse: Not on murder; it don't ever run out.

CLICK.

Me: Hello? Hello?

Approximately ten days later, I made an unscheduled visit to Jesse Henderson's apartment building and waited again for a resident to allow me to enter the brick fortress. When I stepped off the elevator on Jesse's floor, I could see activity in the hallway near his unit. A few steps later, I was peering into the open front door of his apartment, an apartment filled with sunlight and a couple of men with ladders painting the bedroom and the walls in the small living area.

"Where's Mr. Henderson?" I inquired."

"Who?"

"The guy who lives here?" I said.

"Oh, he moved out. I don't where he's gone. You can check with the office on the first floor."

As he said this, he applied a roller full of paint to the wall and continued to talk. "I think they said he'd moved out of state, seemed kind of sudden if you ask me. Most of them move out at the end of a month."

A few days after the Jesse Henderson experience, I stopped by to visit Charles Galbreath at his office in downtown Nashville. When I stepped through the doorway of his ninth floor suite, I was surprised to be greeted by Galbreath himself, and amused to find him pecking away at an old boat-anchor typewriter. But then I quickly realized that his legal assistant was probably out to lunch and that Galbreath was fending for himself in her absence. After a brief re-introduction, I asked him again if he really felt like his former client had been innocent of murder.

"Oh no, he did it. I'm sure of that."[2]

"What? I thought you said you'd bet your house that he was innocent?"

Galbreath stopped typing and looked up at me with a face full of exasperation.

"James Earl Ray? He shot Martin Luther King, no doubt about it. Why would you think otherwise?"

I quickly mirrored his exasperation before responding. "I'm talking about John Randolph Clarke and the Paula Herring murder!"

"Oh, I thought you were talking about Ray.[3] Yes, Clarke was innocent. He didn't shoot that girl."

"Well that's a relief, I thought you were about to tell me that James Earl Ray was with John Randolph Clarke on the night of the Herring girl's murder." As I said this, I recalled the news of Ray's recent death in a Nashville prison in April of 1998, exactly three decades after having murdered King in Memphis, Tennessee. My attempt at gallows humor didn't last long, as I posed an obvious next question to Charles Galbreath:

"You worked with James Earl Ray?"

"Yes, I worked on a contingency basis for him while we tried to get his Mustang returned, and I'm just now cleaning up my files."

When he said the word *Mustang*, I remembered that James Earl Ray had left his white 1966 Ford Mustang in Atlanta, Georgia, within hours of King's assassination. Ray had driven the car from Memphis to Atlanta and then abandoned it in an apartment complex parking lot in order to catch a bus to Canada and escape capture in April 1968.[4]

I quickly moved on to the Paula Herring case. "Mr. Galbreath, hypothetically speaking, is it good news or bad news if I can prove that John Randolph Clarke was truly innocent?" I asked.

"That's good news, because then we can get a pardon for him," he said.

"The governor would pardon him, even if Clarke is dead?" I asked.

"Oh, yes."

"Well, I think I found someone who may have been a coworker of Sam Carlton's. However, at this point I'm not sure what he knows or how helpful he wants to be," I replied.

"You think Carlton and one of his coworkers killed the girl?"

"I don't know," I replied.

"I always thought Sam Carlton knew the girl's mother."

"It wouldn't surprise me," I said. "Jo Herring lived in two places that would have been a short distance to Sam Carlton's house. One was a rental house on Elysian Fields and the other was Timberhill Drive. It wouldn't surprise me at all."

"Well, if you end up getting a confession, we can get a pardon for John Clarke."

"But there's no gun, no fingerprints, no blood, no DNA evidence, no autopsy report, no police files," I noted.

"You don't need the other stuff if you have a witness with corroboration. And when are you going to be finished with your research?"

"It's still ongoing."

After inquiring with his previous landlord, I discovered that Jesse Henderson had exited his apartment on White Bridge Road for a property in the little community of Joelton. You can find Joelton, Tennessee, via an easy twenty-minute car ride northwest of Nashville. It's a pleasant trip through farming country dotted with a few subdivisions.

Without a specific location to search for Jesse, I was back to the proverbial drawing board in hopes of finding the strange little man who appeared to be living life in a solitary confinement of his own making. And I was dismayed to realize that if Jesse Henderson was residing in an assisted living facility, there would be no electric or water bill account as a way to locate him, and my attempts at finding him by telephone ended in failure. The only option I could think of was to attempt to find every retirement home in the Joelton area, then call each one and ask to speak with Jesse Henderson. It was not an attractive chore, but it was one that I would pursue nonetheless.

After several weeks of endless calls and research, my Red Ace gas station worker appeared to have vanished for good. Of the few records I could find for Jesse, most were dead ends until I stumbled upon a notation in a small North Alabama town that a man named Jesse Henderson had been the witness for a couple marrying in front of a judge decades earlier, in 1964. Thinking that the couple might be able to offer some insight into our mutual friend, I began pursuing this new angle, but again without success. Having no luck finding the groom, I began to work backward, starting with the bride's name. A month later, the trail had evaporated, and I could conclude only that the wife had either left town or was deceased.

So I did the only thing I knew to do. I drove to Joelton and started knocking on doors. With a cooler of ice water and snacks in my car, I settled in for a long day. I visited nursing home after nursing home, crisscrossing two counties along the way. At every stop, I parked my car as close to the front door as possible and walked inside to ask two simple questions: Do you have a resident named Jesse Henderson? No? Okay, do you know the name of any other nursing homes in the area?

After a day completely filled with failed attempts, at just after 4:00 p.m., I stopped at a tidy little retirement village about an hour outside of Nashville to pose the same two questions once again. With another no response, I was on my way out of the lobby when a young woman who had been watering plants called out to me as I reached the door to exit the building.

"You know, there's a woman up the road here that rents out to veterans. Have you tried up there?"

"A nursing home?" I inquired.

"No, it's more of a regular house, not like this building."

"Got a name?"

"Grantham's is what I think they call it. No, actually that was the woman's name that owned it. I don't know that there's even a sign in the yard. It don't matter, it's about two miles up this same road, on the left after you go around the big curve. You can't miss it. It's brick, kind of a long brick house. If he was a veteran he might be up there."

I thanked her for her kindness, returned to my car, and navigated the two-lane blacktop in the direction she had pointed. As described, after rounding a large curve, on the left side of the road, sheltered by towering oaks and hickory trees, was a large home that had a pale yellow brick exterior and an oversized driveway littered with too many cars for a regular home, but just about the right number for a business. There was no sign in the yard, and just a large mailbox at the end of the driveway.

After parking my car, I cautiously approached the side door of the building and knocked before entering. A man's voice greeted me.

"You can come on in, sonny. She's in the back cleaning up the kitchen."

When I stepped inside, the lighting was slightly better, and I could see that my greeter was a grizzled old man in a wheelchair, wearing a baseball cap and chewing on an unlit cigar.

"Good afternoon, is the manager or owner here?"

"Lurleen! You got company!" He yelled this message in the general direction of a central hallway that appeared to run the length of the house.

"She'll be up here in a minute, sonny. What brings you out this way?"

"Oh, just looking for a friend of mine," I replied.

A moment later, the hallway was darkened by a tall woman wearing a food-stained apron.

"I'm sorry to disturb you; the folks down at the other nursing home said you might have a friend of mine staying with you. That's why I was stopping by."

"Well, we got about fifteen of them here, mister. What's his name?"

"Jesse Henderson."

"Yep, he's one of ours. He's in the back reading a book, I think. Just follow me. Is he expecting you?"

"No, ma'am, I don't think so. He used to live in Nashville, and then he moved away, and I haven't seen him in a while."

As we walked along the corridor, I resisted the urge to look into the rooms on either side of the hall, out of respect for the resident's privacy. A few steps later, she pointed at a door on my left and said, "He's in there," and then she returned to her kitchen work in the back of the house. I knocked softly on the door, hoping not to disturb the old man in case he was asleep, and then I slowly pushed the door open.

In the small bedroom, I could see Jesse Henderson lying on a twin bed, his head propped up by double pillows, dingy reading glasses in place, and a worn white sheet over him, pulled up under his arms.

On the other side of the room, I could see another twin bed, occupied by an ancient man without hair. The other man was lying on top of his mattress, enjoying an afternoon talk show that was blaring from the small television positioned just above my head over the doorway.

"Mr. Henderson, how are you feeling today?" I asked.[5]

He looked up to see me, then quickly removed his glasses, rubbed his eyes as if seeing a ghost, and finally responded: "Oh, the cheap detective. What are you doing here?"

"I just wanted to make sure you were alright. You left your other place in a hurry."

"Yeah, they just kicked me out is all. Said I was gonna burn the place down. I wasn't supposed to be smoking in my room, but I like a cigar every now and then."

"I hear this place only houses veterans. You were in what, World War II or Korea? Or was it the American Revolution?"

"Ha! I was a Navy man in World War II."

"So how have you been?"

"I ain't buying any green bananas, if that's what you're asking."

I laughed out loud while I looked for a place to sit, but there were no chairs in the room and attempting to sit on the edge of the bed seemed like a bad idea.

"You still writing a book about that Clarke fellow?"

"Mostly doing some research. Hey, I almost forgot, you remember telling me you'd been married. Your wife, what was her name?"

"Oh, you're talking about Betty. She's somewhere in Georgia, I think. I don't keep up with her."

He responded as if I were asking about a missing can of corn.

In an attempt to keep things on a light path, I noted that, "It's hard enough to keep up with one wife, let alone three or five of them, right?" This attempt at humor achieved the desired effect, and Henderson had a good chuckle out of it.

"If I'd had any sense, I'd still be married to Betty, but I liked to drink too much. I drank my way right on down to working for the Colonel and then pumping gas."

"The Colonel?"

"Yeah, the fried chicken place."

"That's funny. How about helping me write up this story about Red Clarke and that tragic accident? You'd certainly have a unique point of view."

"That wasn't no accident. Whoever did that to that girl was mad at her."

"Really? How's your old friend BlueSky doing these days?" I asked.

"I don't know how he's doing. I guess he's around somewhere. You still thinking that Carlton fellow had something to do with that girl getting killed?"

"I don't know. I know Clarke's attorney sure thought he might have been the one who killed that girl," I replied.

"Charlie was getting paid to say it was anybody but Red Clarke. You know none of those defense attorneys ever have a guilty client. Hey, what about those other two guys?"

"I'm sorry, I'm not following you." I said.

"I thought you said there were some guys fighting in the garage when that girl was killed?" Jesse said.

"What? No, I never said anything like that."

At this point, my head was spinning from the number of options that Henderson was introducing into the story. Perhaps that was his goal—to confuse me by introducing a laundry list of suspects for the murder. Or perhaps I was giving him too much credit, and this revolving suspect list was his cloudy remembrance of the baffling crime.

After a few more minutes of conversation, I could hear food trays being delivered down the hall for the early evening meal. I promised Jesse that I would return with a few paperback books on my next visit, and Henderson was either pleased to have me returning as a future guest or pleased that he could keep an eye on me and, more importantly, keep up with any progress on my research.

A few weeks later, I took the opportunity to return to Joelton, bringing a sack full of paperback books in an attempt to gain favor with the old man. But as I pulled into the driveway of the nursing home, my jaw dropped.

No, not again! I said to myself.

I had been so focused on the potential conversation with Jesse, I hadn't realized what was different about the overly large home.

There were no other cars in the driveway or parked on the lawn, the trash cans were overflowing, and all of the interior curtains appeared to be missing from the windows.

After exiting my car and peering into one of the windows, not only were there no people inside, the house was completely empty; not a piece of furniture was to be seen anywhere. At the side entrance door that I had used on my previous visit, I found a utility company note taped to the glass, indicating that power would be shut off for lack of payment. The note was dated two weeks earlier.

"I'm the one you want."[6]

She had a nervous tone in her voice, and, while most of the other people I had contacted about the Paula Herring murder were careful with their responses to me, she was too talkative.

But her opening line sounded eerily prophetic, or so it seemed to me as I wondered how and where she would fit into the story.

"You were in my daughter's driveway, looking for my mother the other day," she said.

"Lizzie?"

"That's my mother's name. But she's not going to be any good to you," she said.

Before I could respond by thanking her for returning my call, she jumped in with another inquiry: "You had some questions about my mother? It freaked my daughter out that you were in her driveway asking questions. My mother had a head injury years ago, and she's not, uh, quite right. Sometimes she makes sense. Sometimes she doesn't. So how can I help you?"

"I'm sorry if I caused your daughter any alarm, I was just trying to find a Lizzie DeVern, and I think she lived in the Music Row area of Nashville, back in the 1960s."

"Is it about her pension?"

"Actually, no, it's not," I replied.

"How did you find my daughter?"

"I'm sorry, I didn't catch your name." I said.

"Gina."

"Well, Gina, I'll confess, basically through a lot of old records and a lot of interviews."

What Gina didn't know concerned my activity for the past half-year. I had traveled down the Jesse Henderson path as far as I could go, and, at the end of that trail, I had taken a different path and met with one of the former and now retired managers of Red Ace gasoline, in hopes that I would uncover a ream of information related to both Jesse Henderson and Sam Carlton. The aged manager remembered Carlton as the company employee who had been reeled into the aftermath of the Paula Herring murder, but as to the manager's personal view, he had nothing to add and no memory of Henderson at all. After this session, I resorted to the only option I could think of, which was to spend hours reviewing the city phone directory to find people who might have lived near Jesse Henderson and his mother on 18th Avenue in 1963 and 1964, and then to discover whether any of those old neighbors could be found decades later.

I found an old man who was still living in the same 1940s bungalow-styled home that he had lived in almost fifty years earlier. This clue earned him an in-person visit on a sunny afternoon in March 2000. As I stood on his front porch asking him about the Paula Herring murder, he had no memory of the event. When I asked about Jesse Henderson, however, he remembered drinking with Jesse on many occasions because both of them had been World War II veterans and had often seen each other at various watering holes around town and even a few parties.

Better than remembering Jesse Henderson, the old man had fond memories of Jesse's girlfriend, a hot little number named Lizzie. When I asked how I could find Lizzie, the old man could not remember her last name, but he willingly offered to walk me through the alleyway between 18th Avenue and 17th Avenue to point out the house where she had lived in the early 1960s. And that was the starting point I used to find Lizzie DeVern.

After my "old records and a lot of interviews" comment, Gina started speaking in a repetitive stream of non-communicators, which accomplished nothing except to fill the air and did not convey any actual information to me. She had a steady delivery of "well, you know" and "in other words" and "the thing about it is" and similar air-fillers. Her topics ranged from 1960s Nashville and all of the high-profile citizens she had known back in the day, to her daily activities in the present. But my new friend wasn't hanging up the telephone, and I sensed that she might be buying time to assess me. *Here's a woman whose mother may be a player in this story, and instead of hanging up on me, or telling me she has no interest in a discussion, she's still on the line. Interesting. Maybe she wants to know what I know?*

"Gina, I'll save us both some time. I'm trying to reach your mother about a former Red Ace gas station attendant that she may have known decades ago in Nashville. The gas station man and his mother lived within walking distance of the DeVern family in 1963. Walking distance, as in, through an alleyway between 18th Avenue and 17th Avenue."

If the temperature of a phone line could physically drop thirty degrees Fahrenheit in a matter of seconds, this one did. A nervous laugh came through the line, and my brain started racing into high gear. "Gina, did you graduate high school in Nashville?" I asked.

"Yes, in the 1960s. That was a while ago."

"So it was you and your family that lived on 17th Avenue?"

"It was just me and my mother. My dad died right about that time. What does this have to do with my mom?"

"I'm sorry about your dad. And that's a fair question, and here's the answer: The gas station attendant, named Jesse Henderson, was good friends with a man who was convicted of murdering a University of Tennessee coed in 1964, and I'm trying to find someone that knew either of those guys or perhaps both of those men. Do you know Jesse Henderson?"

Again the nervous laugh, and she didn't answer my question. *She hasn't asked who I am. She should ask about the murder,* I thought to myself. *It's an obvious next question.*

I decided to offer up the information as if she had indeed asked about the murder. "Ironically, and sadly, I might note, the murder victim was a young woman who graduated high school in 1963."

Silence again, but she was still on the line.

"Gina, maybe we could meet for a cup of coffee? I'm thinking, based on my caller-ID, that you're calling from somewhere in Kentucky. Maybe you could come to Nashville and we could meet. Could you do that for me, please?" I asked.

"My mother may have known Jesse. But the thing is . . . is that I don't even know why you think I would know anything about any of this," she replied.

"That's not a problem. I'm just trying to understand the relationships," I said. "The guy convicted of murder was named John Randolph Clarke. I think there's a good chance that your mother knows this story."

"Maybe, I don't know. That was a long time ago."

"Jesse's an interesting little man. He mostly subsists on cigars, soft drinks, and junk food. As for the murder, it involved a University of Tennessee student home for the weekend in February 1964. The victim's mother, a nurse at Vanderbilt, goes out to dinner that night, comes home around 11:00 p.m., and finds her daughter lying on the den floor, dead. A few days later, the police settle on Jesse Henderson's friend as the best suspect, a thirty-nine-year-old ne'er-do-well named John Randolph Clarke. Trial and conviction follow, and that's the end of the story. At least until I come along a few decades later."

"And Jesse mentioned that he knew my mom?" she inquired.

"No, not exactly. Another thing that intrigued me was that Jesse and another Red Ace employee, a truck stop manager, seemed to have a connection to the murder. I'm not completely sure what the connection means, so I'm hoping your mom can help me better understand that chapter in Jesse Henderson's life."

"I've got to go now. Maybe you could call me back in a few days."

"Gina, was your mother working anywhere when you lived on 17th Avenue?"

"Yes, she was a nurse."

CHAPTER TWENTY-THREE

PRESCRIPTION FOR MURDER

The more I thought about it, the more I wondered if the Paula Herring murder had become an urban legend because it was never going to be anything more. It was an urban legend with multiple solutions conjured up by concerned citizens who had heard, or perhaps even experienced, various parts of the story. And John Randolph Clarke had become the most favored and the most formal solution in the legend, closely followed by the bloody man solution, and the prowler/rapist solution. Perhaps no one would ever know what had really taken place inside the house on Timberhill Drive.

A few days later I was at a well-known eatery on West End Avenue, ready to take a turn at perhaps adding yet another solution to the babysitter legend, albeit one arriving decades late. It was 10:30 in the morning, and I was sitting inside the restaurant, at a table close to the front door, when Gina walked in. I was wearing a baseball cap to help her identify me. And I had never asked how to identify her, primarily because I didn't think Gina actually would show up. But a few moments after our appointed time, a woman of perhaps sixty sat down opposite me. She was tall and thin, with short platinum-blond hair, which, to my eye, was a wig. She was hiding behind fashionable eyewear and carrying a small, well-worn pocketbook with a set of keys attached. Before I could say hello, I caught a brief glimpse of her trembling hand.

"I took the liberty of ordering one coffee and one iced tea. I hope that works for you," I said.

"Yes, thank you. Coffee's fine. I don't have that much time, actually."[1]

"Not a problem. Can I just begin with a few questions? Would that be too direct? Or do we need to spend some time on the social graces?" I asked.

She laughed at my words, and I sensed just a hint of relaxation in her demeanor. I took her laughter as agreement that we could skip the rapport-building phase and just move forward with a few questions. But she beat me to the first one.

"So, the girl who was killed, you said her name was Herrington?" she asked.

"No, actually, I didn't say. But her name was Herring. Paula Herring. You remember the story?"

"I think I may have known her; I'm not sure. We lived in a rental house in the Music Row area," she said.

She offered this in the same tension-edged voice that I recognized from the earlier phone call.

"How on earth would you have known Paula Herring?" I asked.

"I'm just saying kids at that time always hung out at the drive-in restaurants, especially those near Belle Meade. So you're a private detective?" she asked.

"No. I'm just attempting to round up a few answers related to what many describe as Metro Nashville's first big murder case. I'm an amateur researcher; that's probably the best description. Kind of like an investigative journalist but without a journal or any real credentials. How's that?"

At this point, I decided to employ an interview method that I had recently discovered—pretending that you don't know what you actually do know, and then pretending you do know what you actually don't. Rather than pursue the Jesse Henderson topic as I'd done the first time we had spoken, I rolled the dice.

"When did you first meet BlueSky?" I asked.

"Oh, gosh, I don't remember. I knew him before I knew Jesse."

"Is he in town?"

"As far as I know, unless he passed away. His family had money, big money. He and my mother ran around a lot back in the day."

"Got any fond memories of your time with Jesse Henderson?" I asked.

As she gazed wistfully out the window, she said, "I just remember standing on the sidewalk in front of his apartment early one morning and him telling me everything was going to be okay."

"Gina, I need your help," I began. But before I could describe the assistance I needed, she cut me off.

"I know that you think that somebody that we were around knew about the girl dying. But it's like I'm two different people. And right now, the way I'm thinking about that whole thing is that somehow it's in my head and I don't think any of it really happened. Even talking to you about it, it's kinda like it's all a dream," she said.

I gave her a puzzled look and finished my previous attempt at a request. "I need to know BlueSky's real name, and I need you to find him for me," I said. "Today would be a really good day for that, and maybe you could take me to see him. Because I don't think he's dead. In fact, I think BlueSky and Jesse talk pretty frequently, even now. Let's just call it my intuition," I said.

If she was startled at my request, she didn't verbalize it, though she quickly looked out the window at the cars filling up the drive-through lane before responding. I let silence fill the air as long as necessary.

"The thing is, I don't even know why I think I know anything about any of this. I'm about ready to go see BlueSky. I really am about ready to go see him and just tell him that I've just got to have some sane answers from somebody because my mother has driven me nuts through all these years. He'd understand that," she said.

As I heard this puzzling response, I got the feeling that my guest was a million miles away. It was as if I wasn't sitting on the other side of the table from her. So I tried again to bring her back to our conversation.

"Gina, I need his name."

"And I'm not worried about your interest because the thing is, is that I know, I just know that I didn't hurt the girl myself; that I'm sure of. If anybody's got a fear and a hate and a desire not to touch or have anything to do with a gun it's this girl here. I have got a real aversion to a gun."

Why would she say she didn't hurt Paula? Was she in the house on the night of the murder? I tried not to be too obvious as my right hand slowly rose from the table to cover my mouth, trying to buy some time, searching for a question I might ask after hearing this bombshell.

"So your mother, Lizzie, how long did she work as a nurse at

Al Baker (Nashville Public Library, Special Collections).

John Randolph Clarke—all-night interrogation (Nashville Public Library, Special Collections).

Mayor Clifton Beverly Briley (Nashville Public Library, Special Collections).

Eva Jo Herring—midnight interrogation (Nashville Public Library, Special Collections).

John Randolph Clarke escorted away (Nashville Public Library, Special Collections).

Jailhouse prisoners search for missing book (Nashville Public Library, Special Collections).

Herring home exterior—Timberhill Drive, Nashville (Nashville Public Library, Special Collections).

John Randolph Clarke (*center*), Charles Galbreath (in dark glasses), and defense team (Nashville Public Library, Special Collections).

Metro Detective inspecting the crime scene (Nashville Public Library, Special Collections).

Eva Jo Herring—hands-up pose with Evelyn Johnson (from Evelyn Johnson).

Paula Herring Senior photo (from Evelyn Johnson).

Richard Walter—the living Sherlock Holmes (from Richard Walter).

Paula Herring in New West Dormitory (from V. F. Hochnedel).

7-32 (Rev. 4-16-57)

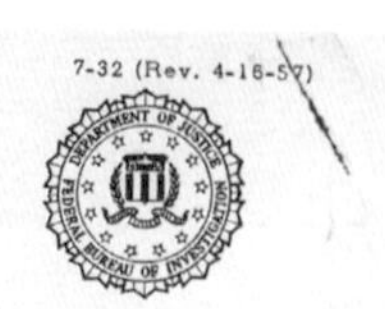

UNITED STATES DEPARTMENT OF JUSTICE

FEDERAL BUREAU OF INVESTIGATION

In Reply, Please Refer to
File No. D-444557 HE

WASHINGTON 25, D. C.

March 10, 1964

Mr. Hubert O. Kemp
Chief of Police
Nashville, Tennessee 37201

John R. Clarke - Suspect;
Paula Herring - Victim;
Murder
(Letter 3/5/64)

My dear Chief:

The FBI Laboratory has received the evidence which you sent for examination in connection with the above-entitled case. A Laboratory report will be sent to you after the examination has been completed.

You are assured of my desire to cooperate in these matters.

Sincerely yours,

J. Edgar Hoover

John Edgar Hoover
Director

J. Edgar Hoover—letter (Metro Nashville Archives, Metro Photographer Record Group).

Herring garage on Timberhill Drive (Metro Nashville Archives, Metro Photographer Record Group).

Lawyers for the prosecution: (*left to right*) John Hollins, Whit LaFon, David Murray, and Howard Butler (*The Tennessean*, September 22nd © 1964, Gannett-Community Publishing).

Eva Jo Herring—Registered Nurse (from Evelyn Johnson).

Wilmer Herring—Baylor University 1949 Yearbook Senior Photo (The Texas Collection, Baylor University, Waco, Texas).

March 2, 1964

Mrs.
West Longdale Drive
Nashville, Tennessee

Dear Mrs.

I am sorry that you have misunderstood my reaction to the conditions and developments in the Crieve Hall area.

Both my office and the Police Department are definitely interested in the safety and protection of all Metropolitan residents. The Police Department has had that area under close surveillance since sometime last fall. We do not believe that the prowler and the murderer have any relationship whatsoever.

On the night Miss Herring was murdered, I was leaving house in Crieve Hall when I heard the report to the Police Department over the shortwave radio in my car. I listened to the entire proceedings, and knew that a police car was at the home within two minutes from the time the police were notified. This indicated that police cars were in the immediate vicinity, in the normal course of duty.

For your information, the Police Department has been hampered in its activities in that area because many of the residents who have reported incidents called a nearby Fire Department of the office of the District Attorney rather than notify the Metropolitan Police. Since the Metropolitan Police Department is considered the local law enforcement agency, calls of this nature should be referred directly to them.

I have many night meetings and conferences which I must attend in performing my duties as Mayor of Metropolitan Nashville-Davidson County. On these occasions Mrs. Briley is left at home alone, since both our son and daughter are married and live to themselves. I have just as much concern for her safety, and that of my daughter, daughter-in-law, and their children, as the men who head the families of Crieve Hall residents. Please be assured that we are striving to give proper attention to all residential areas in our Metropolitan community.

Sincerely yours,

Beverly Briley, Mayor

GS/nl

cc: H. O. Kemp, Chief of Police

Mayor Briley's letter to Crieve Hall resident (Nashville Public Library, Special Collections).

Vanderbilt Hospital?" Gina's mouth fell open slightly, but she didn't try to deflect the question and simply answered, as I had hoped.

"I think a few years while we lived in the Music Row area and then after that at the VA Hospital."

"And when she worked at Vanderbilt, she found a new best friend named Jo Herring."

I stated this as a simple matter of fact, but my guest didn't offer a response. And I didn't say a word, as it was my turn to look at the cars in the drive-through lane outside, all the while hoping that she didn't notice my own hands sweating as I held onto my glass of iced tea as if it were the last stationary object on a boat being slammed by a summer storm.

"I could almost be a split personality. And so right now I know, I know kinda who you are. I don't think I'm in the story—see I don't know what the girl's name is right this minute. I know that she got killed. I know that you think that somebody . . . that we were around or knew about it or were there . . . but right this minute, I don't even remember what we've talked about. Even when I talk to you about it, it's kinda like it's all a dream. The whole accident happened and never even could get to court or anything."

"Do you think all of this in 1964 started out as an accident?" I asked.

"As an accident? If I had to put my druthers on it, I think it just started out as a . . . I don't think anybody meant to kill anybody . . . except that I think Jo's husband was meant to be killed."

"Who was behind that?" I asked, thinking, *This is unreal. This woman is talking about two murders, the father and the daughter? Why? How can she possibly know this?*

"I think Jo Herring was probably behind that," she said, with her now-familiar nervous laugh.

"Now let me tell you, I called BlueSky, and he called me right back."[2]

This was Gina's opening line as follow-up from our coffee shop meeting two weeks prior. Only this time, the conversation was by phone, as she was concerned about meeting again in public. Before we had departed from our first in-person meeting, I had convinced her that we should swap email addresses, and she had agreed. Not only had she agreed, she had asked if I would provide her with a brief summary of the Paula Herring story. Within hours, I sent her a few brief paragraphs, all similar to what she could have gleaned on her own from the newspapers of the day.

"Basically, I got nothing from BlueSky other than the fact that he did think . . . he thought I ought to call the police," she said.

"Gina, that's completely up to you. Feel free to call the authorities and tell them whatever you feel compelled to tell them," I said. "I'm certain they would love to hear from you on this topic, if you know what I mean."

"But then he decided that maybe I shouldn't call them," Gina concluded.

"I'm not surprised," I said.

"BlueSky kept telling me, did I realize his age, and, that was years ago. And I informed him I did. The thing is, I pretty much ran it by him that you were asking questions about Paula Herring and that you had found Jesse Henderson, and I got nothing, absolutely nothing from him in response."

"Well, that's unfortunate. But I still need his name, please. Where can I find him today?" I asked.

"You know that little boy would now be a man about your age."

"You think I'm Paula Herring's little brother come back to town for answers?" I asked.

"Aren't you?" she asked.

"No, I'm not the little boy that was in the house that night, though I'm certainly seeking answers," I said.

"Look, whoever that little boy is that wants to know about his father or his mother? I feel sorry for him. He's better off thinking his mother had absolutely nothing to do with anything and that it was the guy that did it or that it was his buddy that did it or whatever," she said.

"Gina, why don't you tell me what was going on the night that Paula Herring was, um, accidentally shot. Tell me about that night. How about your mom? What was Lizzie doing on that Saturday night?" I asked.

"My mother was not a good driver. Not good at all, really. She was more of a 'bumper in the wall' kind of driver, especially if she was trying to back up."

"Well, that's interesting. So you're saying that your mother had a little automobile accident on the night of the murder?"

There was complete silence on the other end of the phone line. I waited a moment before saying her name to bring her back into the conversation.

"I think maybe a car got trashed out on River Road that night. Maybe it had been out in Crieve Hall that night and it didn't need to be found." She said this in a near whisper.

"Gina, why do you think Paula Herring was killed?" I asked.

"I don't know, Mike; I really don't know. Maybe it had something to do with drugs? And it wasn't like they could tell Paula to drop out of school."

Who would be telling Paula Herring to drop out of school? I wondered.

"I don't see the connection with the victim and drugs. She was an athlete, so why would she use drugs?"

"I know that after my dad died a lot of people would come to our apartment to get meds. Sometimes it was college students and sometimes it was truck drivers. There were a lot of professional wrestlers who were customers. I didn't realize what was going on at first, but I eventually figured out that my mom was selling them right out of our house."

"What kind of meds?" I asked.

"The usual back then, uppers and downers and pain killers."

"You're talking about amphetamines and barbiturates?" I asked.

"Sure. Speed helped you lose weight and you could study for hours. I guess you could drive a truck for hours, too. And the downers and pain killers let you sleep when you wanted to sleep. When you mixed in some booze, it was a pretty good high, or so I was told," she said.

"So, I'm thinking because of your mother's work and her lifestyle, maybe you were exposed to a lot of powerful people when you were growing up in Nashville," I said.

Her voice began to take on a shaky quality with her reply, as if I'd hit on a nerve and a sensitive topic.

"Well, there was this . . . person in town . . . that thought nothing of making a financial arrangement with my mom, and she'd say, 'Well, you know, whatever you work out with her,' and let him go on with what he had planned."

"You mean, 'Here's some money, Lizzie, and I'm gonna try out your daughter Gina'?" I asked.

"Or, 'Here's some money, and since I'm paying your rent, you just sit down over there and be quiet.'"

"I'm so sorry you were used that way," I said, almost in a whisper.

"Well, for your story, I think the only positive thing about it is that hopefully the little boy is alive and he's got a good life to lead, and hopefully he can put some of this behind him . . . and realize it was not his fault and that he could not have stopped it. . . . He might have some guilt that he survived and nobody else did, and . . . well . . . the pleas for help . . . he may have heard something or saw something that even now he will never remember that he saw or heard," she said.

"How's your mother doing, by the way? How is Lizzie these days?" I asked.

"She has good days and bad. When I was growing up, my mom and dad would take off. You know what I mean? They would just vanish for days at a time. My grandmother would take care of me. My mother was, um, a little like Lizzie Borden on drugs sometimes.[3] She could go a little crazy, if you know what I mean? Like, she could have fired those shots in the floor at the house that night."

"The shots fired through Paula's back into the floor?"

"Yes."

At this news, I was certain that my heart had stopped. I had been sitting at my desk in a private office across from the Tin Angel restaurant on West End Avenue when I heard these words, and I stood up, took a couple of deep breaths, and attempted to offer a feeble response.

"So, let me ask you. Has anyone tried to blackmail you over this story?"

"No. Not so far."

"Gina, I really need to meet with BlueSky. Where can I find him?" I asked.

"I can't help you with that. I just can't. Have you talked to Jesse lately?" she asked.

"No, he's gone missing again. Would you know a reason for that?"

"No, I don't, but I'm not surprised," she responded.

"Where can I find our friend, Mr. BlueSky?"

"I've got to go now. I'm sorry."

And then the phone line went dead. But what I hadn't told Gina was that I already had crafted a plan to find her old friend BlueSky, and I really didn't need her help.

CHAPTER TWENTY-FOUR

SINNERS

Before there was a drive-in restaurant at 2501 Franklin Road in Nashville near the Melrose area, there was a hotel at the exact same spot. The York Hotel Court was the official name, though everyone referred to it as the York Motel, and it was a one-story, forty-room motor court. Postcards created by the owner described the property as Nashville's newest and finest, AAA approved and just two blocks south of Nashville's city limit. In smaller print, additional notes informed the potential guest that every room in the York had a telephone, a television, and sound insulation, a feature that may have been in demand on a cold night in February 1964.

While it didn't carry the prestige of the Noel Hotel near Printers Alley, the York Hotel Court was in a high traffic area for those making their way to the mecca of country music, the Ryman Auditorium. In the days of pre-interstate travel, it was two days from Florida and one from Chicago. In fact, Roy Orbison and Elvis Aaron Presley were occasional guests at the York, as were a number of professional wrestlers on the multistate circuit managed by Nick Gulas and Roy Welch.[1]

On Sunday morning, February 23, 1964, the housekeeping crew at the York arrived to find the typical list of to-dos: changing linens, cleaning bathrooms, and emptying ashtrays. They did not expect to find a substantial amount of blood on the floor in one of the guest rooms—enough blood to alert management, who, having read in the morning newspaper about a young coed being slain the night before in nearby Crieve Hall, decided to call the police.

A few days after the bloody motel room was found, John Clarke's defense attorney, Charles Galbreath, visited the motor court to take a deposition from the owner, indicating that Paula Herring's killer may have been so bloody from the slaying that he hid out at the York Motel after unsuccessfully attempting to make a phone call at the Krystal hamburger restaurant just down the street. The distance from the Krystal to the York Motel was so close it could be walked in a handful of minutes, and by car it was just over a half-minute trip from one location to the other.

Forty years later, a bit of research and a couple of phone calls confirmed that the 1964 owner of the York Motel was a man named Jack Spence. Spence, upon being contacted, easily remembered that his wife's uncle, J. J. Richmond, had been managing the motel at the time of the 1964 Crieve Hall murder. When asked about the possibility that the uncle was still alive, Spence said, "Yes, he's in a nursing home near Hartsville, Tennessee."[2]

I asked about the bloody room, and Spence unhappily remembered calling the police, only to find out that they had no interest in his discovery. But defense attorney Charles Galbreath got news of this possible alternate suspect in the murder, and he came to the York to investigate. Spence also remembered having to replace the carpet in the room because an attempt to clean it had failed.

Hartsville is a wide path in the road about forty miles northeast of Nashville. The little town of two thousand residents has the dubious distinction of being neighbors with one of Tennessee's most expensive abandoned properties, a two billion dollar nuclear plant, which began construction more than a decade after Paula Herring had been murdered and then was swiftly abandoned by the Tennessee Valley Authority before the plant ever went into operation.[3]

Not far from Hartsville proper, I turned into the driveway of a country nursing home, a tidy property with a wide front porch and rocking chairs at street level and another ranch-style house running perpendicular at the basement level.

As I walked up the path to the front door, I greeted an old gentleman apparently dozing in one of the rocking chairs. He slowly raised his head as I approached and asked if I could help him unzip the top pocket of his faded bib overalls. I cautiously agreed, and then he asked if I would also reach down into the pocket and see if he had any cigarettes there. My first thought was that the next day's newspaper would tell the story of "man slain by nursing home resident with pocket full of scorpions." I was needlessly worried, as the pocket held neither scorpions nor cigarettes. I could tell he was disappointed, and silently I was hoping that Mr. Tobacco wasn't Jesse James Richmond.

A few moments later, after being allowed entrance into the facility, I carefully made my way down the hall, reading the names of the residents affixed to each doorway and making sure I remembered to smile and say hello to anyone who happened to glance my way.

With a bit of help, I found Mr. Richmond's room on the first floor. He had just finished lunch and was still sitting up in bed, reading the newspaper. He was a large man with an expressive face and a bit of sparse gray hair, and he read without glasses. A quick glance at a note tacked to his bulletin board indicated that he had just celebrated his eighty-ninth birthday two days prior. To me, he looked a decade younger than his actual age.

Introductions were a struggle, as Mr. Richmond's hearing was as bad as his eyesight was good. I kept thinking, *This man must have a hearing aid somewhere in the room,* as I stood at his bedside practically shouting my reason for visiting him. Every time I had to yell the word "murder," I looked toward the doorway to see if a security guard was coming to escort me out of the building, but fortunately no one did. I moved closer to his bedside and directed my much louder than normal voice at his left ear.

"Mr. Richmond, you worked at the York Motel as the night clerk?"

"No, as a manager with my wife."[4]

I produced a copy of the deposition Charles Galbreath had created for the former motel manager to sign in 1964, hoping to refresh his memory and also to interrupt our high-volume conversation.

"You remember that weekend and the girl being murdered?"

"Yeah, I looked out a window and saw 'em."

"Excuse me?"

"Me and my wife lived in a room around back of the motel and we had already changed shifts with the night clerk," he said.

"What time was the shift change?" I asked.

"Oh, we swapped out somewhere around 8:30 p.m. on most nights."

"So who was the night clerk?"

"We used students from that school, where they studied to be a preacher."

"David Lipscomb?"

"No, up on Murfreesboro Road."

I thought for a moment, and then it came to me. "Oh, you mean Trevecca?"

"Yeah, Tu-vecca."

"Why do you remember that night, if you didn't check the guests into their room?" I asked.

"Because they rented a room around back," he said.

This part of the explanation made sense to me, because as was the style of motor courts, at the York Motel you literally parked your car directly in front of your room, so close you were barely two steps from the room's front door. Anyone renting a room on the front side of the building easily could have been seen by drivers and passengers on Franklin Road.

"They rented a room around back?"

"Yeah, and they were making some noise, and I looked out the window and saw 'em."

"How many people?" I asked.

"Two or three."

"Any women?"

"Yeah, a couple of them," he said.

"Did anyone come talk to you about that night?" As I inquired, I tapped my finger on the deposition that J. J. was still holding in his hand.

"That lawyer Galbreath and somebody else I think."

"What about the deposition? You didn't sign it?" I asked.

"No, and I don't remember why I didn't," he replied.

The return visit to Miss Evelyn's home was a lunchtime session, which involved bologna sandwiches, sliced American cheese, fresh tomatoes, and iced tea. Having experienced the regular ringing of the telephone on my previous visit with her, I decided to make good use of my time and jump right into a few questions for my feisty witness as we sat down for lunch at her kitchen table.

"Miss Evelyn, any chance you knew other nurses who might have been close friends with Jo Herring?" I inquired.

"No, none come to mind," she said.[5]

"How about the name Amanda, does that sound familiar?"

As I asked this question, she was finishing the final touches on her sandwich, adding a slice of iceberg lettuce to the stack.

"No, that name doesn't mean anything to me."

"I'm told that Jo might also have been close friends with a woman named Lizzie," I offered.

At the mention of this name, Evelyn's face whipped quickly to the left, away from me, and I registered the invisible slap as a clue.

"There are just some things I don't care to remember," she said, while continuing to look away.

"Why don't we talk about the trial in Jackson," I suggested. "Tell me about staying at the New Southern Hotel."

"Oh, I think they had some fun."

"Really? Wasn't there a murder trial going on that week?" I asked.

"Yes, in fact I roomed with Jo the night I was there, but after my testimony I came back to Nashville. Those people were partying like it was New Year's Eve. I remember Jo got a cab driver to take her to a bootlegger somewhere around Jackson, and she brought back a case of liquor. They partied the whole week. Of course, I had a little fun myself. I remember hiding in a hotel room that one of the DA's investigators was staying in, and after he entered the room he discovered me in his bed wearing nothing but one of Jo's expensive negligees. He was so surprised but also very unhappy about it. I think he was one of the straight-laced guys."

"I can imagine. You say it was one of the DA's men? Did Jo Herring have a pretty good relationship with the district attorney's office in Nashville?" I asked.

"Are you kidding me? She was seeing one of the attorneys." Evelyn said.

I nearly choked at this news, but recovered quickly. "She was dating a lawyer in the district attorney's office?"

"Yes."

"You mean at the time of the trial in Jackson?" The astonishment on my face must have been quite visible at this point.

"Sure. The negligee that I was wearing was one I borrowed from Jo, and it had been a gift to her from the assistant DA. Of course he was married, so it was kept quiet."

I stopped eating, got up from the table in hopes that she couldn't read my face, and walked over to the counter to pour myself another glass of iced tea while staring out the window.

"So who was the lawyer?" I asked.

"I'll just call him a 'big guy,' but other than that I'd rather not say. Let's just leave it at that," she said.

"No problem. I know there were about a dozen attorneys who worked in the DA's office. I don't suppose this, uh, 'big guy' was in Jackson at the trial was he?"

"He sure was."

As she said this, I was shaking my head in disbelief, pondering the implications of this bombshell news.

"They had a few places around Nashville where they could go during the day or whenever they wanted to get away for a little while." She said this as if it was of little importance, though she could clearly see I was hanging on every word.

"You mean something like a secret hideaway or a safe house?" I asked.

"Yes, one was a cabin near Marrowbone Lake, and there was a boat up on Old Hickory Lake they could use," she said.

I remembered Marrowbone Lake as one of the best kept secrets in the area. It was small, beautiful, and remote, and mostly ignored by locals and tourists alike. The lake was near Joelton, where I had found Jesse Henderson.

"And there was an apartment not far from downtown. The apartment had more liquor in it than a liquor store." She laughed as she gave me this news.

"I feel like I should ask who all was involved."

"A couple of low-level police detectives, some lawyers, and some politicians."

"And, let me guess, some nurses, right?"

"Jo and me and one of the other nurses. Now this was a long time ago, Mike, way before I got married. I wasn't that interested in the older guys in the group, I wanted young blood on my body. And it was 1964, and I suppose a lot of folks were doing all kinds of things back then and probably still do."

"So how did you get together?"

"Oh, we'd just make a plan to meet in the middle of the day, or sometimes after work. We'd meet up with a couple of the guys at one of the hideouts, have some fun, and then maybe swap up and have some more fun!"

"But all of the guys, they were married, right?" I asked.

"Sure, but they weren't exactly running home to tell their wives what they were up to."

"I bet not. So where was the apartment?" I inquired.

"You know where Zanies is nowadays?"

"Yes, ma'am. The comedy club?"

"Yes. It was back behind it. Walking distance to Wedgewood Diner back then. And there was a drugstore there before the comedy club," she said.

I thought about this and then continued: "It sounds like this group had setup their own private Printers Alley?"

"It sure was!" she said with gusto.

"Wouldn't your testimony in Jackson at the criminal trial have been just a little bit compromised? I mean there was John Randolph Clarke, on trial for his life, and yet one of the lawyers trying to send him to prison just happens to be having sex with a key witness, the mother of the victim?"

"We had to lie. There was no other option. None."

I was so engrossed in Evelyn's story, I didn't think to ask her why she was willing to be so forthcoming with me. But the answer may have surfaced near the end of our session when I sensed a bit of sadness in my new friend, perhaps the presence of remorse over the tragic events that had taken place decades earlier.

Before Clifton Beverly Briley became Metro Nashville's first chief executive officer—its mayor—a position he held for twelve years, he served twelve years as chief executive of Davidson County, the county judge. Briley was a visionary, and as such he had served as the president of the National Association of County Executives prior to being elected mayor of the new Metropolitan Government. There had been talk of Briley pursuing the governor's office as well, a position he likely would have won if then Governor Frank Clement had vacated the office to run for president.

In January of 1964, during Briley's first year as mayor, he celebrated his fiftieth birthday. During his first fifty years, Briley had accumulated an impressive array of accomplishments. At age thirteen, he was touted as having been the youngest person in Nashville to attain the rank of Eagle Scout, and he had then graduated from Central High School in 1930, at the age of sixteen. Briley also had the good fortune of being noted as a Vanderbilt University graduate, as well as attaining his law degree from Cumberland Law School in Lebanon, Tennessee, and he was admitted to the bar at the impressive age of eighteen. The law school curriculum in that era was an accelerated program of study available for those pursuing the apprentice-style degree in the 1930s.[6]

A bit of research revealed that Cumberland Law School had been sold and relocated to Samford University in Birmingham, Alabama, in 1961. When I contacted the relocated school, they confirmed Briley's achievement. The school also confirmed that Charles Galbreath had completed his law degree there, though he was a bit older than Beverly Briley when he did so.

But the claim that Briley was a graduate of Vanderbilt University was a complete myth. Briley never completed a single semester at Vanderbilt University, let alone earned a degree at the prestigious school. He may have had intentions to earn a degree at Vanderbilt, but instead he enrolled in the accelerated law program at Cumberland in 1930 and then graduated in the early summer of 1932.

Despite this, numerous mentions of the graduation from Vanderbilt University have been recorded in historical records, among them Metro resolutions, such as the resolution by the 10th Metro Council that named the Criminal Courts building in Briley's honor. Briley's son, however, did graduate from Vanderbilt University in the early 1960s.

So I decided to review again a letter I first found in Chief Hubert Kemp's file, written ten days after Paula Herring's murder by Mayor Beverly Briley to a woman who lived in the Crieve Hall area, approximately one mile from the Herring's home.[7] After some research, I found the woman and her husband living in another state. When I asked them about the timeline of the Paula Herring murder, the wife remembered that the week following the murder had been especially tense. She also remembered the postman complaining that homeowners wouldn't answer their doors as he attempted to deliver packages in the neighborhood.

The mayor's letter had been written in response to the woman's complaint that Metro police had not been sensitive to the prowler issue, and that Mayor Briley did not appear to be concerned regarding the safety of Metro citizens. Briley's response had been copied to the metro chief of police, Hubert Kemp.

But therein lay the problem. Not only had the mayor's letter not been received by the couple in March 1964, neither of the stated recipients of the letter had ever voiced a single concern to the mayor's office. Ever. And even more extraordinary, Briley had penned a letter placing himself in the Crieve Hall neighborhood, not only on the night of Paula Herring's murder, but at the time of the murder. Did Kemp know something about Briley's activities on this night, and if so, was this Kemp's method of forcing Briley to explain his presence in writing?

CHAPTER TWENTY-FIVE

RESEARCH OR REINVESTIGATION?

Dinner would be at one of Nashville's oldest steakhouses. And it would be just the two of us: myself and a man named Keller.[1] Keller had spent decades working as a homicide investigator in Middle Tennessee. A jolly man with tortoiseshell glasses, a slick bald head, and a keen grasp of Tennessee's homicide history, he had an extensive background in determining cause of death, both with classroom and field training, as well as on-the-job experience.

In a previous meeting, approximately a year earlier, Keller had provided me with a photo autopsy of Paula Herring.[2] For a couple of hours, he used the crime-scene photographs and the other exhibits in the file, along with an array of magnifying lenses, to examine the images of the gunshot entrance and exit paths through the sweater and skirt of the victim. Then he moved to a review of Paula's physical injuries—the deep bruises on her face, fingernail marks on her throat, and bullet entry and exit wounds on her body—and noted as well the postmortem blood pooling, as evident in the pictures of Paula lying on a metal gurney.

Eventually, Keller's conclusion matched that of Dr. Al Harper, that Paula Herring had been shot three times, twice in the back and once in the front, in the upper chest. He also noted that one bullet was very likely still inside Paula's body. Keller said that the collarbone shot appeared to have been fired into the victim while the victim was on her knees, primarily because of a raised area of skin and discoloration on Paula's lower back that was clearly evident in one of the black and white photographs of her. He noted that the detectives shown in the photo had gone to the trouble of rolling the victim onto her side and then pointing at the area in question.

During the same review, it was Keller who had studied the photograph of the den where Paula had been found and then stated that the unidentified object resting beneath the television set was in fact a little green army man.[3] "I used to play with those," I said. I remembered the two inch tall green, plastic toy soldiers, that kids used to play with.

Even more surprising was when Keller pointed to the photograph of the interior of the Timberhill Drive garage and said, "See that dry spot on the floor near the broken bottle? See how it fans out? It's dry there because whoever got hit in the head with the bottle blocked the splatter. That's a person's outline. Was the Clarke fellow injured during the slaying?" he asked.

"No. But one theory is that a truck stop manager named Carlton might have been hit with the beer bottle," I replied.

At one point during the session, I mentioned that Jo Herring had found her husband, dead, at the Noel Hotel some three years prior to finding her dead daughter at home on a Saturday night, and from all reports, Jo Herring had not even been viewed as a suspect in the two deaths.

Keller asked for the cause of death for Paula's father.

"I found out that he drank rat poison, so it would have been arsenic," I said.

"Do you know how many men commit suicide by drinking poison?" he asked.

"No idea."

"I've investigated more than a thousand deaths in my career, and I can't remember even two of them where a man used poison to do himself in. Poison is a woman's weapon. You say the first person to find the dead man was his wife?" Keller asked.

"That's a fact," I said.

"We had a case a few years ago where a guy stumbled upon a body out in a remote area, miles from anywhere. I mean an area you wouldn't even know existed on a map. It didn't take the detectives two minutes to figure out that the guy who found the body was the guy who did the killing." Keller paused for a moment, then continued. "See the picture of the girl's mother walking down this hallway?"

Keller was pointing at a photograph of Jo Herring and a man walking along an interior hallway of what appeared to be a public building. Jo carried a large purse and overcoat on one arm, wore a high-necked dress, and sported a pair of cat-eye glasses. The man, sporting a flattop haircut, was wearing a white shirt with coat and tie and carrying a notepad in his right hand.

"What about it?"

"That's the Municipal Safety Building, downtown, and the guy escorting the Herring woman is Mickey McDaniel, one of the top detectives in the police department at that time. The point is, somebody brought her downtown, and I'm saying she must have been viewed as a suspect in the murder, from the looks of the photo, and the Metro photographer or somebody took this picture of her."[4]

"If that's true, it didn't make the paper," I replied.

Months later, Keller and I were waiting for our meal to be delivered at the upscale steakhouse, but this time the relaxed and jolly homicide investigator was on edge and seemed nervous. By the time we finished the first course, the source of the anxiety became clear.

"I spoke with one of the original investigators on the Herring case," Keller softly said. "I told him you were looking into it, and he wanted me to ask you something. Are you just doing some research, or are you reinvestigating the murder?"

The large window next to me reflected the color draining out of my face. I quickly reached for a glass of water to buy a few seconds of time before responding. "No, no, not a reinvestigation," I said. "I'm just researching some stories from Nashville's history. It's just interesting, that's all."

I could see Keller's somber demeanor as he refused to look at me and stared down at his salad plate. I took a slow scan around the restaurant to see if anyone was watching our meeting a little too intently. The next hour passed with a mix of non-homicide topics, which included memories of quirky politicians, famous eating places in Nashville, and a police sergeant who ran a prostitution business using nothing more than his squad car to deliver hookers to clients.

At the end of the meal, we said good-bye and went our separate ways into the night. As I walked back to my car, my thoughts were racing: *If I end up dead in the coming weeks, of just about any cause, my wife should probably alert the local district attorney that I was murdered. Could a couple of detectives, maybe the low-level detectives who were part of the group as Nurse Evelyn had mentioned, could those two detectives have helped clean up the crime scene on Timberhill Drive before the 11:00 p.m. call was made to the police dispatcher? Who better to do the deed, threaten Jo Herring, and then cover it up at the same time?*

PART IV

HOUSE FULL OF HELL

. . . and be sure your sin will find you out.

—Numbers 32:23, Old Testament

CHAPTER TWENTY-SIX

SHERLOCK HOLMES

With Gina's reluctance to aid the cause, and with Jesse Henderson's apparent departure from society, not to mention the lengthy challenge of tracking down his old friend BlueSky, I was almost ready to attend a séance in hopes of communicating with one of my childhood heroes, Sherlock Holmes. But a fictional detective was going to do little to help me, so I did the next best thing: I tracked down the man described by many as the "Living Sherlock Holmes," Mr. Richard Walter.[1]

Richard Walter, a brilliant forensic psychologist and one of the pioneers of criminal profiling, spent more than two decades and thousands of hours studying and working with convicted felons in the Michigan prison system, one of the largest populations of violent criminals in the United States.[2] In this "laboratory" setting, Walter honed his considerable talents with treatment and daily interviews of criminals of all varieties: serial killers, rapists, pedophiles, and more. And after a period of time, he began to share his findings and his insights with the academic community, as well as with law enforcement agencies.

Walter's insight was routinely requested for seemingly unsolvable cold cases and the most difficult of investigations, in part, because Richard Walter abhorred the routine and the outdated homicide investigation model, and instead preached a new gospel of recognizing and modeling the artistry, symbolism, and motivations of the criminal's own mind in order to solve cases. Eventually, he became an international consultant to law enforcement agencies, including Scotland Yard, where he was tagged with the "Sherlock Holmes" nickname he came to loathe, and he also provided consulting expertise to America's FBI and other agencies.[3]

In 1990, Richard Walter was one of the three founding members of the Vidocq Society, an organization named in honor of the famous French detective, François Vidocq, an eighteenth-century French criminal turned cop. Vidocq's ability to catch criminals was legendary, and he is credited with creating the first private detective agency in Paris in the early 1800s. Vidocq also had the foresight to hire former criminals to help with his new crime-solving enterprise.

With the founding of the new Vidocq Society, Richard Walter and his colleagues had a standing offer to provide free assistance to law enforcement personnel, especially if the case involved unsolved deaths and other major crimes. And, for the past twenty-five years, the best forensic minds in the world gather monthly for a meal in Philadelphia at the Union League to review, debate, and solve the unsolvable cases presented to its membership.[4]

A book about its founding members, *The Murder Room*, by Michael Capuzzo, was the catalyst behind my attempt to reach out to Walter. I hoped that he might listen to the story of the eighteen-year-old babysitter and perhaps provide a fresh perspective on a homicide investigation that was not so much unsolved, given John Randolph Clarke's 1964 conviction, as it was, perhaps, incorrectly solved.[5]

In November of 2011, while awaiting a flight from Providence, Rhode Island, back to Nashville, my cell phone rang, and a phone number that I did not recognize appeared on the screen, followed by a man's voice that I didn't know. When the speaker identified himself as Richard Walter, I remembered having left a voice message for him several days prior. His voice and speaking pattern was formal and distinct, a clipped enunciation of every word, with an occasional "my dear fellow" added to the conversation.

Richard Walter told me that he was preparing for a presentation at Drexel University as a panelist on the topic of Jack the Ripper,[6] but he wanted to know more about the research I was doing.

Over the next several minutes, I quickly told the story of the 1964 murder and the little boy who slept through the tragic event. I noted the missing paperback book, Jo Herring's secret lifestyle with powerful men in the community, and her close relationship with a nurse named Lizzie. I then noted my personal involvement, including the assistance of Dr. Al Harper of the Henry Lee Institute in Connecticut. I was careful not to include any of my own assumptions along the way, but instead I attempted to let the facts, as reported in 1964, be presented for evaluation.

Perhaps my mention of Dr. Harper was confirmation that I was committed to finding the truth with regard to Paula Herring's slaying. After stating that I had no law enforcement or legal background, I was relieved to hear Walter say that he knew Dr. Harper and that he wanted to learn more about the slaying of the babysitter. And thus began an enlightening exchange with a world-class expert.

"Did the mother try to recruit the daughter into the partying lifestyle, the secret group in other words?" he asked.

"Not that I know of, and I don't think the daughter would have been open to it." I said.

"Do you know the mother's sexual preference? Many times the unusual interest in servicing men, whether for money or power, reflects other than heterosexual tendencies. Might she have had such a relationship with the nurse named Lizzie?"

"I don't know about that."

"Was the victim sexually assaulted in this crime?" he asked.

"Well, that's an interesting question. Technically, John Randolph Clarke, the man ultimately convicted of the crime, was initially charged with murder in the first-degree and also rape on the body of Paula Herring. But somewhere between the grand jury's indictment and the trial itself, the prosecution dropped the rape charge. The medical examiner testified that the victim had not been sexually assaulted, and I have no new information to cause me to disagree with that assessment."

"So, if a sex fiend did this, then what did he get out of it?" he asked.

"I don't think I can answer that," I replied.

"We'll come back to that in a moment. Was there an insurance policy in play?" he asked.

"Yes, with regard to the victim's father, found dead in 1960, and no, or at least unknown, with regard to the eighteen-year-old daughter," I said.[7]

"What about the cause of death for the victim's father?"

"Funny you should ask. His death was attributed to suicide, and the official cause noted as ingestion of rat poison, what I understand to be an arsenic-based solution. A bottle of it was found in his hotel room. Oh, and something else, want to know who discovered the body? His wife did, and she brought another nurse friend with her. And then, three-and-a-half years later, the widow discovers another dead family member, her eighteen-year-old daughter, but this time at home," I noted.

"My dear fellow, poison is a woman's murder tool. That's how women usually do murder. And, they almost always bring a witness when they, shall we say, 'discover' the crime. That's a red flag. We call that a 'clue' for investigators."

I started laughing and had to cover my mouth to keep from making too much noise. I then apologized to my new friend on the phone. His dry wit was a nice break from the seriousness of the conversation, and I had not been expecting it.

"Were there any facial injuries on the victim, or defensive wounds? And how would you describe the room where the victim was found?" he asked.

"A lot of facial trauma, bruises, bloody nose, no apparent wounds on the hands or forearms. If the victim was engaged in a fight to the death, as I assume she was, the room was surprisingly 'in order,' with nothing in disarray except, of course, for the dead girl on the floor, the girl's sweater wadded up on the end of the couch, and a little toy army man underneath the television," I said.

"What was the official cause of death?" he asked.

"That would be two gunshots in the back, from a .32-caliber pistol, and noted to have been while the victim was lying facedown on the floor, either unconscious or semi-conscious, at least according to statements by the medical examiner."[8]

"And you say a child slept through the gunshots being fired in the house?"

"That's the story," I said.

"Do you understand how deafening that would be?"

"I'm familiar with firearms, so yes, I do."

"I assume you have a copy of the autopsy report?"

"Actually, I don't, because no autopsy was performed at the time," I said.[9]

"That's highly unusual. Can you get a hold of the medical examiner's records?"

"I made an attempt. They were left with the medical examiner's family after the old doctor passed away, but I'm told the family destroyed the records after a few decades, thinking they didn't want to take a chance on any of the information getting into the public realm. I can't say that I blame them for that. I do have the crime-scene photographs from the case, and they include some stark black and white photos of the victim as if she was being prepared for an autopsy, but no autopsy was performed," I said.

"At some point, it would be helpful for me to review those records. But in the interest of time, and given that you've got a plane to catch, let me offer some initial insight for your consideration."

"Thank you; I'm making notes," I said.

"Investigators tend to wander afar. This lead or that bit of information leads the investigator farther and farther away from the central issue."

"I can relate to that," I replied.

"Thus we go back to the central issue. There lies the person. Who has the closest interest? The victim was not sexually assaulted. She's not undressed. The room is not disturbed. Yet, she was murdered in her own home. If a sex fiend did this, what did he get out of it? So you have a purposeful killing, in your own home, with minimal cleanup."

"Purposeful?" I softly asked.

"There was a purposeful reason for the murder. And that could be this: It's likely what the girl knew, and what she might tell, ensured that she was going to die. Does that help you?"

"Yes, sir, most definitely. Thank you. I'll get a letter out to you over the weekend, and it will include some of the exhibits and other documents for review at your convenience."

"Good, let's stay in touch," he said.

CHAPTER TWENTY-SEVEN

CONTROLLING THE VICTIM

While driving through western North Carolina a few weeks later, my cell phone rang and I heard the unmistakable voice of my new friend Richard Walter. After a brief exchange and enough time for me to exit the road I was on, I pulled into an abandoned store's empty parking lot, whereupon Richard Walter proceeded to stun me with his initial assessment of the package I had sent to him.

"I reviewed your notes and photographs, and I have a few questions for you," he said.[1]

"Go ahead, I'm ready."

"What was John Clarke's defense on the witness stand?" he asked.

"That he didn't do the crime, had never met the victim, and was not in her neighborhood on that Saturday night. However, he had certainly met the mother, in the biblical sense, some two weeks prior to the eighteen-year-old victim coming home for the weekend. And he willingly testified for five hours on the witness stand during the week of the criminal trial in 1964," I said.[2]

"I see that the defendant's father was a judge. Did he support his son's defense? Provide bail money perhaps?" Walter asked.

"I believe the bail money was ultimately arranged through Clarke's wife. Basically, Clarke's father-in-law pledged some property in a nearby county as collateral to bond him out."[3]

"So Clarke's father saw the murder the way the state did?" Walter's voice lifted a half step with this question.

"No, I didn't mean to imply that. In fact, Clarke's father paid for a very good defense attorney from East Tennessee to be a part of his son's team at trial. The team was made up of four attorneys. And I did manage to meet with John Randolph Clarke's ninety-two-year-old stepmother in his hometown in East Tennessee. She may have been ninety-two, but she moved and acted as if she were fifty-two. We met in a church building in Jonesborough, and she told me straight up that there was no way John would have had the nerve to kill anyone. No way. He was more about fun and games than anything violent. At least that was her viewpoint of her stepson," I said.

"And you say there was no autopsy?"

"Correct."

"In one of the photographs of the victim, I think I see evidence of bruising on her neck consistent with the type of bruising left by a belt or strap, approximately one to two inches wide," he noted.

"Uh-oh. That hasn't come up before."

"It would explain some things," he said.

"How so?"

"With a strong athletic girl such as this victim, in this type of murder you have to control her. That is easily accomplished when you attack the victim from behind, using a belt or strap around the neck. It can be placed around the neck before the victim even realizes what's happening. With pressure, in just a few seconds the victim would lose consciousness; no oxygen flow to the brain, and you're out."

"Thirty seconds?" I asked.

"Actually less than that would do the trick," Walter said.

"Just like the Boston Strangler; that was his methodology," I replied. "Not with a belt. He used the crook of his arm to create a lever to accomplish the same thing, like a wrestler's sleeper hold," I mused aloud.[4]

"My dear fellow, this was a purposeful killing. That's an intentional word, meaning this wasn't some random event in the neighborhood that took place. There's no rape, and there's no robbery. I would view this as a bit of a mix between a Power Assertive murder, with evidence of Anger Retaliatory, though not completely anger in motivation. The victim is left dead and posed in a classic Anger Retaliatory pose. She could have been controlled with a belt or strap, moved into the den, and then finished off, though I must say it appears to have taken some effort to kill her."

"It's just chilling to hear you describe it," I said. All was quiet for a few moments as I thought about the visual Richard Walter had painted. I sat quietly in my car, staring toward an orange sun slowly dropping behind the mountain range west of Asheville, North Carolina. From the background research I had done on Richard Walter, I knew some held him up as the father of modern criminal profiling, and, together with Dr. Robert Kessler, he had proposed a more useful model for profiling killers. As for the Power Assertive type that he mentioned, I learned that it simply meant that the murder was most likely unplanned but part of controlling the victim.[5] Then, Walter surprised me with another question.

"Would you be able to come to Philadelphia and present the case to the Vidocq Society? Normally, we only look at unsolved cold cases, but this is a unique set of circumstances, if I may say so. A few times per year we have a formal presentation of a case during the monthly meal. Members will be asking you questions and sometimes arguing with each other over the interpretation. I can help you with the presentation. You can travel for this, yes?"[6]

I wanted to say yes and thank him for even considering the Paula Herring murder as a possible topic for the world's best investigators, but I knew how the invitation would eventually resolve itself, so I said the words I hated to say to the man I least wanted to disappoint.

"I can't tell you how helpful that would be, and I'm flattered that the case would be considered, but if I understand correctly, your bylaws say you only take cases presented by law enforcement or a related party, but not private citizens."

"You're not connected to a law enforcement agency?"

"No, sir, I am not. Just a private citizen with a commitment to discovering what really happened to the babysitter."

"Well, that would have been an interesting presentation. Let's see, I'll be in Atlanta at the American Academy of Forensic Science Conference in a few weeks. Can you meet me there? I'll have some additional notes for you by then, and I'll have some insights regarding the little boy who slept through the murder," he said.

"I'll find a way to be there, and I look forward to it."

I could not foresee that, a few weeks later in Atlanta, Richard Walter would also explain a mystery that I had previously decided was unknowable, the reason that Jo Herring had purchased not one but two burial plots hours after her daughter's murder.

CHAPTER TWENTY-EIGHT

AMERICAN VETERANS

Now I had two important missing people I needed to find—Jesse Henderson and BlueSky. Unknown to Gina, I had already devised a roadmap of sorts to BlueSky. My plan was a simple one, I just needed to find Jesse Henderson's daughter. My thinking was that if BlueSky truly was an old friend of Jesse Henderson, then he also might have a World War II background, perhaps another Navy man. After mulling it over, I came to the conclusion that there were only two possible people on the planet whom Jesse Henderson would keep track of at his advanced age. His daughter was one. And BlueSky was the other.

I did not know the daughter's name, nor how old she was, if she had ever been married, or if she had been married five times. I did remember being told that she might be living in North Carolina, and I got the impression that Jesse Henderson might have been in contact with her because he always spoke glowingly of his only child.

Since I didn't know where Jesse Henderson was living, I wasn't going to receive any help from him in finding his friend BlueSky, nor was I going to get an assist from Gina. But I realized that a mother most likely would know where her daughter was living. And if the daughter could point me toward the missing Jesse Henderson, then maybe I had another shot at finding BlueSky.

Unknown to Jesse, I previously had found his former wife, Betty, almost a year earlier, living exactly as Henderson himself had described, in the mountains of North Georgia. Our conversation had taken place in a nursing home where Betty's mother was a patient. The discussion went rather well, except for the times when Jesse Henderson's former mother-in-law accused me of being the devil and told her daughter to kick me out of the room.

In exchange for insights into her ex-husband, the former Mrs. Henderson made me promise that I would not, under any circumstances, alert Jesse that I had found her or had met with her. And I kept my promise.

She explained to me that, in the early years of the 1960s, Jesse had quite a track record of checking himself into the VA hospital when he needed to avoid creditors or the consequences of some unflattering behavior.

When I asked her point-blank if she thought her ex-husband would have had the capacity to kill an eighteen-year-old college coed in 1964, she thought about her reply, and then said, "Yes, he might have been able to do it, but he'd never be able to shut up about it."[1]

A year later, I called Betty again to ask if she could put me in touch with her daughter, because I was sure the daughter could help me find the now-missing father.

"Can you help me with the city and state where she currently lives. And her last name?" I pleaded.

"No, I cannot," she said.

Ignoring the silence, I said, "I'm grasping at straws here; I really am."

"I can only say she doesn't live in Tennessee."

There was silence on the other end of the line, and then she said the words that I needed most:

"Try 'Daggets' near Black Mountain, North Carolina. That's the best I can do for you."

I breathed an audible sigh of relief, and said, "Thank you."

A few days later, on my way toward dialing every "Daggets" in and around the Asheville, North Carolina, area, a man answered his home phone in the middle of the day.

"Good afternoon, my name is Michael Bishop. I'm calling to reach the daughter of a Mr. Jesse Henderson, a man who lived in the Nashville, Tennessee, area, and may still live in the Nashville area, but that's what I'm trying to confirm by speaking with his daughter."

"What's the nature of your business with Mr. Henderson?" he asked.

"That's a good question," I said, while smiling and silently fist-pumping an *I've found her!* "I got to know Mr. Henderson years ago, and he was helping me with a story of the early days of Metro Nashville, and then, just like that, he vanished. The nursing home he was living in closed down, and the residents were sent elsewhere. I could never find him after that."

"Must be an important story," he responded.

"Yes, sir, it is. I'm hoping his daughter can help me find him. It would mean a great deal if she could call me, please."

"If you leave your number, I'll pass it along to her, but don't expect a call is all I'm saying. Okay?" he said.

But within twenty-four hours, she did call, and she was more than intrigued. After a lengthy conversation that involved me doing most of the talking and her vetting my motivations, I explained my need to speak with her father as soon as possible.

"I don't know you," she said.[2]

"You certainly don't," I responded.

Her reply was unexpected. "He's in a better place now."

My heart sank, and I bowed my head, knowing what was coming next. "He's dead, right?"

"Oh, no. He's doing just fine," she said.

"Really?"

"Yes, but I want to know the story that is so intriguing that you wouldn't give it up. And how is my father involved?"

I took a deep breath, switched the phone to my other hand, and thought about the reply for more than a few seconds before responding.

"Here's the deal. The story involves your father and the first big murder case to take place in Metro Nashville history. The murder was that of an eighteen-year-old college student. The girl's little brother slept through the tragedy, which took place in their ranch-style brick house in the suburbs of Nashville. Your father knew some of the . . . well, let's just say your father knew the man convicted of the crime and leave it at that. That's why I need to speak with him."

"You think my father was involved in the murder?" she said.

"No, I'm not saying that at all."

"If it's this important to you, there must be something wrong with the outcome and that's why you're on it," she said.

"You're a very smart woman. That is what I believe, and I also believe your father may know the other players involved," I said.

"I'll speak with him and ask if he's willing to see you. Is that fair enough?"

"It's more than fair; it's gracious of you," I replied.

"And you say he'll remember your name?"

"I have no doubt; just please tell him that the Cheap Detective wants to stop by and say hello."

A day later I was in New England in a hotel room, preparing for a work meeting with a client, when my cell phone rang. I walked across the room to look out at the Boston skyline as I answered the call. A team was sculling the Charles River across from Harvard University in the late afternoon sunlight.

"I was hoping that was you," I said with a smile.

"It is. My father will see you."

"That's wonderful news. Thank you. How is he and where is he?"

"He's in a new nursing home, because the last one, if you can call it that, kicked all of their residents out on the street and closed down."

"I'm sorry to hear that, though I can't say I'm surprised," I said. "When I went back to visit Jesse, the place was empty and looked like an abandoned house, which I suppose it was. Your father has had a tough life, I take it?"

"Yes, his father took off when he was young, and his mother raised him while she worked as a nurse in Nashville. He used to tell me that one of his girlfriends would put out her lit cigarettes on him while he was sleeping. Not exactly a happy life," she said.

I let this last comment go by without a response and pondered why I had never asked Jesse what his mother did for a living. "Where do I find him now?" I asked.

"Oh, no, you're not getting off that easily. I want to hear the story."

"Why is that?" I asked.

"My father said he witnessed a murder, and that's why you're after him."

✧ ✧ ✧

Exactly one week after hearing Jesse Henderson's puzzling confession through his daughter, I was allowed to enter a locked nursing home facility south of the Davidson County line. It was a hot steamy day in late July 2011, and I was taking an early lunch hour in hopes of visiting my favorite local World War II Veteran.

After signing in, I asked the young man at the receptionist desk if Mr. Jesse Henderson was available. I was met with the usual suspicious facial expression that implied I was either a lawyer stopping by to take a deposition from one of the residents regarding some facility malfeasance or perhaps a state inspector, so I quickly cut to the chase.

"I'm an old friend of Mr. Henderson. He's expecting me, and I haven't seen him in years." Moments later, I was at Jesse's doorway, looking inside at the same kind of image I had seen a few years earlier—a very thin man lying in bed on his back reading a book, a white sheet pulled up under his arms. He had an ancient pair of reading glasses riding at a sharp angle on his nose in an attempt to increase the magnification of the lenses.

He was due for a shave, as his white beard had a few days of growth, and his short white hair was as wild looking and uncombed as ever. His hospital bed was propped up at an angle so he could read, and he had a private room with a good window to see the outside world.

I wasn't without sympathy for the old man; his daughter, who obviously cared a great deal for her father, had told me that he had spent a life filled with anxiety and post-traumatic stress disorder. I had no reason to doubt any of it. She remembered that he would write poems and songs from time to time, though the subject matter of his creative side was too dark for any commercial success.

"I thought you'd left the country," I announced.

He looked in my direction. "Who's that?"[3]

I walked over to his bedside and stuck out my hand. "It's your old friend, the cheap detective. Remember me?"

He offered a weak hand; his long thin fingers seemed even longer, with yellow nails that had not been trimmed in many days.

"Yeah, my daughter said you'd be coming to see me. You finished writing that book yet? What was the name of that guy that shot that girl?" he asked.

"No book yet," I said. "I did speak with your daughter, and she helped me figure out what happened to you after you left Joelton."

"She's my pride and joy," he said.

"So they kicked you out on the streets after they closed the place down in Joelton. That wasn't very nice of them. Getting good treatment here, I hope?"

"Yeah, can't complain. What can I do for you?" he asked.

"After I lost track of you, I was certain I'd never meet up with you again. It's been a while. It's good to see you."

He adjusted his reading glasses and then fumbled with the book now resting open on his chest.

"Jesse, you ever speak with your old friend BlueSky?" I asked.

"No, I reckon he's dead," he replied.

"You're probably right. He'd be getting on up there in years if he were still around. You too, for that matter," I noted. At this point, I considered pulling a chair up near the bed, but I decided to just stand on his right side and chat for a few minutes.

"You know, I never met BlueSky or spoke with him when he was alive," I stated.

"His family had money. He had an uncle who was rich as anything," he said.

"Jesse, it's been about a half century since you and BlueSky and Lizzie made the trip for them to get married in front of a judge in Alabama. Did you realize that?"

"It was that long ago? Not much of a marriage, I don't reckon."

I had wondered whether Jesse Henderson would take the bait, and he had.

"How did Lizzie's first husband die?" I asked.

"I reckon he drank himself to death," he said.

"You know Paula Herring's father drank rat poison, and then his loving wife was the first one to find him."

Jesse Henderson looked directly at me and asked, "You think that was the first time she ever did that?"

My puzzled facial expression must not have been enough, so I asked, "Did what?"

"Went to look for her husband," he replied.

"Just my opinion, but I bet she couldn't have cared less where he was any other time," I said.

"I imagine she went looking to make certain he was dead, don't you?" he said.

I could sense that Jesse was in a talkative mood and was enjoying dribbling out little gems of information, so I moved the conversation along with a political question.

"Didn't you tell me you were a veteran?" I asked.

"Yeah, and I used to hang out with a bunch of them down at AMVETS."[4]

"Like American Veterans of World War II, that group?" I inquired.

"Yeah, me and Red Clarke, BlueSky, the mayor, a bunch of us used to hang around there and drink a cold one from time to time," Jesse said.

"You're talking about Mayor Briley. He was dead and gone before I ever moved here," I said.

"We were all Navy men. During the war I was on an oiler, and the mayor was on a destroyer.[5] Plus, they'd leave the mayor alone in there. He could get out of the office a few hours without being bothered," Jesse said.

Without missing a beat, Jesse Henderson looked out the window at the sun-filled parking lot full of cars. "Hey, who was paying for that girl's tuition? You reckon her momma paid for it with insurance money?" he asked.

I turned my gaze to the window as well, "I don't think so. That insurance money paid for a house on Timberhill Drive."

"I'm thinking a government official might have been involved with that Herring woman."

"Now, why would a government official be paying for Paula Herring's tuition?" I asked.

"I used to know a patient at Vanderbilt Hospital who'd keep whiskey in his locker over there."

"Yeah, I know of more than one politician who spent some time drying out at Vanderbilt," I said.

Jesse Henderson was on a roll, and I was content to let him guide the conversation. The hallway behind me had little noise, and no one was bothering us at this point.

"Wonder what caused that girl to get killed anyway? You think it might have been drug related?" he asked.

"I've actually heard that once before."

"I thought they kept pretty good track of those medicines," he said.

"I guess it depends on who's counting them," I said.

"Lizzie used to have a key to the medicines when she worked at the hospital. She could be vicious. No evidence that the Herring girl was involved with drugs, was there?" Jesse asked.

"Paula Herring? Nothing in my research indicated that she was," I said.

I heard a noise behind me, and a young nurse with a medicine bottle and paper cup in her hand entered the room. I introduced myself as an old friend of her resident and then stepped to the other side of the room while she gave Jesse the medication.

As she fussed over the old man, I could see his sense of humor was having a positive effect, and she seemed to enjoy his witty personality.

After she left the room, I suggested that Jesse was getting treated like royalty, attempting to tease him in a friendly way, but his response surprised me.

"I wonder why they treated that Herring woman like she was royalty?" he asked.

Before I could respond, I glanced at the old man and realized that whatever medicine the nurse had just administered, it was having a fast impact. Jesse's eyes were closed, and his breathing rate was slowing down. I knew my time with him was at an end for this visit. So I said goodbye and told him I'd be back in a few days with a handful of books for him to read.

Before I turned away, he opened his eyes, looked up at me, and then slowly moved his hand in my direction. "You know, sometimes, they're innocent. You know that, right?"

I smiled back at him, and said, "I know. I'll see you later."

But six days later, Jesse Henderson was dead.

CHAPTER TWENTY-NINE

COACH AND PLAYER

Jody Ellis, a former Nashville Central High School star athlete in the late 1940s, helped coach the Donelson High School boys' basketball team to a state championship in 1964.[1] In 1965, he coached the Donelson High football team to the Clinic Bowl championship by beating a neighboring rival, Lebanon High School, twenty-eight to zero, whereupon he was named Coach of the Year, in Tennessee.[2]

In 1963, Jody's wife, Dorothy Ellis, was teaching and coaching at the new John Overton High School in the southern part of Nashville. With the impending departure of the first graduating class of seniors at Overton High, Dorothy Ellis decided that the timing was right to move on to other challenges with fond memories of her favorite girls' basketball team, the one led by Captain Paula Herring.

After Paula Herring's class graduated from Overton High, Dorothy Ellis took a teaching job at another Metro school, while her husband stayed at Donelson. The husband and wife coaching duo were still relatively young adults in 1964, with Jody Ellis barely age thirty-five at the time of Paula's tragic death.

When I caught up with Dorothy Ellis by phone several decades later, she was still haunted by the murder of one of her favorite players.

"I can hear a sad note in your voice," I said.

"Yes, I was so distraught over that for such a long time. Paula was a dear person. Her whole life seemingly wrapped up in basketball and her little brother. It was tragic. Is Paula's mother still living?" she asked.[3]

"No, she passed away in 1976 in Texas. I'm told it was alcohol related," I replied.

"I got a call early that Sunday morning that Paula had been killed. I thought I was dreaming at first, I was so distraught and caught up in the bitterness of the whole thing."

"I'm sure that was not a call you were expecting," I said.

"Detectives called me, or at least one of them did, or maybe it was an investigator, but they wanted to know if Paula had long fingernails. I answered everything as best I could."

"Do you remember anything else about that weekend?" I asked.

"That night, Saturday night, my husband was taking me out with another couple. The four of us were going to a basketball game. We were supposed to go a tournament, but I'm not sure where the tournament was. No, I remember, it was Donelson girls versus Overton girls, but the game was in Madison, Tennessee."

"But you were not the Overton girls' coach at that time?" I asked.

"No, I left Overton when Paula's class graduated in 1963. But Paula had called that day. She had come in from the University of Tennessee for the weekend. This goes back a while, but I remember it like it was yesterday. Paula wanted to go to the game," she said.

"Excuse me? You don't mean on Saturday night when she was killed, do you?"

"Yes, I do. She wanted to ride with us to the tournament on Saturday night. I wasn't sure we were even going to go, because I didn't feel well, but we did go with another couple, just the four of us. And we didn't have room in the car. I remember thinking, 'Oh if only she had gone with us.' But she ended up babysitting I guess."

"I'm so sorry," I responded.

The coach continued: "I adored that whole team, and they were full of fun, too. I was showing one of the girls how to tape her ankle, when a mouse got loose in the house, and I jumped up on a table. What they had done was to make me think one of the girls needed her ankle taped, and instead of a mouse they stopped by and let a hamster out in the room while I did the taping.

"Paula was a sweet girl. Basketball was everything to her. She could be a lady and she could play tough. I remember Paula adored her little brother. It was so sad; Paula had her whole life ahead of her. Let me ask you something, what about the man convicted of the murder?"

"John Randolph Clarke? He's dead."

"He was the mother's boyfriend, right?" she inquired.

"Apparently, yes," I said.

"And his wife was a teacher, I think?" she asked.

"Yes, she was. Callie Clarke taught in Metro, and by all accounts was a very good teacher."[4]

"I heard she gave up her life savings to pay for her husband's defense, to help him."

"Yes, ma'am, I understand that to be true also. And I'm told she visited the prison every week. She believed her husband to be innocent of the charges," I said.

"Well, Paula was all muscle. She must have had a real struggle with the man that did it. She would've put up a big fight. It was on my mind for years."

"You may have had one of the last conversations with Paula," I said sadly.

The phone call came in early on a Friday morning. And it came from a woman who was traveling through Nashville later that day, a woman I had previously assumed I would never find, Carmen Lee. In the years since I had been to Clarksdale, Mississippi, I had done the only thing I knew to do. I repeatedly dialed a number that no one ever answered. About every tenth call a voice messaging system would pick up, but it only asked the caller to leave a message and never confirmed where I was calling. My only hope was that whoever owned the phone would eventually get tired of my messages and actually return my call. And she did.

Part of the reason I was never going to give up my search for Carmen Lee was found in an inscription from Paula Herring's high school yearbook, an inscription Paula's brother, Alan, had graciously provided to me after I sent him the trial transcript. I frequently quoted from this note whenever I left a message for Carmen via the phone number I had received in Clarksdale, Mississippi:

Dear Paula,

What can I say? You are absolutely great!!! I can't begin to tell or even start to write what your friendship has meant to me. I can't express it in words. I hope we will always be close and closer than we are now. Basketball was great. I don't think I'll ever get as much pleasure from the sport again. We've had some hilarious times together that will never be duplicated. I can't imagine you graduating this year—but next year will be mine!! Maybe we'll go to college together!!

I hope I've meant something along your road of life and now that the road is ending in high school I hope the one in college will be just as successful! I am sure it will.

You know I'll never forget every time you, Mrs. Ellis, and I went everywhere and really had a time. I wish you all the luck in the world and I'm very serious. If there's ever anything you want me to do—let me know—I'll be there.

As ever,
Carmen[5]

Instead of the in-person meeting that I longed for, due to a delayed flight and a short layover, Carmen and I spoke by phone. What she had to say about her friend Paula Herring, though, turned out to be worth the multi-year wait.

"I've probably thought about Paula Herring nearly every day for years. She was my best friend in high school. So how can I help you now?" she asked.[6]

"I'm curious why so long to respond?"

"I've moved quite a lot with my work, and your note was eventually forwarded to me long after you sent it."

"The weekend that Paula was murdered, you were in Nashville, still attending Overton High School, your senior year, would that be about right?" I asked.

"Yes."

"Did you know Paula was at home that weekend?" I inquired.

"Did I know? She came to our house for breakfast on Saturday morning!" she said.

I looked toward the ceiling and grabbed for my chin, thinking that the breakfast memory was probably a mistake, just a confusion with many such Saturday morning events while the two were in high school together. "I never heard that she visited anyone that weekend," I countered.

"She came to our house on that Saturday morning, the happiest I had ever seen her," she replied.

"Was she by herself or with her little brother?" I asked.

"No. She was alone. We were literally still eating breakfast when she knocked on the door. She stayed for about an hour. My parents always enjoyed her company, and it was fun to catch up."

"Would Paula have walked to your house for breakfast?"

"No, she drove their family car," she said.

With this news, I recognized another perjury dilemma. During the questioning of witnesses in the criminal trial, Jo Herring had been certain to mention that she had worked first shift at Vanderbilt Hospital on Saturday, February 22, 1964. And first shift at Vanderbilt meant starting at 7:00 a.m. and ending around 3:00 p.m. So how could Paula Herring have had the family car on Saturday morning at the Lees'? Jo Herring would have driven the car to work, or at least she testified that she had.

While I was in mid-thought, Carmen offered another gem.

"It was February and plenty cold, I remember that. We were making plans for that night."

"What plans?"

"She was coming to the basketball tournament that night in Madison. We were in the tournament, playing against Donelson High. And then I was going to ride home with Paula after the game to spend the night with her," she said.

"You were going to spend Saturday night at Paula Herring's house?" I asked.

"Yes."

I could only imagine the tone of incredulity in my voice as I continued. "I'm sorry, I must have misunderstood. We're talking about the night Paula was killed? Did you in fact go to her house after the basketball game?"

"No, when she didn't show up at the game, I just assumed she'd found something else to do, and the game was over late, so I went home, went to bed, and the next morning my parents woke me up to tell me the news," she said.

"Oh, I'm so sorry. That must have been some kind of shock," I said.

"It. Creeped. Me. Out. I was scared out of my mind after her murder. For the rest of the school year, I slept in my parents' bedroom. I was seventeen years old; it was awful."

"I can only imagine the shock if you had gone on over to Paula's after the game. I guess it goes without saying that the two of you were close friends?"

"I was probably her best friend. The plan was that when I graduated in May of 1964, we were both going to be at the University of Tennessee at the same time."

"Let me guess, after Paula's death you went to school elsewhere?" I asked.

"Exactly."

"How well did you know Paula's mother?"

"Looking back on it, it was kind of funny. I didn't know much about her mother, her lifestyle. I knew her, obviously, but I also didn't know the scoop on Paula's dad until later, after Paula had died," she said.

"Apparently, not many knew about Paula's dad, either. Paula told her college friends that her dad had been killed in a car accident. Carmen, did the police ever question you about your plans for that Saturday night with Paula?"

"No, the police never questioned me about anything, the plans, nothing."

"How about your parents? Did they get a visit? Were they questioned?" I asked.

"No, never."

"Anything else you can remember?" I asked.

"Well, I remember Paula was crazy about her little brother, and I adored him as well. He was a cute little boy. But there is one thing I should probably mention," she said.

"Sure, please do."

"Paula's mother called me to come over to her house. It was a few days after Paula had been killed, maybe that same week, I think. And Paula's mom obviously knew about our plans for that Saturday night," she said.

"Well, just so you know, Paula's mother kept your visit quiet. She never told the police about the plans you and Paula had made. And she clearly wanted to see you in person to learn what you knew about Paula's state of mind the last hours of her life," I said softly.

"Paula's mom asked me a lot of questions. And I hadn't been there too long when she asked me if I wanted something to drink. I was sitting at their kitchen table, and I could see that she already had a glass of lemonade or something made up, but I could only see one glass on the counter."

"Uh-oh," I replied.

"Yeah, I just had a gut feeling. And I started getting scared, and I said, 'No, thank you.' I practically ran out of that house. When I got home, I told my parents that there was something wrong with her. I was scared of Paula's mom after that kitchen episode," she said.

"So what happened after that?" I asked.

"I never went back to that house again, ever."

CHAPTER THIRTY

CLEAR BLUE SKY

On a day when my mind was still puzzling over Jesse Henderson's comments to me, I wondered if "Lizzie" was actually named Elizabeth and "Lizzie" was her nickname. It was a short trek, mentally speaking, to the first time I had stumbled upon a courthouse citation in North Alabama where a man named Jesse Henderson had been a witness at a wedding where the bride was named Elizabeth Smith. At the time, I had copied down the particulars of the event but had lost my notes and never revisited the topic.

But now my gut was screaming to me that the bride just might be the Lizzie my research had uncovered, Gina's mother and Jesse's former girlfriend. And the guy she married could be Mr. BlueSky. Was it possible?

I quickly made the trek back to North Alabama, copied down the details again, and raced back to Nashville to spend a day tracking the groom through the old city directory at the downtown library. But this time, instead of moving forward from the date of the wedding, I went in reverse year after year after year. I discovered that the groom, Carl Raylee, had been a lifelong resident of Nashville until the end of 1964, when he and his bride had vanished. This time I noticed that their Alabama wedding date had been mere days after John Clarke's conviction in Jackson, Tennessee.

After my library work confirmed the last street address available for Raylee, the next morning I was standing on the front porch of an abandoned house situated within walking distance of Vanderbilt University and West End Avenue. Using my laptop computer and cell phone, it took less than an hour to find the owner of the property, who confirmed that a man named Carl Raylee had rented the house from her for years but had finally moved to an assisted living facility somewhere in the area. She was very fond of her friend Carl, and she remembered that he had a brother in Charleston, South Carolina.

The third attempt was the right one. "Hello, I'm calling from Nashville, Tennessee. I haven't spoken with you before, but I'm hoping you can help me find an older gentleman named Carl Raylee." I quickly added, "Mr. Raylee's former landlady told me that he has a brother living in South Carolina, and that's why I'm calling this number."

"I believe I can help you. Why are you looking for Carl? He's my older brother."[1]

"It's an honor to speak with you, sir. I'm a good bit younger than Mr. Carl, but he and I are mutual friends with a World War II veteran here in the Nashville area named Jesse Henderson, and unfortunately Mr. Henderson just passed away. I was trying to contact Mr. Raylee to let him know that one of his old buddies had passed, and I'm not sure how to do that, though I'm certain he would want to know about his friend."

"Well, I just spoke with him yesterday afternoon. You said you live in Nashville?" he asked.

"Yes, sir." I was holding my breath at this point, hoping for a location that would be an easy drive, and I got my wish.

"He lives close to Nashville in one of those assisted living places. You ever heard of Spring Hill, Tennessee?" he asked.

"Yes, sir. It's a little town about thirty miles south of the city. I know it well. Would it be okay to visit with your brother and pass along the news about Mr. Henderson?" I inquired.

"Certainly so," he said.

"Mr. Raylee's health pretty good these days?" I asked.

"Oh, you know, he complains about minor aches and pains and such, but his mind is good," he said.

"That's excellent. I will certainly tell him I spoke with you, of course. Any chance you'd have the name or address of the facility where he's living?" I asked.

While I copied down the name and general area of town, I remembered to ask a couple of questions that had haunted me for a long time. "I assume Mr. Raylee is retired, but what kind of work did he do back in, say, the 1960s era?"

"Oh, let's see, I know he worked for Vanderbilt Hospital, the university hospital, there in Nashville for many years. I'm not sure about any other work," he said.

"You don't say, the hospital?" I asked.

"Yes, he was a buyer, a purchasing agent for the hospital for several years. Oh, let's see now, that was in the 1950s and 1960s. He used to tell me he bought all manner of things. Some days it was medicines and hospital supplies, some days he'd buy live animals for their laboratory research."

"Was he a married man?" I asked.

"He did marry late in life, but oddly enough I never met the bride. I don't think it worked out, sad to say."

"Well, I do appreciate your time, and I'll let him know that we spoke, and I thank you, again."

"Tell him his family said hello."

"Yes, sir. I certainly will," I replied.

A quick drive to the little hamlet of Spring Hill put me in the parking lot of a nursing home just off the main road through town. I had charmed many a receptionist throughout the Paula Herring journey, in part because I was usually dressed like a state inspector carrying a leather portfolio, or else I carried nothing and looked like a family member or friend checking in on a patient.

Either way, I was always warm and friendly when asking for the room of the person I wanted to interview. And without prompting I would also offer a single reason for my visit, which was always the same honest statement: "I'm hoping to visit with Mr. or Ms. John Doe so they can help me with some old Nashville history." I always made certain to enunciate "old"—as in, interesting but harmless. I usually failed to mention that the old Nashville history I was interested in included one of the biggest murder cases of the last half century in Tennessee.

After walking through the glass door security system, I could see that it was set up to allow entry, but anyone trying to exit the building had to have electronic assistance from the front desk.

After multiple visits to nursing homes, I also had learned that, as a general rule, late morning was the time when the residents were most awake and lucid. They'd had some breakfast, their medication, a cup of coffee to get their nervous system cranked up a bit, and perhaps a bath, and they were usually out of bed and dressed for the day. So I usually arrived around 10:30 a.m. and hoped for the best.

After signing in with the front desk clerk, I asked how to find Mr. Carl Raylee, and they sent me on a winding tour of the facility toward a long hallway on the south wing, filled with multiple staff members and more than one housekeeping cart.

Stopping outside the last doorway, I saw two names listed; one of them was Carl Raylee. I peeked inside and saw two residents, both elderly men, both sitting in wheelchairs. But which one was my mystery man? While I paused to think about it, a female staff member dressed in a white nurse's uniform stepped around me and asked if she could help me with anything.

"Yes, ma'am, I'm here to visit with Mr. Raylee," I said.

"Sure, I'm going to take Mr. Kennedy here to the atrium for some fresh air, and you and Mr. Carl can visit all you want," she said.

"You're so kind," I heard myself say, and then I watched to see which one of the two men she chose.

She chose the man closest to the door, a wiry, little gentleman with thick, black glasses and a full head of hair, who appeared to be half asleep but with an active leg shake. The other man didn't seem to be too interested in my appearance in the doorway. He was the much larger of the two residents. Dressed in dark blue warm-up pants and comfortably seated in a large wheelchair, one foot was wrapped in a compression bandage, while the other was in a large running shoe, the type with Velcro for straps instead of shoelaces. He also wore a faded, gray t-shirt.

As the staff member moved Mr. Kennedy from around the bed through the doorway, I tried to get a better assessment of my interviewee. Even as an octogenarian, this was a large man. He had a thick chest and large shoulders, but he wasn't overweight. He had big hands, a bull neck, and a very short haircut, less than a half inch of gray hair all over his head, balding a little at his temples. He was not wearing glasses. If he was standing, I estimated he would be over six feet tall.

In his comfortable attire, Carl Raylee looked like an old boxer, a man who had just spent the previous hour punching a heavy bag in the gym and then retiring to his room while he cooled off and waited for his glass of six raw eggs.

"Good morning, Mr. Raylee. How are you feeling today?" I asked. I had heard my brother-in-law, a minister and nursing home executive, use this same greeting with the elderly, and they seemed to enjoy the opportunity to describe their physical state to anyone taking the time to ask.[2]

"Good morning," he replied. "I'm alright, I reckon."[3]

His speech was clear but gruff. He looked up at me with his head cocked at an angle and one eye half closed, as he sized up the stranger before him. I decided to make it easier for our discussion and grabbed a chair, positioning it in front and to the side of his wheelchair.

"We haven't met before. My name is Michael Bishop."

I offered a handshake, in part to gauge his strength, and he offered a huge right paw in return, a strong one.

"Good to meet you."

"I spoke with your brother in South Carolina earlier today, and he said to tell you hello," I offered.

"That right?" A lift of the chin, and a nice smile drifted across his face like a passing cloud.

"Yes, sir, I did." I thought it might be useful to move the conversation back to the 1960s era, so I added, "Your brother said you grew up in Nashville."

"Yes, we lived out on Central Pike, in a big old house."

"That was a long time ago, wasn't it?" I said.

"Sure was."

"You lived by yourself?"

"No. I lived with my parents and grandparents. I had to help out with them," he said.

"You're a good man. You worked for Vanderbilt Hospital for several years, according to your brother, back in the 1960s?" I stated.

The old man nodded.

I pushed on. "Nashville was a fun place to be back in the sixties. The city was growing so fast; there was wrestling at the Hippodrome, and all the good places to grab a hamburger or barbeque and a beer, right?"[4]

"It sure was; a lot of fun," he said.

"Well, one of the reasons I'm here is to pass along some news about one of your friends from back in those days. Do you remember Jesse Henderson? He might've been a drinking buddy of yours?" I asked.

A chuckle and a smile were the quick response, followed by a yes and another nod. Given his age, I wondered if he really remembered, but then he floored me with his follow-up.

"Jesse was a character. Always wanted to go out and get a beer or a drink. Course, I paid for most of them. He'd find me, had to get rid of him sometimes, but he'd chase you down."

"He said he always called you BlueSky. Is that right?" I asked.

"Yes, that's right," he replied.

As he spoke, I could see he was drifting back to my desired decade, and then he looked directly at me. I was ready.

"And what about Lizzie, Mr. Raylee?"

"She was something else," he said quietly.

"You knew her, too?" I asked.

"Yes, we ran around a lot and eventually got married, but I haven't seen her in a long time."

"How did you meet her?" No sooner had I spoken than another worker entered the room. I introduced myself to her and asked if I was interrupting anything scheduled for Mr. Raylee, such as therapy or medication of some kind. But the friendly staff member had only stopped by to drop off clean clothes from the laundry for Mr. Kennedy. She was gone in less than sixty seconds.

"How did you come to meet Jesse and Lizzie?" I asked.

"That was a long time ago. I don't remember. Trouble followed them," he said.

"I don't understand. Are you talking about Jesse and Lizzie?" I asked.

"Yes. Trouble always followed them."

"I have some bad news about Jesse Henderson. He passed away a few days ago. I actually saw him just days before he died. I'm told he passed peacefully in his sleep. We talked about you and Lizzie when I was with him."

I continued. "Mr. Raylee, I'm hoping you can help me unravel a mystery that has been going on now for almost fifty years. Do you think you can help me?"

"I'll try. What is it?" he said.

"Back in 1964, when you were working at Vanderbilt University Hospital, there was a young girl tragically murdered in the Crieve Hall area of Nashville. The girl was eighteen, a University of Tennessee student home for the weekend in February. Her name was Paula Herring. Does that name sound familiar to you?"

"No, it doesn't," he responded.

"Take your time, it's important," I said.

As I said this, I realized I sounded like a trial lawyer gently coaching a key witness through critical testimony. I turned around and looked at the doorway to make sure no one was listening.

"It's foreign to me," he said.

"I don't understand."

"That name, I don't know it." He seemed to have more conviction in his gruff voice.

"Do you remember John Randolph Clarke, Red Clarke, or Jo Herring?" I asked.

A dark, red cloud appeared on the old man's face. I could see he had a great capacity for anger, and it was beginning to focus on me.

"No! It's foreign to me. Don't ask me about that!"

I could see his hands were now gripping the arms of the wheelchair, strongly enough to turn his knuckles white. It was at that exact moment a flash of insight came to me, spurred by the cryptic comment by Jesse Henderson regarding two guys fighting in the Herrings' garage.

"Mr. Raylee, when I was with Jesse Henderson, he told me that, on the night of Paula Herring's murder, you and he were in the dead girl's garage fighting with a truck stop man named Sam Carlton. Can you help me? Please?" I was almost begging him at this point.

"No, don't ask me."

And with those words, he repositioned his wheelchair away from me and turned himself to look out the window at a pleasant view of green grass, flowers, and manicured shrubbery. For all practical purposes, Carl Raylee had objected to the questioning and called his own mistrial for my final session of court.

Moments later, looking at the floor, I negotiated my way past the nursing station as they unlocked the front door from within and reflected on the fact that I had spent more than a decade hoping and praying for a chance to finally meet with Carl Raylee, and in a matter of minutes that opportunity had been lost. I was sick to my stomach knowing that I had been stonewalled and the game was over, a complete shutout in the Paula Herring solution contest, with the "cheap detective" on the wrong end of the score.

Deep in thought on the way back to my car, I reached into my pocket for my car keys with the idea that I would simply sit in my car in the parking lot and try to figure out a way that I could turn this major setback into something other than a loss. I was stumped.

If I went back inside to see Carl Raylee, the old man could simply say that I was harassing him, and I would be escorted out of the building for good, likely forever. If I waited a few weeks, or even a few days, and then returned, Carl Raylee could pass in the meantime from this life into the next, and he'd take the answers I needed with him. Not a pleasant thought. Not after the Jesse Henderson experience, and not after the journey that had brought me here.

With keys in hand and ready to open my car door, I glanced at the luxury sedan next to me, a Cadillac, and at that moment I thought of Jesse Henderson and his statement to me that John Randolph Clarke had driven a Cadillac in the winter of 1964. I smiled as I now began to wonder if Jesse had been toying with me, in an attempt to see if I could figure who actually owned a Cadillac that might have been a part of this story. Perhaps the owner in 1964 was the man I had just met? Instead of opening my car door, I opened my trunk and retrieved a leather portfolio. I almost broke into a trot heading back to the entrance of the nursing home, and I didn't slow down as I flew by the front desk and tossed a "Forgot something, sorry" in the direction of the receptionist.

When I arrived back at his room, Carl Raylee was still positioned to look out the window. I said, "Mr. Raylee, I forgot to ask you one question. What kind of car did you drive when you worked for Vanderbilt?"

He turned his wheelchair toward me, looked up, and replied, "I always drove a Cadillac."

"What color?" I asked.

"Black. My grandmother had a black Cadillac, but she couldn't drive anymore, and I started driving it and never drove any other brand."

Thank you, Jesse Henderson, I thought to myself.

For the moment, it seemed like we had reconnected and gotten past the previous stalemate. I opened my leather portfolio and retrieved photographs of the 1964 crime scene.

"Do you remember getting married to Lizzie in Alabama? You and Lizzie brought Jesse with you to be your witness. And you drove your grandmother's Cadillac for the trip, right?"

"Yes."

"Do you remember waiting to see if John Randolph Clarke was convicted before you two got married?" I asked.

"Yes."

"That way you wouldn't have to testify against each other about what happened to Paula Herring, Jo Herring's daughter. You're still married to her, aren't you, Mr. Raylee? I bet you haven't lived together in decades."

As he turned his head to look away at the sunny view outside his window, I thought to myself that Lizzie would have easily chosen Raylee and his family money over Jesse Henderson, no matter how Jesse may have felt about it.

"Tell me about Lizzie; can you do that, please?" I asked softly.

"She could get angry in a minute. Jesse, too."

At this last response, I produced the graduation photo of Paula Herring, so that he could see her face.

"Mr. Raylee, this is Paula Herring, as she looked in 1964."

"Pretty girl," he said.

"Yes, sir, she was," I said. "Unfortunately, her life ended in a tragic death in Nashville in February 1964. Do you remember being at her house the night she died?"

He quickly looked away. It was a classic sign that the words had registered with him as strongly as a slap in the face. I then showed him one of the large photographs of Paula lying on the den floor at Timberhill Drive.

"I need your help, Mr. Raylee. Can you tell me about the girl and why this happened? Can you do that for me, please?" My words were soft.

I placed my hand on his arm, and it startled him a bit. He looked up at me. As soon as he did, I dropped to one knee beside him. "Can you help me, please? There's nothing anyone can do for her now. She's gone. And so are her father and mother. They're all dead. I know you know. Help me, please?"

Carl Raylee sat quietly, staring at the photograph. I swapped it with one of Paula Herring lying on the floor, on her back. You could see her eyes focused on the ceiling while detectives worked over her. It was a cruel thing to do to the old man, but I needed his help.

Suddenly, a high-pitched squeal seemed to be emanating from the wheelchair. It was so odd and out of human vocal range that I couldn't believe it was coming from the old man seated next to me, but it was. He was looking at the photograph, holding it with both hands, and the sound lasted almost a half-minute, as if he'd held his breath for fifty years waiting to exhale. It was as if he'd gone back in time to the night of the murder.

When he looked up at me, his mouth was slightly open, his eyes were red and wet, and he was visibly shaken. I wondered if I needed to call one of the staff members in case he needed medical attention.

"Mr. Raylee, are you alright?" He didn't respond, but he didn't appear to be in pain, so I continued, hoping that I would not be interrupted for the next few moments. "The night that this happened was a Saturday night. You were driving your grandmother's Cadillac, right?" I said.

"Yes, but I wrecked it," he said softly.

"Do you remember where?"

"Out on River Road, toward Pegram," he replied.

Then he looked up at me, "We turned it over going around a curve."

"Anyone hurt?" I asked.

"Nah, just shook up a bit."

'What about the car? You had to get it towed somewhere?" I asked.

"No, it landed back on the wheels and I drove it home. My uncle fixed it for me and never asked me about it."

"How did you come to be at Timberhill Drive on the night of the girl's murder?" I asked.

"We had dinner," he said.

"I don't understand. Who had dinner, you and Jesse Henderson?"

"Yes, and the nurses," he responded.

"When you say nurses, you mean Lizzie?"

"Her mother, the girl's mother," he said.

At this news, I stood up and paced the tiny room for a moment, quickly realizing that Vanderpool and Meadows, the men who supposedly had been with Jo Herring on the night of Paula's murder, had been substituted for Jesse and BlueSky as part of the cover up. Vanderpool would have been an easy recruit in exchange for keeping his massage parlor business open and uninterrupted, and Meadows would have gotten the building material he sought at a bargain price.

"You, Jesse Henderson, Lizzie, and Paula's mother were eating dinner after Paula's mother got off of work on that Saturday night?" I asked.

"Yes."

"Where? The Wedgewood Diner?" I continued.

"No, at the Krystal drive-in," he said.

"You mean the Krystal hamburger place out on Franklin Road near Melrose and Rhea Little's garage?"

"No, on West End near Vanderbilt. They had a drive-up, where you could sit in your car. They brought out hamburgers in little baskets with French fries."

I could not remember hearing or reading that there was a Krystal near Vanderbilt in the 1960s. This important fact had never once surfaced on my radar screen.

"And after that, you followed Jo Herring out to her house on Timberhill Drive?"

"She didn't look like that when we left," he said.

"I don't understand," I said.

He pointed at Paula's photograph. "She didn't look like that when we left."

I glanced at my watch and decided that someone would soon come to get my witness and wheel him down to the cafeteria for lunch. *I don't have long,* I thought.

And then I reminded myself that this was real. I was hearing, in person, an old man confessing to being part of a felony murder that had taken place a half century earlier. And no matter how little or how much Carl Raylee had or hadn't done to Paula Herring, as a criminal defense attorney had once told me, "When you're in for the part, you're in for the whole."[5] And Carl Raylee had just put himself in the house on Timberhill Drive the night Paula Herring had been murdered.

No matter that, by all appearances, he was probably a big teddy bear at heart, because of his status and apparent access to wealth, he had been pursued religiously by Jesse and Lizzie whenever someone else's money and assets were required for a night of drinking and partying. He had just put himself at the scene of a fifty-year-old homicide. Carl Raylee mumbled a few words.

"Did you say something?" I asked.

"Looks like she had an accident." He was still staring at the photo of Paula.

I responded by quoting the words that Jesse Henderson had spoken to me once: "'That wasn't no accident, whoever did that was mad at her.' Mr. Raylee, had you ever been to Timberhill Drive before that night?" I asked.

"No, never was out there before."

"When you got to the house that night, Paula was angry?" I asked.

"Yes, there was a fight."

"What happened?"

"She bit her," he replied.

"The girl bit one of the women?"

"She bit Lizzie real bad, and Lizzie shot her."

I stopped breathing for a long moment.

"No one called the police, and no one took the girl to the hospital to get help. Is that right? Even though a couple of nurses were in the house at the same time, no one offered to help her. Mr. Raylee, is that right?"

"That's right."

"You drove away and left the little boy in the house with his dying sister?"

"Didn't know about the boy until we went back."

"Where did you go?"

"A motel for a little while and then back to the house."

"Why did you go back?"

"The gun was on the floor, and we had to go back and get it," he said.

"And somewhere during that timeline you ended up fighting with Sam Carlton in the Herring's garage?" I asked.

"I didn't know who he was."

I knew from a legal perspective that I was leading the witness at this point, but I also knew that the witness wasn't going to lead me anywhere or voluntarily incriminate himself. I was on the verge of leaving, when I thought of additional questions I needed to ask.

"The police didn't come find you after that night?"

"Never did."

"Mr. Raylee, did you keep on working at Vanderbilt Hospital or did you have to leave after the girl's murder? The reason I ask is that Paula's mother, Jo Herring, the nurse, she was fired from Vanderbilt right after her daughter was killed. They said she was addicted to medication and impaired on the job. Did you have to leave Vanderbilt as well?"

"I went to Oak Ridge," he said.

"You mean Oak Ridge in East Tennessee. I think I know the answer to this question, but I'll ask it anyway. Did you ever work for the VA Hospital system after you went to Oak Ridge?"

"Yes, I was a hospital inspector for them. It was a good job," he replied.

"And that's how Lizzie eventually got a job with the VA? You hired her?" I inquired.

"Yes."

I placed my hand on his shoulder and gave it a squeeze. "Mr. Raylee, thank you for helping Paula Herring today. I've been trying to find you for years. You get some rest, okay?" I continued holding onto his shoulder as I stood up to retrieve the newspaper from his lap, and then returned it with the photographs to my portfolio.

As I walked down the main hallway to exit the building, I realized I knew of one person who could verify what I had just heard, and I had no time to waste to get to her. Moments later, I exited through the heavy glass security doors, and then broke into a dead run back to my car.

CHAPTER THIRTY-ONE

HOUSE FULL OF HELL

She was as feisty as ever when she answered the door for me an hour after Carl Raylee had confessed to the role he had played in the Paula Herring slaying. She was dressed in a cloud-blue bathrobe and fuzzy slippers, and her dark hair was taking on a distinctly gray hue.[1]

"How have you been, Mike?" she asked.

"Doing fine Miss Evelyn, and you look well."

"Do you need a drink of water? You look like you've been out running this morning," she said.

After taking a seat on her sofa, I explained why I was back to see her. I began by stating the facts that I had just uncovered. And I wanted an insider's view of the Herring family, of Paula and her mother's relationship. My reasoning was quite simple: in more than one interview, and also on the witness stand in Jackson, Jo Herring had made certain to describe Paula as happy and enjoying her college life, especially so on the weekend of her tragic death. But Evelyn had a different view, one she delivered with surprising intensity.

"They fought all the time, all the time," she said.

"Paula and her mother?" I asked.

"Oh, my, yes, it was a house full of hell. Jo was on her every day, and Paula gave it right back."

She paused a moment for a sip of coffee from a large mug, which she held in both hands while sitting in a gray recliner rocker. "And the neighbors felt sorry for Jo. They knew she'd lost her husband to that Noel Hotel incident."

"And Paula was doing a lot of babysitting with her little brother when she was living at home?" I asked.

"Babysitting?" she snorted in my direction. "She was the one taking care of that boy; it sure wasn't Jo Herring," she said.

I continued, "And Jo is watching her daughter become prettier than her mother, and now the eighteen-year-old is off to college, having a great time. She's becoming a leader, she helps start the first snow skiing club at the University of Tennessee, and she's about to join a prestigious sorority.[2] Life was probably better than it had ever been, at least for Paula," I said.

"And Jo was jealous," she replied.

"Well, and something else," I added. "It cost a lot of money to pay for college and all of those skiing activities and having fun in Knoxville."

I didn't want to give away my next topic too easily, but I had decided this was the best way to potentially introduce the money aspect. It was a baited segue that Evelyn eyeballed like a wary brown trout in a Smoky Mountain stream. She looked hard in my direction with a steely gaze as she offered a response.

"Jo was cold. She'd do anything for money," she said.

My eyes narrowed, and I looked long and hard back at Evelyn, thinking she might be opening the door to a motive that I had never mentioned before, primarily because it was a motive too terrible to comprehend.

"Let me come back to that topic in a minute and ask you about your work at Vanderbilt Hospital. Actually, let me ask you about Jo Herring's work at Vanderbilt. What shift did she work back then?"

She thought for a moment, then said, "She used to work first, but she'd been on second shift for a good while when we worked together."

"What hours would that be?" I asked.

"She worked as a floor nurse, from 11:00 a.m. to 7:00 p.m., second shift. Did you know she took care of some of the bigwigs that came to the hospital?"[3]

"I'm not sure what that means," I replied.

"When some of these guys had to dry out, they had to do that discreetly, if you know what I mean. I'm talking about some prominent folks." she said.

"Jo Herring was the person who was their nurse and kept her mouth shut, is that what you mean?" I asked.

"Yes, and she liked that kind of work, too. It let her get to know some powerful people. And Jo was willing to help them out with whatever they needed, don't you know? Of course, no one else at the hospital knew what she was up to," she said.

"Like maybe providing them with something other than medication?" I asked.

Miss Evelyn nodded her head in agreement and took another sip of coffee. "And some entertainment later on," she added.

"You say powerful people?" I asked.

"I'm mostly talking about Bev. He made trips to Michigan to rehab, but in town they'd just drop him off at the hospital to clean up and dry out from time to time."

"You mean Beverly Briley, the mayor?" I asked.

"Right. One of the Vanderbilt doctors was trying to help him with his addiction problems, but I don't think even the doctors could compete with Jo Herring and her ways."

"So in the group of people you told me about previously, the ones meeting up at these secret hideaways, like the cabin on Marrowbone Lake, the boat on Old Hickory, or the apartment near Wedgewood Diner, the mayor was part of that group?"

"Of course," she said.

"I think I'm beginning to see the big picture." As I shook my head, I asked a follow up question. "Jo Herring much of a drinker?"

"Are you kidding? She could get loopy-legged every day. I thought she was far too smart to be drinking so much, but she could drink anyone under the table."

As she said this, she rolled her eyes. She pushed her rocker back a little and then cocked her head and asked, "Why are you still interested in all of this anyway, like it was yesterday morning's newspaper?"

"Because I think Paula was going to accomplish some things. She had big plans," I said.

"Her daddy sure talked to her that way. He wanted the best for her."

"I just think with all of the lies that were told, in court and everywhere else, that the truth should be told for Paula's sake. And even if I tell Paula's story, there's going to be plenty of people who will say that John Randolph Clarke or Sam Carlton the truck stop manager or some unknown Nashville prowler did the killing. But you and I both know that's a bunch of hogwash." I continued, "If no one else, I think Paula Herring at least deserves the truth, no matter how bad it may be for some people to hear it."

"I do, too," came her soft reply.

"I need your help, Miss Evelyn. I don't know how much time any of us have on this earth, and nearly fifty years have already passed since this whole sordid mess took place."

"What kind of help?" As she asked, she leaned forward out of her rocker and placed the empty coffee cup on the small kitchen table, but this time I could see she was ready to dispense with the friendly banter and move on to the darker aspects of her friendship with Jo Herring.

"Jo Herring was working as a nurse, and apparently spent money faster than she could make it; does that sound about right?" I asked.

"Jo would do anything for money, she could never get enough of it," she said.

"At the trial in Jackson, I know Jo Herring was asked about being addicted to drugs. Would you know about any drugs in the house on the night that Paula was killed? Jo could have made some extra money that way, right?"

She nodded. "I thought the reason Jo called me the night Paula was killed was to help her get the drugs out of the house before the police arrived."

"So how did the drugs get in the house in the first place?" I asked.

"She brought them home from the hospital." She said this with an air of some exasperation, as if I were too dense to see the obvious.

"So she stole them from the hospital?" I asked.

"Well, technically she was stealing them from patients."

"What kind of drugs?" I asked.

"Jo was stealing anything that could be sold. Amphetamines, narcotics, pills, inhalers, and plenty more," she said.

"I thought all of those drugs were locked up in the pharmacy," I said.

"Not back then. The medicine carts would be in the hallways on each floor. All you had to do was not give a patient their pill, or give aspirin or something like that instead of what had been ordered. You would just sign on their card that you gave the pill to the patient and then keep it instead. It was no problem, I assure you. And a lot of nurses got fired over addiction problems."

"Just like Jo Herring got fired from Vanderbilt Hospital?" I waited a moment before asking my next question.

"So what was Paula's frame of mind on the night she was murdered? Care to offer an opinion?" I asked.

"She was still angry about her daddy, and she wanted revenge. That's what I think." She offered this with an edge to her voice.

"You think Jo had something to do with Paula's murder?"

"She was the first person they hauled downtown to the police station that night!" Miss Evelyn almost spit the words out as she leaned toward me.

I nearly fell off of the couch before I eventually responded: "I'm glad you said that, because I don't think it took the cops anytime at all to figure out that the best suspect in the Paula Herring murder was the woman who found Paula in the den, do you?"

"They took Jo to the police station around midnight, and I followed them in my car. I wasn't sure what was going to happen to her but they turned her loose around daybreak, and I drove her back to Crieve Hall and dropped her off. Some of the cops thought from beginning to end that Jo did it, even after that Clarke fellow was convicted," she said.

"So yet another babysitter enters the picture," I muttered to myself, remembering that Miss Hattie had said she walked to the Herrings' to babysit Alan when Jo returned at sunrise.

"Babysitter?"

"Yes, it appears there was a never-ending supply of them on the night of the murder. The Herring's next-door neighbor was the first babysitter, while you were downtown with Jo, then apparently a neighbor named Hattie early on Sunday morning when they turned Jo loose, and then, well it doesn't matter now," I said. "Do you know anything about the book that went missing?" I asked.

"I thought that was Jo's book."

"I'm talking about the paperback that everyone was searching for after the murder, you know, *All the King's Men*. It was supposed to be the killing clue."

"I know what you're talking about, and I'm pretty sure that was Jo's book," she said.

"By the way, I've got a picture of Jo Herring in the old Municipal Safety Building from the night of the murder." As I said this, a look of horror came over Evelyn's face.

"Am I in that picture?" she asked.

"No, ma'am, it's just Jo and a couple of investigators," I replied.

"Good. None of that was supposed to be in the newspaper. I don't know who took care of that; Bev calling in a few favors, I'm sure. I just didn't want to see my face on the front page of the paper back then, and I still don't."

"Yes, ma'am."

CHAPTER THIRTY-TWO

GRAVEYARD DEAD

"We need to meet tomorrow morning. I have a story you're going to want to hear." This was my opening salvo to Gina, shortly after my final session with Nurse Evelyn had ended.

"I don't think I can make it."

"I think you should try. It's important, really important."

I wasn't certain that my directness would be well received, but after a bit of negotiating around the meeting time, Gina did arrive the next day, promptly at 11:00 a.m., at the same eatery as our prior session, and once again I had pre-purchased two drinks. This time, the wig had a reddish hue, and I noticed that her hands were shaking even more than when we had first met.[1]

"You said you had a story to tell me?"

"I do. It's a short story, and you may have actually heard it before." As we sat at a table for two near a window, I took another look around the coffee house to see if anyone was a bit too perfectly positioned to hear what I was about to say.

"I discovered that years ago, decades actually, two women who were nurses and working at the same hospital just happened to have daughters of the same age, and both nurses were, shall we say, unhappily married."

I paused a beat to ensure that she was paying attention. Satisfied that she was, I continued. "These two nurses discover that they have the same interests and hobbies. They like to drink. They like to dance. They like Printers Alley. Maybe they both like using narcotics? They certainly like using men for fun and pleasure, and lo and behold, they discover that they like each other. A lot. Are you with me so far?"

"Yes."

"So one of the nurses decides to do away with her husband in the summer of 1960. Let's call that person 'Nurse Jo.' And let's call the other nurse, 'Elizabeth.' I don't actually know if Elizabeth was involved in any foul play in her husband's death, but this much is certain, Elizabeth's husband dies about three or so years after Jo's husband." I glanced across the table at my guest, and she was staring out the window, unblinking, lost in a memory.

"Which brings us to the two daughters. One of the nurses begins to recruit her daughter into a lifestyle that I can only describe as unreal. A lifestyle where the mother eventually begins pimping out her daughter to powerful men, men with money, men who can pay the rent, men who can take care of their needs. And through what I might describe as systematic use and abuse, this daughter goes along with the plan. Are you getting the picture?" I asked.

Gina didn't speak but nodded her head affirmatively, still staring out the window.

"Maybe this daughter buries her pain in the arms of these powerful men, and she finds this exciting. Maybe she's treated well, for a while, but of course that doesn't last. It can't. And maybe on the outside it appears to everyone that this daughter is doing just fine. But on the inside? I wonder if that daughter might have vanished years ago, and it's possible that no one has seen her since then?"

I paused to sip from the iced-tea I had purchased, and I could see that Gina's eyes were now moist, but she was still staring out the window, not moving a muscle. I wasn't sure she was even breathing.

"The other daughter, let's call her Paula. She wants nothing to do with her mother's lifestyle. She rejects it and goes in a completely different direction. She leaves home, goes to college, becomes a leader, helps start the first snow skiing club at the University of Tennessee, gets an invitation to join a prestigious sorority, and eventually plans to go to law school. Oh, and something else, she wants justice for her father. But before she can get started down that path, guess what happens? Paula ends up murdered, her life taken from her in a tragic way, and she ends up graveyard dead, outside of town, without so much as a headstone to mark her lonely resting place."

Across the table, I could see a trembling lip, and I asked Gina a question I had been holding back: "Does that seem fair to you? One daughter is murdered. The other one survives."

After a second, I saw a tear rolling down her cheek. I leaned in and lowered my voice. "Gina?"

The whispered response took a while to formulate and was almost inaudible, as she covered her eyes with one hand.

"I wanted to be a nurse," she said.

Now I had a lump in my own throat, and I turned my face toward the window so she couldn't see the tear forming in my own eye. We sat silently for a few minutes, both of us staring out the window, before I whispered softly to her: "There's help if you want it, Gina."

When I turned back to face her, my glance was met with a look of deep sorrow. And then she whispered words I had not expected to hear: "I'm sorry. I'm so sorry. Can you please tell that little boy for me?"

I don't know how much time passed after this poignant exchange. There was another period of silence for what must have been several minutes, before the aroma of freshly roasted coffee began to find its way to our table, along with the sounds of a customer ordering drinks.

"What can I do for you, now?" Gina finally asked, her voice having regained some strength.

"I need your help. Paula Herring knew your mother. I think I'm right about that."

"Yes, but they hated each other. I think at one point Paula threatened her if she ever came to their house again."

"I think I know how that turned out," I said. "So on the night all of this went down, you weren't there?"

"No. My mom got hurt somehow, and she tried to get me to bring a doctor's bag to her. At the time, I didn't know if my mom had been shot or stabbed, but I wouldn't do it. I knew something bad had happened, I just didn't know what it was, and I didn't want any part of it."

"You found out later?"

"Jesse finally told me bits and pieces. When my mom got home that night, she had a pillowcase wrapped around her leg, with a piece of wire holding it in place. I'd never seen her like that, and she wouldn't talk. She packed a bag and left, and I didn't see her for almost a year."

I shifted modes, ready to assert what I wasn't confident in, pretending that I knew what I actually did not. "How about a different topic: why don't you tell me about Beverly?"

She turned to the window again.

"Mom and Jo spent a lot of time with him on the boat."

"And the apartment? The one near Wedgewood Diner, or I guess now you'd call it behind Zanies?" I asked.

"So you know about that?" she asked.

"I do. Anything you want to tell me about it?"

"No," she replied.

"Do you know whatever happened to John Clarke's pistol?"

"It wouldn't surprise me if it ended up at the bottom of Old Hickory Lake."

"That's what I would have done with it," I replied. Pausing a moment to think about what had just been confirmed, I returned to a more personal question. "Gina, do you need help? There are people in this town who can help you, you know that?"[2]

"I'm not ready. I'm just not."

CHAPTER THIRTY-THREE

SHERLOCK IN ATLANTA

Attempting to savor my food during a lengthy discussion of murder and suicide was a challenge for me, but not so much for my two esteemed forensic guests, who seemed inured to such topics when we met for dinner during the American Academy of Forensic Sciences Conference in Atlanta, Georgia.[1]

A few minutes before our meeting time, it had been a relatively easy quest to ferret out the living Sherlock Holmes amidst hundreds of CSI enthusiasts filling up the massive lobby of the Marriott Hotel in midtown Atlanta. I simply looked for a man in a blue suit who could double for a tall, thin Basil Rathbone, wearing steel-framed eyeglasses, sporting a bit less hair, and indulging in one of two possible pleasures, tobacco or fine wine.

Basil Rathbone was the actor most associated with the Sherlock Holmes role for film and radio in the World War II era and again in the 1970s, when the films were rereleased. But whereas the fictional Sherlock Holmes might normally be found contemplating a problem while enjoying a pipe full of tobacco, Richard Walter preferred cigarettes, the Kool brand, as well as a fine glass of Chardonnay.

After introductions, I had the pleasure of sharing a meal not only with Richard Walter but also with one of his international colleagues, Dr. Klaus Neudecker, a physician and forensic psychiatrist from Bavaria, in southeast Germany. Walter explained that he had prepped Klaus with some minimal details about the babysitter murder and asked if the good doctor might join us for dinner.[2] I welcomed the additional expertise. We found a quiet table in the back of one of the hotel restaurants, away from the main flow of guests, so as not to impact the dining experience of anyone seated near us.

"You're enjoying the conference?" I asked, after we had all been seated.

"It's rather good, yes. Especially today's presentation on suicide by water, where the victim drank so much water a chemical imbalance occurred and the person died, a rather clever way to off oneself," noted Richard Walter.[3]

"That's interesting. How did the two of you come to meet?"

"Let's see, I believe that was over a sadism consult, wasn't it, Klaus?" Walter asked.

"Yes, it was," the German psychiatrist replied.

As he spoke, I quickly remembered that Richard Walter had used his research to model a helix of evil, a sort of roadmap to hell, one that could literally predict the progression path of a peeping Tom to the eventual depths of his psychosis, with all of the intervening steps along the way. It was not unusual for "sociopaths in training" to attempt to sneak into one of Richard Walter's presentations in hopes of learning how to make faster progress toward their perverse enjoyments. Unfortunately, those enjoyments were usually at the expense of the rest of free society. It was as if Richard Walter knew their future crimes before they could commit them.

"So, how was the Jack the Ripper conference at Drexel?" I asked.[4] "And by the way, I figured out who the Ripper was based on your model."[5]

"But I didn't say who he was."

"No, you didn't, but I studied your learning model and applied it to the suspect list, and it seems obvious that the young man found floating in the river, the Druitt fellow, was Jack the Ripper," I stated confidently.

"Well done. You are correct. The Brits don't much like to hear such definitive assessments, however, as it cuts into their tourist trade. They like to keep the mystery going. Why don't you tell Klaus the babysitter story," Walter suggested.

And so I did, and along with the story, I produced supporting documents, crime-scene photographs, a few of the detective magazines from the era, telegrams from J. Edgar Hoover, and more, all from my leather portfolio. Klaus reviewed each of these carefully as I progressed through the narrative, carefully describing the night of the murder, including the phone calls answered by the little boy and his sister. It was as if I were presenting the case before a modern-day Dr. Watson and Sherlock Holmes, only this time, they were named Neudecker and Walter.

A half hour later, with pauses for questions and clarifications along the way, I reached the end of the story and brought the timeline to the present dinner meeting in Atlanta. Richard Walter posed the initial follow-up question to his colleague.

"So, Klaus, who murdered the girl?" Walter asked.

"Clearly, it was not the judge's son. Not the Clarke fellow," he replied in a Bavarian accent.

"Might you posit the hand of the girl's mother with this event?" Walter inquired.

"Yes, most certainly. But how did the mother escape notice? It seems the odds of finding two dead family members would be almost incalculable."

I jumped in with the answer: "The mother had made significant investments in the power structure of Nashville. With her work as a nurse, she was in position to encounter some powerful people with addiction problems, starting with the mayor of Nashville. Eventually her circle included police detectives, an assistant DA, and more. I'm certainly not an expert, but it seems to me that the mother could spot human weakness like a hawk can spot a three-legged rabbit." This latter statement elicited a chuckle from my new friends, and I continued.

"There were two nurses in the house on the night of the murder, and I was told that the other nurse actually fired the gunshots that executed the girl, but the mastermind of it all was the victim's mother. She was bad news. Those two nurses were providing sexual favors, stolen drugs, and entertainment of a kind you couldn't find just anywhere, to the group. If I had to characterize the players, I'd call them drinkers, philanderers, politicians, power brokers, maybe even addicts. Whatever you want to call them, it seems they were all cooperating with each other to get their cravings satisfied. And unfortunately, that's just the way Nashville rolled fifty years ago."

"The mother was all about power. She was a Power Assertive personality," noted Richard Walter. "In a typical sexual homicide, which this murder is not, the perpetrator wants to feel the victim. He wants to feel the percussive impact of the assault. He will ejaculate into the victim. Not so with the Power Assertive personality. They are eliminating threats and taking names. They will talk about it. Brag about it. They're sending messaging about the crime. They are in charge, and the murder is over and done when they say it's over and done. And the letter that the mother sent to the chief of police, that's more messaging. That's hardly the act of a grieving mother over a lost child."

As we reached this portion of the discussion, our waiter began to deliver an array of food: barbeque ribs and cold beer for the German doctor; a seafood dish with a glass of Chardonnay for the tall, thin man, and a Caesar salad with flatbread appetizer for the layman, me. After a long sip of his chilled wine, Walter repeated the poignant questions that I had heard previously, only this time they were directed to his colleague.

"What explains this case? There's a murder in the home, in a constricted area, and it's mostly undisturbed. There is no rape, no robbery. But there is staging of a type to misdirect the investigation. The mother likely viewed this as a perfect crime," he said.

I picked up a photograph from 1964 showing Jo Herring in the hallway of the Municipal Safety Building on the night of Paula's murder.

"Not exactly the look of a grieving mother," I heard Walter say.

"No. She looks like she just won a prize fight, and she's ready to take on all comers," I said.

"Klaus, we were going to present this case to the Vidocq Society, but my talented friend here is not a member of the law enforcement community," Walter said.

"I'm a private citizen. What can I say?" I shrugged my shoulders and turned my palms upward.

Walter turned to me with a question I hadn't expected: "Tell me, what happened to the relationship between the two nurses, what eventually transpired?"

"Within days of the criminal trial verdict, the other nurse involved in the slaying, I'll call her Lizzie, married one of the two men who came to the house on that Saturday night. That newlywed couple moved away and stayed off of the radar screen for years. In part, I think they wanted to avoid any retribution from the Clarke fellow who was convicted. And getting married prevented them from testifying against each other," I said.

"So the partnership, however you want to describe it between the two nurses, that didn't continue?" Walter asked.

"No," I replied.

"Klaus, you see what happens, it has to change. After the murder, the relationship will, of necessity, decay."

"And something else: after the slaying, the dead girl's mother moved back home to work in a hospital in Waco, Texas," I added.

"That's what I call a return to Normalville," Walter responded.

"What do you mean by that?" I asked.

"The mother is now facing life without a husband and life without her daughter, notwithstanding the fact that she had a direct hand in the reasons for both. The other nurse, Lizzie, can't very well continue being with her. And once the men in the group realize the actual relationship between the two nurses, and who was really involved in the murder, they stop seeing her as well. So she will eventually commit suicide over time. It's just the way the psyche works," Richard Walter said.

"By all reports, she abused alcohol and cigarettes, and by the time her son was eighteen years old, she was dead," I noted. But this led me to a mystery that had haunted me from the early days of the research, when I had visited Paula's gravesite in Gallatin.

"So the victim's mother purchases not one but two grave plots within hours of murdering her daughter. One body, two graves. Why two graves when only one is needed? Would that have been because she might have committed suicide herself in the days right after the murder?" I asked.

Neudecker placed his utensils aside, took a sip of his drink, and injected a clarifying follow-up to me: "How did she purchase the plots?"

"She paid ninety dollars for each, cash, hours after the Saturday night murder," I said.

Richard Walter was staring at me with hawk-like intensity. "My dear fellow, that second grave was for the little boy. Not for herself. She was already making plans to do him in. She would have killed him within hours, certainly that next week, if he had presented any threat to her at all."

My mouth was open, and I didn't make a sound. I could see that Neudecker was nodding his head in agreement.

Walter continued, "The little boy probably would have met with a most unfortunate accident. That would have been her plan."

"I never thought about that potential," I said. "That's just evil."

"His own survival instinct must have told him, strongly told him, to simply remember nothing from the night of the murder and to park that conscious knowledge elsewhere. He was lucky to survive."

Neudecker used the silence to ask where Alan Herring was living and I replied that he was hundreds of miles from Timberhill Drive.[6] "I don't imagine he's coming back anytime soon. Who could blame him, really?" I said.

Moments later, we returned to the topic of motivation, especially as it related to Jo Herring's motivation concerning her daughter and little son.

"The Power Assertive personality will simply eliminate any threat to the ego. It doesn't matter if it's an external threat or one from inside the home. And it's not the first time a powerful and controlling psychopath was hiding behind the clothing of a Florence Nightingale. She was simply using sexual domination and manipulation to get what she wanted. And in this case, she wanted to eliminate a threat from within, her own daughter, and the son would have been next," Walter noted.

"The girl was doomed," Neudecker injected.

"Once the daughter expressed any potential to point a finger at the mother for the father's death, it was just a matter of time, or in this case, a matter of about three and a half years," I said.

We paused for a moment, while our waiter delivered slices of chocolate cake to the table. At this point, I was just eating mindlessly, with no thought of the taste of the food or even that I was actually finishing a meal.

Richard Walter looked toward the ceiling, as if recalling a lost cloud formation, before delivering another facet of the crime. "Don't look past another motivation. And that would be the elimination of a threat to the rest of the group. She might say to the politicos involved, especially if they were married, and I would bet all of the male members were married with wives and families, 'See what I did for you? I killed her. She's not going to be a problem. Game over.' A smart nurse would have drugged the child while she went about her work that night. It would have been easy enough to do with a simple sedative or depressant," Richard Walter said.

"I'm told she knew more about medications than the doctors she worked with, plus she had a large supply of stolen meds in her home," I replied.

"And one of those phone calls that the boy heard may well have been his mother answering the phone, not his sister answering. It may have been the other nurse calling back to the house to say that she was safely elsewhere with a ready alibi and the mother could go ahead and call in the discovery of the crime," Walter said.

As I gazed across the room, the living Sherlock Holmes made an observation about me: "You are no doubt dazzled by the personalities of this story, and the political aspect as well. It seems the young woman was on a path to rise above her circumstances. You plan to write the book, yes, to honor her?"

"Yes, that's my plan," I said.

"I would buy that book," noted Neudecker.

"You should do it," echoed Richard Walter.

Within hours of the unforgettable meal with my new colleagues, I returned to Nashville, knowing that the next step in my plan was to pen the final solution to the babysitter murder. In a multi-hour session, fueled by caffeine and adrenaline, I would tell the incredible story of Paula Herring and her date with death, from the moment she stepped off of a plane at the Nashville airport in February 1964, until the arrest of a scapegoat named John Randolph Clarke a week later. Only this time, the story would include the secret players, their motives, and how they participated in covering up the murder of an eighteen-year-old college student, a young woman who planned to tell her own story of murder, a plan that ultimately took her life.

CHAPTER THIRTY-FOUR

BAD NIGHT IN NASHVILLE

It is certainly possible that the wheels of justice that swept 'round and 'round Metro Nashville in the frantic hours after Paula Herring's murder did indeed gather up the one true suspect in the slaying, John Randolph Clarke. Though if Clarke did the deed, he nearly committed the perfect crime, because other than the matching bullet found near an 18th Avenue sidewalk, and a few fibers helped onto his clothing by a compromised investigator, no other physical evidence existed to convict him. No eyewitness, no bite marks, no blood stains, no noisy car, no scratches.

But let us leave Mr. Clarke alone for the moment and consider a story that just might provide a more satisfying narrative for a jury and also involve real physical evidence, as well as the motivations for those individuals potentially involved in the slaying. I present to you a Bad Night in Nashville.

Life could not have been better for Paula Herring on February 21, 1964. With a mountain full of snow in Gatlinburg, on Friday morning she made a quick trip to the little resort town to ski with fellow club members and enjoy the wonderful, fresh powder that had fallen hours before.[1] And it wasn't just the thrill of skiing that was making Paula happy. She had been dating the newly elected president of the ski club each of the previous three weekends. By late afternoon, she was at the regional airport just outside of Knoxville, smiling and laughing with her future sorority sisters as the small group boarded an Eastern Airlines flight traveling to Memphis, Tennessee.[2]

When the flight made a scheduled stop in Nashville, Paula Herring stepped off the airplane and flagged down a cab driver to take her home to Timberhill Drive. Instead of finding her mother and little brother at home, though, Paula found an empty house waiting for her. Having spent her money on a lift ticket earlier that day, she had no money to pay for taxi service. But a quick dash next door ended with Becky Wexler's mom writing a check for the cab fare.[3]

Unknown to Paula, her little brother, Alan, was just up the street visiting with one of Jo Herring's neighbors. A few miles away, Paula's mother was sitting at a table at Wedgewood Diner, drinking beer after work with Billy Vanderpool, A. J. Meadows Jr., and one of her nurse friends from Vanderbilt Hospital, a woman named Evelyn. After Jo and Alan finally did arrive home, the conversation likely turned to snow skiing, college life, and the invitation to join Alpha Omicron Pi, the prestigious sorority membership that Paula coveted.

On Saturday morning, Paula drove the family Ford a few blocks up the street to her best friend Carmen Lee's house, and over breakfast and nonstop stories from the University of Tennessee, the two girls hatched a plan to meet at the basketball tournament being played in Madison, Tennessee, that evening.[4] After the game, Carmen would ride home with Paula and spend Saturday night at the Herrings, staying up late into the night, whispering, laughing, and making plans for the future.

Attending the basketball game also would allow Paula the rare opportunity to surprise some of her former Overton High classmates, as well as the coaching duo representing Overton's competition that night. The previous year, Dorothy Ellis had coached her favorite team, the one led by Paula Herring, before resigning her teaching and coaching duties at Overton High School. And the irony could not have been sweeter now that Dorothy Ellis's husband, Jody, was the head football coach for Donelson High School, and powerful Donelson was playing Overton in a winner-advance or go-home game, which Paula desperately wanted to see.[5] It was a game not to be missed, and Paula had traveled many miles to be courtside and cheer on her friend Carmen in hopes that Overton would win.

When Paula Herring left John Overton High in June of 1963, she was more often than not engaged in some athletic activity, which invoked both the "tomboy" description and the word "Fish," the moniker given to her in high school due to her last name, but the girl who would be entering the gymnasium on this Saturday night would not be the Fish that many remembered. This Paula Herring was an attractive blond. She had swapped her eyeglasses for contact lenses and would be dressed in a new sweater and wraparound skirt, with penny loafers and knee-length socks to complete the coed ensemble. It was also the first opportunity for Paula to announce that she was joining a most prestigious sorority, Alpha Omicron Pi.

More than that, this Paula Herring had a beautiful smile on her face and the glow of a college student who was more than anxious to see the surprised looks on the faces of friends and classmates as they realized the transformation that had taken place since they had last seen her. The transformation was not confined to just her outer appearance but reflected a newfound confidence, showing that Paula Herring had discovered her place in the world and was on a journey to make a difference in it.[6]

After an hour or so of visiting with Carmen and her family during breakfast, Paula returned home so that her mother could take the family car to work at Vanderbilt Hospital. Jo Herring had worked the previous day, Friday, from 11:00 a.m. to 7:00 p.m., before stopping for the drinking session at the Wedgewood Diner.

Her mother's work schedule was important to Paula because Jo Herring was planning to come home early enough on Saturday so that Paula could drive the family car to the basketball game. But sometime on Saturday afternoon, Jo Herring must have spoken with Paula by phone and informed her that a new plan was now in play, one that did not involve Jo arriving home early enough for Paula to use the family automobile. Perhaps Jo told Paula that she had to work late into the evening and there was nothing she could do about it. Perhaps she told Paula a sympathy-inducing tale of having to work a double shift or an unexpected hospital incident that required Jo Herring to stay late and provide her expertise as a caregiver. It is likely that Paula expressed disappointment and then told her mother she would have no trouble finding a ride for herself and Alan to go to the basketball game.

Paula may have even thought it would be a great opportunity to ask her favorite teacher and former coach for a ride, only to discover that Dorothy and Jody Ellis already had made plans to attend the game with friends and could not help her. Even more disappointing, her friend Carmen was already en route to the game with her teammates from Overton High.

About the time Paula Herring was reeling from the potential of actually missing the game she had so hoped to attend, John Randolph Clarke was getting dressed for a night of prowling, while leaving his schoolteacher wife at home alone. He knew Jo Herring would be clocking out of her hospital shift around 7:00 p.m., and Clarke knew where the little registered nurse would likely appear, at Ruth's Diner or at one of the many watering holes in the area. His thirty-ninth birthday had been the previous day, and he wanted another chance to rendezvous with the alluring nurse.

At some point in the early evening, Clarke made his way to Ruth's Diner and began drinking beer with his friend Al Baker.[7] With no sign of his favorite nurse, Clarke stepped away from the bar and used the diner's pay phone to call the Herring home. When he returned, he would utter words that would eventually seal his fate with future jurors. He bragged to Baker that he was going over to Timberhill Drive to wait for Jo, and that in the interim he would try his hand with Jo's daughter, whom he had just spoken with, learning that she was home from college for the weekend.[8] Not long after mentioning this macho plan, Clarke left the diner, but he didn't follow through with his boast. Instead, he began searching for his favorite nurse at other drinking spots.

On this Saturday night, Jo Herring never made an appearance at any of the watering holes she normally frequented because, unknown to John Randolph Clarke, Jo Herring was sitting in a car within walking distance of Clarke's home. At approximately 7:00 p.m., Jo had clocked out of Vanderbilt Hospital and was picked up at the curb by a man behind the wheel of a black Cadillac. In the back seat of the Cadillac was a Red Ace gas station attendant named Jesse Henderson, along with Jo Herring's best friend and coworker, Lizzie. The Cadillac's driver was also a Vanderbilt Hospital employee, a tall, thick-chested man named Carl Raylee.[9] After the car left the hospital, the foursome turned their attention to finding food to go along with the adult beverages in the car.

Carl Raylee was not just any employee at the hospital, though; he was a purchasing agent, a man who could requisition drugs, medicines, and equipment, and, most importantly, a man who could reconcile shortages of drugs and who could revise purchasing records if necessary. Nurse Lizzie and Jo Herring were keenly interested in currying favor with the big man and also ensuring that he had a very good time on this Saturday night in February 1964. Unknown to Carl Raylee, it was about to become a night he would never forget.

After the black Cadillac pulled away from the hospital, it ended up a few blocks away, on West End Avenue, parked in one of the car stalls at the Krystal hamburger drive-in restaurant, where the foursome ordered curb service and received ten-cent hamburgers served in red plastic baskets with French fries. As they chatted and munched on their burgers, downing multiple beers that Jesse had brought along for the ride, a plan was hatched to drive to Jo Herring's house, where Jo and Lizzie would change out of their hospital scrubs, and then the two couples would go out on the town for a night of drinking and partying.

Near the eight o'clock hour, Carl Raylee eased the big Cadillac through the back parking lot of the drive-in onto Elliston Place and back to Vanderbilt Hospital, where the two nurses transferred to Jo's Ford and led the Cadillac to Timberhill Drive. Thus began a bad night in Nashville.

Certainly the two men following Jo Herring's car had no indication that they were about to be in for the worst night of their lives. But confirmation of this point came moments after the foursome entered the Herring home. To Paula's surprise, her mother was not at the hospital working late. And, to Jo's surprise, instead of finding an empty house, Paula was still at home, and she hadn't found a ride to the basketball game as planned.

The more troubling and darker element was that Jo Herring had walked in the door with a woman Paula Herring despised and hadn't seen for months, Nurse Lizzie.[10] The thirty-five-year-old Lizzie was also a widow, just like Jo Herring. To Paula's astonishment, visibly angry at her mother and loathing her mother's best friend, these two nurses had the gall to stand before her, turning what should have been one of the happiest nights of her life into what was about to become the worst night of her life. This was the beginning of the end for Paula Herring.

From the perspective of what Paula knew or didn't know, it's certainly possible that Paula may not have known the full scope of her mother's lifestyle and the powerful men she entertained at secret hideaways, but she was very intelligent and could connect the dots. Maybe she didn't know about the stolen drugs in the house, but Paula had experienced her mother's chronic alcoholism for years. Maybe Jo hadn't tried to entice her daughter into using powerful men for sex and profit, but Paula Herring had experienced enough of her mother's lifestyle, and the random men that she brought home, to reject it completely and to be on a very different journey than her mother.

For every personal achievement that Paula Herring reported from college life in Knoxville, Jo Herring's resentment and jealousy must have increased exponentially. Paula was younger, prettier, a good student, a great athlete, and a leader. There was no way that Jo could ignore Paula's success, and the invitation to join an exclusive sorority was proof positive that her daughter was in demand and on the way to becoming everything that Jo Herring was not.

So what must Paula have felt when on Friday evening she arrived from Knoxville to an empty house? Jo Herring had paid for the plane ticket, certainly not the chronically broke college student, and Jo would have known when the flight was scheduled to arrive, but instead of a mother excitedly meeting the flight at the airport gate or waiting at home for her daughter, what did Paula Herring experience?

She experienced a mother who had chosen to go out drinking on Friday night after work, while thumbing her nose at her daughter's return.[11] The Friday night situation was actually worse than Paula realized. Jo Herring wasn't rushing home to see her daughter, she was meeting with a man who owned a massage parlor, a brick and mortar front for a prostitution business.[12] As for Saturday night, Jo could have hurried home and enjoyed an outing with Paula and Alan, but instead Jo Herring chose to reject her daughter yet again and spend a second night out on the town, with plans for drinking and partying with her partner, Nurse Lizzie, and the two men. To make matters even worse, the house full of hell on Timberhill Drive wasn't about a battle over borrowed clothing or missed curfews, it was a war, with the darkest of undercurrents, about the death of Wilmer Herring.[13]

While fifteen-year-old Paula Herring may have been devastated and confused by the mysterious death of her father, the eighteen-year-old version of that young woman appears to have been free from such doubts. According to one of Jo Herring's friends, Paula was an unlit fuse, biding her time until she could do something about her father's death. Or as one of Wilmer Herring's relatives noted for me, "Paula knew that the bottle of rat poison had come from their house and her father hadn't been suicidal."[14]

With the latest round of Jo Herring's rejections, and the double-barreled impact of facing the two nurses, it doesn't require much of a leap of faith to assume that this was the moment when the fuse was lit and the violence began. And while the two male visitors may have initially found some perverted entertainment value in the fight, they quickly realized the level of threats being exchanged and had every reason to believe that something terrible was about to happen.

And unfortunately, there was a gun available to make matters worse. When John Randolph Clarke had been at the Herring home on February 10, giving Alan Herring a "horsey back" ride to bed, he would have removed his pistol and shoulder holster to avoid having the child kick or accidentally discharge the gun. After a couple of rounds in bed with Jo Herring, and in Clarke's inebriated state, he must have left the gun behind and returned home without it. Which is why Clarke's gun, but not the owner, was in the house this night and why Charles Galbreath had asked Jo Herring on the witness stand if she knew where the gun was.

In the midst of the early altercation it seems reasonable to assume that indeed a belt was slipped around Paula's neck from behind, in an attempt to take the powerful athlete to the floor, where she might be more easily controlled.[15] Paula Herring must have instantly realized her life was in danger, and as she fought back she delivered a vicious bite to the younger nurse. In an act of rage, Lizzie fired Clarke's gun at Paula; the bullet entered the coed's collarbone area and eventually came to rest in Paula's lower back.

Indoors, on a cold winter night, the sound of a gunshot would have been deafening. The firing of a .32-caliber pistol would have produced an explosive sound, approaching 150 decibels or more and for everyone in the room, and everyone in the house, their ears would have been ringing, and their adrenaline flowing. With a mortally wounded coed lying on the floor, chaos and anger begin to reign. The two nurses had an opportunity to come to their senses and provide aid to the girl. They could ask the two men to place Paula in the Cadillac and rush her to Vanderbilt Hospital for emergency medical care. They could do everything to save Paula, but, instead, they chose to save themselves. They left the house and drove away, leaving Jo Herring's daughter dying in the den, certain that she would not survive for long.

In a quiet house of horror, with Paula Herring's lifeblood leaving her body, the telephone rang once again. And again it was John Randolph Clarke hoping to find his soul mate, Jo Herring, who likely viewed him not only as a sexual partner but also as a source of income from the stolen drugs. But this time, instead of Paula answering the telephone, it was a terrified little boy who would truthfully say that his mother wasn't home, and in a few short hours would eventually describe his sister as lying on the den floor with "tomato juice in her hair."

Clarke, having called from one of his regular watering holes, would continue looking for Jo Herring for the next hour, making visits to Brown's Diner, Chico's, back to Ruth's, and more, but at some point after 9:00 p.m., he would call it a night and drive to a liquor store at 16th and Broadway, where he would purchase a pint of bourbon before going home.[16]

On Timberhill Drive, however, the two nurses and the two men were cursing at each other as they raced away in Raylee's Cadillac, hoping the neighbors hadn't bothered to look out their windows and notice them. Moments later, and needing a place to formulate a plan, they passed the Krystal hamburger restaurant on Franklin Road and then quickly decided that a room around back of the York Motel would be the best hideout while they figured out what to do next. After checking in, it didn't take them long to realize that they'd not only left the incriminating murder weapon in the house, but the nurses likely realized that the cache of stolen drugs had to be removed as well.[17]

Jo Herring made a couple of phone calls, and one of those appears to have been made to her friend Evelyn Johnson, asking Evelyn to come to the Timberhill Drive home.[18] Perhaps Jo was already planning to repeat the same scenario of having a friend with her as she "discovered" a body, as she had with Wilmer Herring's "suicide." It's also possible that Jo Herring could see an even better solution to her problem, and that would be to invite an unsuspecting neighbor such as Sam Carlton to her home, and then use Clarke's gun to kill the neighbor who had broken into her home and had been "sexually assaulting" her daughter while Jo had been at dinner.

After the calls, the foursome decided the best option available was to return to Timberhill Drive to retrieve the gun and get the drugs out of the house. It was a simple plan, quickly formulated, with no time for a lengthy debate about its merits or those of any other option. But the most important element was the part that no one could foresee. What if Paula Herring was still alive? What then?

With the headlights of the Cadillac turned off as they again navigated up the driveway, the foursome inside the car were still cursing at each other and threatening each other in low voices as they parked just outside of the garage. Jesse Henderson and Carl Raylee were not about to go back into the house. They hadn't touched anything, hadn't fired a gun, hadn't struck a blow against the girl, and had no reason to retrieve anything from inside the den of horror.

When Jo and Lizzie crept back into the house, to their amazement Paula Herring was not dead. She was still lying on the floor right where they had left her, her face turned to the side, eyes focused on her assailants. But the two women were more than capable of putting aside any emotion and simply focusing on doing what was necessary. And what was clearly necessary in their view was to execute the young woman on the floor. But before they could do that, Jo Herring needed to sedate the trembling little boy in a back bedroom. This only required the proper dose of medication, readily available for the boy's mother to administer.

Meanwhile, in the den, Nurse Lizzie retrieved Clarke's pistol and watched Paula to see if she would draw a last breath. Still enraged over the bite she had received, Lizzie tried to hasten Paula's demise by stomping on the fallen girl and then slamming the butt of the pistol into Paula's face. But Paula Herring would not die. Jo quickly returned to the den with a pillowcase full of stolen drugs and, with the precious minutes ticking away, Paula's sweater was used to muffle the sound of two gunshots fired into the girl's back straight through her heart, silencing Paula Herring forever.

Just moments before this execution, the nervous men in the car were running out of patience, and they went back into the house to tell the nurses that they were leaving and that there was no time to spare. At least that was the plan until just before opening the den door, when the men heard the unmistakable sound of a car engine outside. Before the men could alert the nurses, the gunshots from the den sent adrenalin roaring through their veins, but now they were stuck in the garage.

Sam Carlton got out of his parked car, still puzzled over the invitation to Jo Herring's house. With an unopened bottle of Sterling beer in his hand, he confidently stepped through the outer garage door into the darkened room, only to be attacked by two men who were frantically trying to escape the scene.[19] In the blink of an eye, one of the men shattered the quart bottle of Sterling beer over Carlton's head. His torso blocked the spray as it splattered onto the garage floor. A dazed Sam Carlton was on his knees, woozy from the blow.

In the meantime, Nurse Lizzie had fled through the front door, Clarke's gun in hand, a pillowcase of drugs in the other, racing down the sidewalk to the Cadillac parked in the driveway. Lizzie quickly started the car and floored the gas pedal, and the Cadillac launched backward into Carlton's Chrysler. This event broke one of the Chrysler's headlights and damaged the radiator and front of the Chrysler's engine.

But Lizzie's two male companions had similar ideas, and as soon as Carlton was knocked down, the two men exited the garage and ran back to the car, only to discover that Lizzie was attempting to leave them behind. Cursing at her, Carl Raylee opened the driver's-side door, and pushed Lizzie away from the steering wheel, while Jesse Henderson jumped into the front passenger seat from the other side of the car. Raylee maneuvered the big automobile around Carlton's damaged vehicle, and the trio raced away from the horrific scene.

Moments later, as Sam Carlton tried to regain his senses, he wobbled toward the den door. As soon as he saw a young woman lying on the floor, blood pooling around her, he became instantly alert. After a few seconds surveying the scene, he realized that he had been setup for murder, and now he couldn't flee the house fast enough. He returned to his car and also drove away, his damaged vehicle emitting the distinctive metallic scraping sound heard by neighbors that night.

Carlton, enraged, didn't drive home but instead drove his car toward the city lights of Nashville. It was cold and dark and, based on the noise coming from the Chrysler's engine, he needed to find a garage quickly, or at least a place where he could inspect the damage, just in case he became stranded on the road in his blood-stained and beer-soaked condition. When he arrived in the Melrose area, he saw a familiar eatery and steered the damaged Chrysler into a parking space at the Krystal hamburger restaurant. Unknown to Carlton, Henry King was also driving toward the Krystal, looking for a hot cup of coffee while his wife was recovering from surgery in a Nashville hospital.

Once parked, and still furious over the potential setup to frame him with murder, Carlton raised the hood of the Chrysler, inspected the damage to the car, and looked across the street at Rhea Little's service station. Carlton and Little knew each other because both were in the gasoline business, and Rhea Little was the man Carlton now wanted to call for repair help and a late-night favor. Carlton could see that the service station was closed, but the Krystal hamburger restaurant never closed, so he decided to use the pay phone in the Krystal and call the owner at home with his request for help. Carlton walked into the Krystal hamburger restaurant, fumbled with the telephone directory, and was offered assistance by a concerned night manager. But just as quickly, the big man changed his mind and strode out of the restaurant to return to his car.

A few feet outside of the doorway, a startled Henry King said hello to Sam Carlton as they passed each other near the entrance. When King expressed concern over Carlton's all-too-apparent distress, the truck stop manager told the concerned King that he had been hit in the head and attacked by two men and that he was going home to get his gun and kill them.

Unknown to Carlton, the two men who ran out of the Timberhill Drive home after attacking him were now on their way to 17th Avenue, where they would drop off Lizzie DeVern and then race to the other side of Nashville, looking for an alibi location miles away from Timberhill Drive. Twenty minutes later, the black Cadillac was speeding into the night on River Road in West Nashville, and, after rounding a curve, the car skidded off the slick roadway, rolled over, and landed back on its wheels. The duo inside were shaken up but not injured, and the car's engine was still humming. A few minutes later, Carl Raylee delivered his passenger to a gasoline station where he could catch a ride home, and Raylee drove the damaged Cadillac home to Central Avenue, where his uncle would repair it a few days later, no questions asked.

Back at Timberhill Drive, Jo Herring had changed clothes and was waiting for Nurse Evelyn to arrive. Evelyn would later realize that her role was to help Jo "discover" the horrific scene in the den. But Evelyn stopped for gasoline on Murfreesboro Road and was delayed by a few precious minutes. At about the same time, a couple of Jo Herring's Metro friends arrived at the Herring home and began to work on damage control. It was no coincidence that the men who arrived were part of Jo Herring's inner circle and just happened to be members of Metro's law enforcement community. It was very likely that they were concerned that one of the group members, be it a detective, an assistant DA, or an even more powerful member of the group, was in fact responsible for the young woman lying lifeless on the floor in the den.

Somewhere in the approximately ninety-minute window between Nurse Evelyn's arrival and the phone call to the police dispatcher at 11:00 p.m., the decision must have been made to replace Jesse Henderson and Carl Raylee with the two men from the Friday night drinking session at the Wedgewood Diner in the story the police would be told. There is simply no other way to explain the presence of two men who were not actually present that Saturday night. When I spoke with A. J. Meadows Jr., in October of 1999, he admitted that he hadn't actually been at the Timberhill Drive house on the night of Paula Herring's murder. He had been there the night before, Friday night, and, even then, he had never been in the garage or even entered the home.[20]

After more than an hour of chaos, shortly after 11:00 p.m., the Herring home was finally ready for an official visit from Metro detectives called out to investigate yet another Crieve Hall Prowler event. But this time the attack would appear to have escalated into murder. Upon arrival, the real detectives initially found a hysterical mother, sobbing and incoherent. The widowed nurse could barely muster enough words for the investigators to understand how she had discovered the pretty blond college student lying in the den. As experienced detectives, they quickly separated the hysterical mother from her young son and begin asking questions about the chain of events that took place before they arrived.

With a house filling up with policemen and investigators, it didn't take long for the lead detectives to realize that the story the widowed nurse was telling was highly suspect. Around midnight, the next-door neighbor who had paid Paula's cab fare the night before was brought over to babysit Alan Herring while detectives took Jo down to the police station for some intensive questioning. Nurse Evelyn followed the detectives' car to the Municipal Safety Building, where she would wait for Jo Herring until the break of dawn, when Jo was released to return home.

It isn't possible to know every detail of what transpired while Jo Herring was being interrogated during her midnight to dawn session. But it is possible to know what Jo Herring needed to keep hidden from the investigators. Her first order of business would have been an attempt to make herself look completely innocent of the slaying, while hiding every motivation for the murder, along with its participants. Jo Herring had at least a three-hour window of opportunity, perhaps longer than that, to concoct a story that would hopefully allow her to walk away freely from any charge of murdering her daughter. Did she telephone her lawyer for help—the compromised assistant district attorney?

We do know that Jo Herring described her Saturday night activities as the outcome of a gracious daughter strongly encouraging her mother to have a night out on the town, as if such an event were so rare as to be celebrated when the opportunity arose. It was this cold and calculating lie that likely served as the foundation of Jo's attempt to walk away. She embellished it even more by attributing a quote to Paula in support of the plan: "Mother, take the night off while I work on a book report." It was this deceit that allowed Jo Herring to misdirect investigators from seeing one of the motives in her daughter's wrongful death. In fact, the lie made it seem that Paula could have gone anywhere she chose that night, but instead chose to focus on her school work and stay home cuddled up with Robert Penn Warren's classic tale of political corruption and murder.

Rather than admit to the actual relationship she had with Paula, in an attempt to divert suspicion, Jo Herring must have gone out of her way to describe what a close bond she had with her daughter and how proud she was of her college coed. Jo must have also realized that she would have to keep quiet about Paula's anger at being unable to attend the district basketball game; otherwise it might speak to another element of motive in the slaying. And certainly there would have been no reason to bring up any discussion of Wilmer Herring's 1960 death or the identity of the trio who had entered the house with her hours before.

At some point during the interrogation, Jo Herring must have played her eventual trump card. It's doubtful that she would have played it with rank and file detectives, and more likely that she delivered her bombshell news to one of the chiefs of police. It would have been only a matter of time before Chief Hubert Kemp would have received the news and been forced to make a decision. The trump card would have been a devastatingly simple declaration: "I'm close friends with Mayor Briley. Very, very close, if you understand what I'm saying to you? Can you get him on the phone and ask him to come down here? Now." A winning move by the brilliant nurse. Game. Set. Match.

After a couple of phone calls, all Hubert Kemp would have been able to do was to let her go, wondering if in forty-eight hours he would be sending a detective back out to arrest her. No one knows what the mayor might have said during his conversation with Hubert Kemp, but two things took place after the phone call: Jo Herring walked away from the Municipal Safety Building at daybreak on Sunday morning and, sometime the next week, Kemp asked the mayor to explain why he had been in the Crieve Hall neighborhood on the night of the murder. And Briley dutifully penned a letter in response.

Perhaps unknown to Briley, Hubert Kemp's brother lived in Crieve Hall, and the chief used his brother's next-door neighbor as the reason for the request to Briley for an explanation. Though

Kemp may have been viewed as "too dumb to steal" when he was chosen to lead the police department after the Printers Alley housecleaning, he wasn't too dumb to trick Briley into placing himself in Crieve Hall at the time of the murder.[21]

At some point during the night, whether when arriving or departing, Jo Herring strode down the hallway of the Municipal Safety Building, purse and coat hanging on one arm and eyeglasses awkwardly in place, and a newspaper photographer captured the moment on film. Neither the photograph, nor the fact that Paula's mother was the prime suspect in her daughter's murder, would ever make a newspaper or television account in Nashville, and it wouldn't be revealed until decades later. With news beginning to spread that a murder had taken place in Crieve Hall, authorities were on high alert. And especially so on West End Avenue, where two patrolmen stopped a speeding car at daybreak on Sunday morning and, in a tension-filled scene, captured two Vanderbilt University students at gunpoint, one of whom had just fired shots from the passenger's window into the cold morning air using a .32-caliber pistol.[22] The Vanderbilt students were taken to jail and held for questioning as first alternates in Paula's murder. In a bit of irony, just as Jo Herring was leaving her interrogators, her replacements arrived in the form of the two Vanderbilt students.

Sometime on Sunday morning, John Randolph Clarke loaded a collection of paperback books into his car, and he and Callie Clarke began driving to Tullahoma, Tennessee, where they would spend the day with Callie's brother and family. And, on the other side of town, on Sunday afternoon, an angry Sam Carlton, knowing that his noisy car might bring unwanted attention, gave away his damaged Chrysler automobile to a professional wrestler, a man he hardly knew.

On Monday, a concerned Al Baker told a policeman friend that Red Clarke might be a "red hot suspect" in Paula Herring's murder. By the end of the week, Baker's other acquaintance, Jesse Henderson, would check himself into the VA Hospital's psychiatric ward. But before doing so, Jesse discovered that a single bullet was all that was needed to tie a murder weapon to the investigator's chief suspect in the Paula Herring slaying, John Randolph Clarke. Even better, the bullet needed only be found next to the sidewalk in front of Jesse's apartment.

It seems reasonable to assume that Jesse Henderson telephoned Lizzie, instructing her to fire the pistol into a soft target where she could retrieve the bullet. And, within a few short hours, Jesse received a .32-caliber gift that could quietly be dropped into the unguarded digging site. On the Thursday morning after the slaying, the bullet was magically discovered lying on top of the dirt, nose touching the concrete sidewalk, its shape unaltered. This event sealed Clarke's fate via ballistic-matching by a TBI firearms expert later that same day.

On Thursday evening, during a 10:00 p.m. television newscast, Mayor Beverly Briley announced a break in the case to the terrified citizens of Metro Nashville. An announcement that some might view as a cryptic admission regarding the slaying in Crieve Hall: *"We know who's guilty of this crime, we are certain. . . ."*

CHAPTER THIRTY-FIVE

QUEEN OF METRO

On a rainy fall afternoon, not long after my last visit with Nurse Evelyn, I again read *All the King's Men,* the book that played a substantial role in Paula Herring's murder investigation.[1] Students of the book can easily recount a number of themes running throughout this classic American tale: Willie Stark's alcoholism, his episodes of serial adultery, his willingness to use blackmail as a means to an end, as well as his unbridled lust for power and a secret lifestyle that eventually helped destroy him. Ironically, the books famous author, Robert Penn Warren, visited Nashville in the days just prior to Paula Herring's murder, a visit chronicled by one of the local newspapers.

There were only two items known to have been taken from the Herring home immediately after Paula's murder, the murder weapon and the paperback book. What was it about the little paperback that warranted removing it from the den as if it were as incriminating as the gun used in the slaying? And why had Jo Herring used the phrase "a date with *All the King's Men*" in her fictitious description of Paula's Saturday night plans?

As I pondered this secondary mystery, I was reminded of what a world-class liar Jo Herring had been at every opportunity following her daughter's murder and during its subsequent investigation. To one reporter, she had described Paula's last visit home as a wonderful surprise. It was hardly a surprise since Jo had paid for the plane ticket. To another, she told a loving tale of the close relationship between mother and daughter and how Paula had been homesick and just wanted to spend the weekend with her mother and little brother. To yet another reporter, she said she didn't know John Randolph

Clarke.[2] To the detectives working her daughter's murder investigation, she described in detail how Paula had urged her mother to take the night off and go to dinner with friends. But all of these descriptions were lies, self-centered, self-protecting, self-promoting lies.

In retrospect, there was little that came out of Jo Herring's mouth that wasn't deceptive or manipulative. So if Jo Herring's tale about Paula volunteering to stay home and babysit on that fateful night was pure fiction, then why should we believe her when it comes to the book report? Answer: we shouldn't. Here's the rest of the story that I believe was missed between the night of the murder and the arrest of John Randolph Clarke.

A close look at the timeline reveals that the tale of the missing paperback book arose at some point on Sunday, February 23, 1964, and was reported by Jim Squires in the Monday morning edition of the *Nashville Tennessean*:

> Mrs. Herring said her daughter, a freshman student at the University of Tennessee in Knoxville, was reading a book when she went out to dinner, leaving Paula with her 6-year-old brother, Alan. The girl was scheduled to make a report on the book in class today.[3]

But this was yet another lie. Jo Herring hadn't been at home to see or experience anything that had gone on that Saturday night, at least not until she arrived home with Nurse Lizzie and the two men. And there was nothing in the university records to indicate that Paula Herring had been taking any class that would have required a freshman English student to compose a critique of an American classic. A salient point made by Paula's classmates at the time.[4] So what happened?

I believe what happened is this: When Jo Herring walked out of her midnight-to-dawn interrogation, after having played her "mayor's mistress" card, and after having been treated as royalty—thank you, Jesse Henderson—she surely must have known that law enforcement would still be looking at her as a possible suspect in her daughter's slaying. And she couldn't simply call a meeting at her home and invite her paramours over for a late Sunday brunch and a discussion of possible alibis she could use. I believe she did the only thing she could do, and that was to send a message to the King and his Men, All of them.

Jo Herring must have been keeping her eye on a ticking time bomb in her home, from the day that Wilmer Herring died until Paula followed him in death, some thirty-nine months later. If Paula Herring had been angry over her father's death and had blamed her mother for it, then a house full of hell would have indeed evolved and Wilmer's demise would have become the undercurrent in any future battles. With Paula's announcement that she planned to attend law school, it's easy to see how Jo Herring might have been even more concerned about the future.

This likely accounts for the unusual number of powerful men that Jo Herring added to her "get out of jail" plan.

If a fifteen-year-old girl couldn't find it within herself to point a finger at her mother for potentially murdering the girl's father, what could a twenty-five-year old woman, a freshly minted attorney, do instead? Answer: a lot. How many of Jo's inner circle knew of Wilmer Herring's unusual demise? All of them? Some of them? If no one else, at least two of the men must have known. The assistant district attorney and the mayor. For the mayor to have been involved with not one but two nurses (read mistresses), with two eighteen-year-old daughters and two dead husbands, he had to have been aware of the risk, if for no other reason than his own political self-preservation. And if anyone was a student of history, especially American political history, or American literature about American political history, it seems that person would have been Clifton Beverly Briley, the mayor.

Through the secret and sexual relationships in what John Hollins had described as "a drinking group," Jo Herring had become one of the most powerful figures in Metro Nashville, albeit a player behind the scenes. Let's just call her the Queen of Metro. Her rolodex of powerful men was an impressive one. One that included married men who had been playing with fire, only to find themselves beholden to Jo Herring. If she needed to send a message to the mayor, to get his attention and remind him that she could burn down his political kingdom with a single phone call, or an inopportune confession, all she had to do was figuratively waive a copy of the little paperback book in front of a local newspaper reporter, and the message would have been transmitted in crystal clarity to the King and his Nashville Men. It was that simple. I think she did exactly that.

It would have been a chilling reminder that Jo Herring was the person who actually held all of the trump cards in her daughter's murder investigation. In the words of Richard Walter, it would have been more messaging. The district attorney was the only one who could move such a presentment forward, toward a grand jury indictment or, worse still, a trial. And if anyone would have wanted to avoid having Jo Herring defend herself against a charge of murder, exposing her secret friends in the melee that would follow, well, that would have been the mayor and the rest of the powerful little group.

So how did the paperback book get from the den to the ditch, where it was discovered a few days after the slaying? It is possible that Paula Herring did bring a copy of the book home for the weekend, but either way, assuming Nurse Evelyn was correct, Jo Herring had her own copy available.

Would that knowledge have driven Jo to toss the paperback book in a ditch sometime after Paula was killed, in an attempt to use the "missing book" story to her strategic advantage? I'll leave that for the reader to decide.

Perhaps the best thing to have happened to the new Metro government after Paula Herring's slaying would have been if Jo Herring had been exposed as Paula Herring's killer along with Nurse Lizzie. Perhaps justice might have prevailed? Maybe a number of those involved in the horrific tale would have been forced to focus on their personal issues by seeking addiction counseling, while others, with perhaps less obvious problems, could have provided healthier oversight of the new government. It is ironic that, in an area known as the buckle of the Bible belt, Nashville quietly became one of the leading centers for the treatment of sexual addiction in the United States, a status that continues at the time of this writing.

More than fifty years have passed since Metro Nashville was born at the stroke of midnight on April Fools' Day 1963. And more than fifty years also have passed since the biggest homicide case took place in the early formation of the new Metro government, the Paula Herring babysitter murder.

It is certainly possible that John Randolph Clarke did, in fact, murder Paula Herring on a Saturday night in February 1964. And in doing so, he was able to beat a young woman nearly to death and finally did kill his victim by shooting her three times with a .32-caliber handgun, without incurring even so much as a scratch or a bite mark or collecting a single drop of the victim's blood on the clothing he wore that evening. If he did, then he failed his Sexual Assault 101 class, because his victim wasn't sexually assaulted.

It's certainly possible that a registered nurse could indeed stumble separately upon two dead family members in a matter of three-plus years and it simply be an odds-defying, blind piece of unfortunate luck, where one death was completely unrelated to the other. It's unlikely, but possible. Perhaps Eva Jo Herring led a transparent, consistent, and exemplary life at home, at work, and in the community. Or perhaps it also is possible that she was hiding behind the personality of a caretaking Florence Nightingale, covering a startling shallowness in her depth of emotion and connection to others, and simply harboring an appetite for whatever she desired.

The opportunity for Paula to leave Nashville behind and start over in Knoxville may have been both a blessing and a curse for the young woman. The feelings of being trapped at home by her mother may have been fading away as her experience at the University of Tennessee, the new friends, and the sorority plans were rebuilding her confidence. Jo Herring probably could see what was coming. And all of those major issues—Wilmer Herring's questionable suicide, the men coming around and harassing Paula, the drugs, the alcohol, the neglect of Alan, the war over money needed by Paula for school, skiing, and the future sorority membership versus how Jo Herring was spending it, appear to have eventually loaded the literal gun. And the trigger was pulled when Jo Herring's daughter missed the opportunity to display the "new Paula Herring" to her friends at the basketball game, and the two women who were the reason for the missed opportunity entered the den of the Herring home on that tragic Saturday night.

It is more than just possible that Jo Herring was taken in for questioning as the first suspect in her daughter's murder, and she had the clout to outwit and outmaneuver her interrogators. And there was apparently nothing that Metro's finest could do about it except to release her and go back to the street to find a more suitable suspect to arrest. Two Vanderbilt University students were the next ones hauled to jail, followed by the twenty-five-year-old mental patient who had walked away from Central State Psychiatric Hospital and admitted to peeping into homes, and then finally John Randolph Clarke.

From a counting perspective, there were four different attempts at finding the right suspect. Four suspects hauled in and four suspects released, if you count the Vanderbilt duo as one team. Only later in the week did the authorities come back to Clarke as their final choice, aided by the magic bullet found near the 18th Avenue sidewalk and the doctored fiber evidence sent to the FBI. But let the record show that their first suspect, Jo Herring, was their best suspect, along with her unseen partner, Nurse Lizzie.

It is also possible that Jo Herring merely had an affinity for men who worked in law enforcement and also for men who had high earning potential as lawyers. It is ironic that her list of male acquaintances, paramours if you will, when mapped to an organizational chart, just happened to cover the gamut from a couple of police detectives, an assistant DA, the mayor, the son of a former Tennessee Chief Justice of the Supreme Court, and John Randolph Clarke, who just happened to be yet another man with a well-placed judge for a father. It was as if she could see into the future and perhaps see a need to use her rolodex of compromised men as a "get out of jail free" card. Perhaps it is just coincidental that, when Jo Herring needed to call in the favor of favors, several of these men were all too willing to come to her aid. Frankly speaking, they may have been terrified not to.

If Jo Herring had been arrested for murdering her own daughter in February 1964, and especially if she had been tried and convicted for murder, a number of political careers in Music City would likely have burned to the ground. She was that powerful. Chief of police Hubert Kemp appears to have come to this realization when Jo was brought in for questioning on the night of the murder and then apparently used Briley's influence to walk out of the Municipal Safety

Building free as a bird. It certainly helped that no photograph or mention of her midnight-to-dawn interrogation ever made its way into the newspaper. Thus, perhaps it is fair to wonder why Harry Nichol, the district attorney general, who, early on, stated that he personally looked forward to prosecuting Paula's killer, instead decided to step away and let his team deal with the explosive case when it came time for trial.[5]

In hindsight, it didn't take much to have John Randolph Clarke indicted and convicted for Paula Herring's murder. Clarke's comment to Al Baker, the tampered fiber evidence, the matching bullet, and one thing more did the trick: a concerted effort to keep Jo Herring and her activities hidden from view. The more this was achieved, the easier it became to sell Clarke's guilt.

Speaking of courtroom drama, I remember the trial of O. J. Simpson after he pled "absolutely 100 percent not guilty" to the charge of murdering his ex-wife, Nicole, and her friend Ronald Goldman in June of 1994. Simpson's criminal trial ran from late January into early October 1995, more than thirty weeks in duration. But the biggest murder trial in the South in the fall of 1964, the one covered by newspapers from the Mississippi River to the hills of East Tennessee, from Alabama to the Ohio Valley, and picked up by the Associated Press for national distribution, that trial started on a Monday morning, and the verdict was rendered on Friday afternoon of the same week. Could some officer of the court have known the topics to avoid during the trial so that no one came close to shining the light of day on the lifestyles being led behind the scenes? It's possible.

And what could Charles Galbreath and his defense team have known about the plan? It is possible that Galbreath was well acquainted with Jo Herring's powerful "friends" and was resigned to the fact that, no matter how strong a defense, or for that matter, how little of a defense he put on for his client, John Randolph Clarke was likely going to be convicted for murdering an eighteen-year-old girl. It's also possible that Galbreath had a clear understanding of the guilty party when he asked Jo Herring in open court if she knew where the gun was located.

Perhaps that is why Jo Herring and some of the "King's Men"

were partying into the wee hours of the morning during the trial week spent in Jackson. As long as Clarke was convicted and did the time, they were happy to accommodate him and escape the consequences of informing the public of their secret lifestyles.

It appears to have been well known among Jo Herring's powerful circle of friends that she may have been involved in at least one and possibly two murders and that she escaped criminal consequences for both. Either way, the viewpoint held by most of the King's Men was that Jo Herring was untouchable, not because she had carried out the perfect murder, but because she appeared to have absolute power over the Metro monarchy. And no matter how emboldened Paula Herring may have felt in an attempt to avenge her father's 1960 murder, she was still just a little "Fish" in a big Metro pond.

CHAPTER THIRTY-SIX

CLASS OF 1963

Fifty years after Paula Herring graduated as part of the first senior class of John Overton High School, her classmates got together to host a fiftieth reunion on a Saturday night in September, at a country club location just north of Nashville. It's one thing to celebrate the passing decades, the triumphs, joys, and sorrows shared by a group of people remembering such milestones, and it's entirely another thing to crash such a party and ask everyone to spend time focused on one of the worst events in their school memories, the cold-blooded murder of a classmate.

So I did the only thing I could think of; rather than intrude on their celebration, I wrote a one-page personal note to the attendees, asking for remembrances of their fallen classmate, and one of the class officers graciously left copies of my note on a table for anyone to review or ignore as they preferred. No pictures, no newspaper headlines, no brutal descriptions of Paula's murder for the attendees to dwell on.

A few days before the actual reunion, on a warm September afternoon, I made a drive to beautiful Center Hill Lake, about an hour east of Nashville and near Cookeville, Tennessee. After stopping to ask directions more than once, I finally located the stunning lakeside home of a man I'll call Joshua Prince.[1] He met me on his front porch as I handed over fifty copies of my note and thanked him for his assistance.

Joshua was tall and friendly, with a full head of salt and pepper hair and a tiny set of wire-rimmed glasses hanging from his shirt pocket. After a few moments of friendly conversation regarding his ski-boat manufacturing business, I was on the verge of returning to my car when I remembered to ask a question regarding his former classmate.

"Mr. Prince, do you remember what you were doing the Saturday night that Paula Herring was murdered?" I asked.

"Don't think I'll ever forget it, or that weekend either."

"Why's that?"

"I spoke with Paula on that Friday night, not too long after she came in from Knoxville," he replied.

"Well, that would be a piece of information I've never heard before. In fact, I've never found anyone, and I mean any of her high school friends or neighbors, that ever said they saw or spoke with her on that Friday night. Why such a clear memory for you?" I asked.

"Because I had been dating her next-door neighbor."

At this point, my mouth was hanging open, and I was speechless as my brain raced through the implications.

"Do you know Becky Wexler?" he asked.

Before I could answer, he said, "Well I guess she'd be married with a different name now, right?"

"Ah, Mr. Prince, I do, indeed. She's Becky Brewer now. In fact, ironically, I used to do business with Becky and her husband before I had ever heard of Paula Herring."

"I was at Tennessee Tech in Cookeville in my first year of college, and I came home that same weekend hoping to have a date with Becky on Saturday night, but Paula said Becky had left town Friday afternoon. Becky and I were dating pretty heavily during the previous summer," he stated.

"You saw Paula in person on that Friday night?" I asked.

"No, spoke with her by phone."

"Becky had gone to the Daytona 500 stock car race with her dad," I said.

"Right. You know this was before the age of cell phones. Before Paula got on the plane in Knoxville coming home, she called Becky to see if she'd be here, but that's when she found out Becky was on her way out of town," he said.

"What kind of mood was Paula in when you spoke with her?"

"Oh, a good mood. Paula was always in a good mood," he said.

"You lived close to the Herrings?" I asked.

"Sure, we lived within walking distance, just up the street from their house."

"I just thought of something to ask you. Do you remember anyone driving a hot rod, a red sports car, around the neighborhood about the time of the murder, even that very weekend?"

"I drove one," he said.

"Really? What kind of car?"

"It was a 1958 Plymouth with glass pack mufflers and a gear shift that was actually a piston. You know, Richard Petty won that same Daytona 500 driving a 1964 Plymouth. He blew the field away!"

"Well, you just answered a question I've been trying to answer for more than a decade. Did you know the cops were looking for a young man driving a red hot rod through the neighborhood?" I asked.

"No, never heard that, but a couple of detectives came to our house that night around 1:00 a.m. to talk to me."

"I don't think I can leave until I hear this story."

"My dad was terrified when we got the knock at the door at 1:00 a.m. It was Saturday night, so I guess really it was Sunday morning just after midnight. And it was two men, a couple of investigators. Since it was just us guys, I'm in my underwear standing at the door with my dad, and these two detectives are really looking me over, really looking me over, and they told us a neighborhood girl had been killed, but they didn't say who it was."

"You know why they were inspecting you, don't you?"

"No."

"They were looking for blood on your underwear and scratches on you. Paula was left in a bloody condition, lots of bruising and facial trauma. And there was a rumor that she'd bitten her attacker, but I doubt they knew that at the time," I said.

"Well, I told the detectives that I'd been to a party that night and described where I was and who I was with, and they left right after that. We learned it was Paula the next morning. It was awful."

"You realize you were one of the first suspects in the murder? One of the detective magazines a few months after the murder described your hot rod car being in the neighborhood on the day Paula was killed," I said.

"No, I never heard that. I remember that they got the right man. Some guy Paula's mother had been dating, I think?"

"Well, that was the story reported in the newspaper. But the real solution to Paula's murder looks a little different now, some fifty years after the fact."

"Oh, really?"

"I'm afraid so. Let's just say the detectives didn't arrive at your house by accident. They had Paula's mother downtown from midnight until daybreak Sunday morning, interrogating her. She must have known about your Friday night phone call to Paula and your name must have come up. That's how the detectives came to be knocking on your door so soon after they hauled Jo Herring downtown."

Just hours after the John Overton fiftieth reunion had taken place, I received a phone call from another attendee and member of the class, Bill Beasley. Beasley had read my handout the night before, and he and his wife were driving back to Florida where they lived. He was keenly interested in the research and provided a unique perspective of being a Vanderbilt University freshman driving through the Crieve Hall neighborhood within hours of that tragic Saturday night in February 1964.[2]

Not long after we began talking, Bill handed his cell phone to his wife and without missing a beat she said, "I'm not from Nashville, but the first story my husband ever told me about growing up there was the one about his friend Paula Herring. I'll never forget it."[3]

Moments later, her husband was back on the phone, and he described attending the memorial service for Paula and standing in line to offer condolences to Jo Herring at the funeral home three days after the slaying. "I had never been to a funeral for a friend, and Paula was a good friend. I vividly remember Paula's mother saying to me and everyone who came through the line, 'Just find who did this.' I thought that was such an odd thing to say to people paying their respects."

"You were talking to her," I said.

"Pardon me?"

"Paula's mother, she was issuing you and everyone else a challenge. And I'm saying that you were talking directly to Paula's killer when you were in that line."

"I was going to my grave thinking the Clarke fellow did it! Her own mother? How did she get away with it?"

CHAPTER THIRTY-SEVEN

FINAL RESTING PLACE

I had always wanted to visit the hill country of Texas, and so it came to be that, on a blue sky winter day, fifty years after Paula Herring's murder, I found myself driving through the rolling landscape of central Texas looking for a gravesite. Jo Herring's obituary indicated that she had been born in 1923 in Texas, and that she had spent the last decade of her life living with her family in the Lone Star state, where she had been buried in the summer of 1976. And I wanted to see her resting place.

I don't know how the Texas hill country looked in October of 1923 when Jo Herring was born, but I suspect it had the same scruffy appearance as it did on this January day. It was mostly brown pastureland, more populated by cattle and deer than people, with a rolling landscape broken up by small stands of Texas live oak and an occasional cedar tree. In their winter mode, the oak trees looked gray and lifeless, hunched over as if they had spent their entire lives battling the southwest winds, and in the process had developed paralysis of the limbs and spun off hundreds of arthritic fingers.

Nor was I surprised to see a few lonely oil derricks marking time with cattle that had long since gotten used to their mechanical neighbors, though most of the derricks that I saw were silent and stationary. There were signs of recent industrialization, however, as the cattle had new homesteaders in their midst, gas wells, which appeared to have been recently drilled by energy conglomerates and were marked as "field number XYZ" or similar. These miniature silos had all been painted bright white and were a regular feature of the landscape, all the while taking up no more space than a large SUV.

I traveled south from Personville, Texas, for about five minutes on FM 39, a farm-to-market road, as I occasionally glanced at a Texas roadmap lying next to me on the passenger seat of my rental car. Throughout the Paula Herring research project, there had been a few instances where the hair on the back of my head and arms would stand at attention, somehow letting me know that the next few moments were going to be important. It was like a prelude to time slowing down to a point where you could actually see and experience things in slow motion, as if the universe was carefully managing all of your sensory data, so that you could capture it all before being placed back on the conveyor belt of reality.

That was the experience I was having as I slowly negotiated my rental car onto a narrow road toward Oakes Cemetery, a historic resting place that I had been told was hidden from view and seldom visited by anyone but family members. After a hundred yards of blacktop, the pavement ended and became a gravel path eventually narrowing to a trail of packed grass and dirt.

When I looked to my right, I saw a scene straight out of a Texas hymnbook, an old wooden church chapel, with one large room and a low front porch, standing sentry over perhaps a hundred plus graves with the aid of a dozen oak trees. The church itself, save for the roof, had been completely covered in many coats of white paint, including the window panes. The burial ground appeared to have been used so infrequently that the only place to park was on the grass lawn in front of the sanctuary.

After parking my car, I decided that I would have to work quickly and methodically to ensure that I visually inspected every grave plot. If Jo Herring were indeed resting here, I suspected I might only find a foot marker similar to Paula's burial site in Gallatin, Tennessee.

Deciding to press on, I mentally tossed a coin and started carefully walking through the rows of graves, reading each headstone for any sign of the Herring name. After a few minutes of this pattern work, I realized that I was approaching the last of the markers to be read, and I began to mentally prepare myself for the conclusion that I had been misled as to the correct burial site for Jo Herring. But as I turned to walk back to my car, I found myself face to face with the grave of Wilmer Herring.[1] My breath caught in my throat at the realization, and I stood frozen in place.

The larger surprise was realizing that Jo Herring's body was lying next to Wilmer's.[2] With that sobering realization, I closed my eyes for a moment and took a deep breath, as my chin fell to my chest. It felt like a long journey had just ended.

When I looked up again, I could see that both headstones were actually one large piece of granite at the base, as wide as the two graves but with separate pieces for each headstone and a narrow ledge between them. On the ledge between the headstones was an actual granite vase, large enough to hold a small bouquet of flowers, though empty at the moment.

I took in this scene for more than a few minutes, not knowing exactly what to do next, all the while wondering to myself if Wilmer Herring was comfortable with this arrangement. A cold wind suddenly came through the graveyard, and I wrapped my arms around myself in an attempt to create some warmth, but with little success.

Not knowing how long it had been since someone had last visited their graves, I looked for a flower or plant that I could leave in the empty vase. Scanning a nearby fence row, I spied a plastic flower, and after retrieving it I carefully shaped its stem so that it would stay upright in the granite container. A few minutes later, I was back on FM 39 driving north to Mexia and then on to Dallas.

They say the subconscious will always find a way to express itself, and over the years I've come to believe that mantra as surely as anything I know. I hadn't traveled more than a handful of miles when I remembered a story that I had been told under the guise of anonymity, by one of Wilmer Herring's relatives, one that I initially had dismissed as rumor but which now seemed to be relevant, if not perhaps explanatory in its nature.

As the story goes, when Eva Jo Ainsworth was growing up in the little Texas town nearby, her mother had run her own prostitution business. Notwithstanding the moral implications, apparently it was a shrewd business decision, given the influx of thousands of men, many flush with cash, seeking their own oil fortunes. More than this, Eva Jo's father had been his wife's pimp, and their reputation was known far and wide. According to the family relative, this was Eva Jo's traumatic past, a past that she could never escape, though the family member thought Eva Jo may have tried to recover from it in the years before she died.

I quickly pulled the car off the road and sat staring out the windshield as the car's engine hummed quietly. Shaking my head from side to side, I eventually maneuvered the car back onto the highway and was comforted by the thought that Jo and Wilmer Herring would have all of eternity to work out their differences, especially if my visit just happened to resurrect old wounds. As one of Wilmer's relatives so eloquently noted, "In our faith, we're taught to forgive, as we are forgiven."

I hope somewhere that the topic of forgiveness has entered the "discussions" of Jo and Wilmer Herring and their daughter Paula, wherever they now reside after death. Perhaps in time, those still living, such as Alan Herring and Lizzie's daughter Gina, and the terrified citizens of Nashville who lived through this dark period of Metro's early history, will also be able to participate in this same attempt at forgiveness, and more than that, perhaps redemption.

As I made the drive back to Dallas, I thought about how much Nashville and its surrounding communities have changed in the past fifty years. The music business is still going strong and is more diverse than ever, and certainly so is the publishing industry, but now healthcare is leading the way, as we are home to some of the largest hospital corporations in the world. In contrast, Printers Alley is a minor tourist destination, but without the illegal entertainment aspect; it is often overlooked, as visitors flock to enjoy NFL football games, professional hockey, a world-class symphony hall, a sparkling new Country Music Hall of Fame, the Frist Center for the Visual Arts, and a food experience rated among the best in America.

I should note that the corruption that took place in Music City some fifty years ago, though highly publicized by the media, was primarily the work of a few well-placed members of law enforcement and their willing accomplices in Printers Alley and beyond. And those individuals unfortunately tainted the excellent work done by many policemen, detectives, investigators, and sheriff's deputies of that era.

In the case of Paula Herring, the number of participants involved in her miscarriage of justice was much smaller, but sadly included even more powerful representatives from additional offices of Metro government. For those citizens who lived through the Paula Herring tragedy, they will forever remember the fear running through the community and the concern that the Metro consolidation experiment might fail. But, fortunately, Metro Nashville is still going strong at age fifty-plus, and continues to be a great place to visit, a great place to live, and it is, in my humble opinion, still America's best and biggest small town.

If Paula Herring were counted among the living today, perhaps she would be a mover and shaker in the new Nashville, or perhaps she would have carved out a life of her own in Knoxville with her beloved Volunteers or become a national officer in the Alpha Omicron Pi sorority. Tragically, she is gone. I pray that this story will finally allow her to rest in peace, and that it might also provide answers to the little boy who survived a house full of hell on the night that he slept through his sister's murder.

EPILOGUE

WHERE ARE THEY NOW?

Crieve Hall Prowler: He was never caught. One theory was that he cut his hair soon after being described in the local news as a "bushy-haired" rapist. Another was that he began serving in the military and was using his weekend leave to return to the area that he knew well, and that the black scuff marks found near some of the crime scenes were evidence of military-issued shoes and shoe polish.

The Paramours of Jo Herring: After narrowly escaping the destruction of a few political careers, as well as marriages, the number of men and women involved with Jo Herring quickly fell to zero after Paula's murder. A combination of events beginning with Jo's firing from Vanderbilt University Hospital, along with the arrests of the sheriff and several high-ranking police officers in springtime 1964, essentially brought activities to a halt.

Jesse Henderson: Deceased, 2011, and per his wishes he was "planted" in the Veteran's Cemetery in Nashville.

Carl Raylee: Worked for Vanderbilt University Hospital and the VA Hospital system. Died in Spring Hill, Tennessee, almost fifty years to the day that Clarke (or Baker?) fired a bullet into the ground on 18th Avenue.

Nurse Lizzie: After a "no-stone-unturned" search for her whereabouts, a surprising discovery was made: extended family members confirmed that Nurse Lizzie died circa 1992 and was cremated by a local funeral home. She was aged sixty-four at the time of cremation.

Gina: Two years after Paula Herring's murder, Gina gave birth to a little girl, and became the frequent recipient of groceries from a highly placed public official in Nashville's Metro government, a man rumored to be the child's secret father. Gina still lives in Southern Kentucky. It is unknown whether she sought counseling help.

Al Baker: Collected reward money from the John Randolph Clarke conviction of at least $7,480.00 dollars. Deceased.

Sam Carlton: Wrongfully accused of the slaying of Paula Herring. Successfully escaped being murdered himself on the night of February 22, 1964. Sam Carlton died of a heart attack near Chicago, Illinois, in 1987, while driving a tractor trailer rig. He was sixty-years-old at the time of his death.

Edward Tarpley, MD: Deceased, 2006.

Charles Galbreath: Deceased, 2013. In the final analysis, Galbreath was correct: his client didn't kill Paula Herring. In my humble opinion, Galbreath had the makings of a mistrial in 1964, one of epic proportions.

John Seigenthaler, Sr.: Newspaper icon. Deceased, July 2014.

The Allmans: Gregg died May 27, 2017, as this book was about to go to press. He was aged sixty-nine.

W. B. Hogan: Died in 1998. Had his health remained strong, he would have eagerly helped investigate the Paula Herring mystery.

District Attorney's Office Staff: All of these men are now deceased. John J. Hollins Sr., led the prosecution in *State of Tennessee v. John Randolph Clarke.* Routinely voted one of America's top lawyers, he retired from practice in 2011 after more than fifty years of service and died in January 2016. Harry G. Nichol Sr. left the DA's office a few weeks before John Randolph Clarke finally reported to prison to serve his sentence in November 1966. Harry Nichol died in November 1984.

Metro Investigators: Many attempts were made to interview the investigators in the Paula Herring murder case. Some were willing to be interviewed and offered gracious assistance and remembrances. For others, when the topic of the Paula Herring murder was presented, the firewall response was "that was a long time ago, and I don't remember much about that case, sorry." Most of these men are deceased as of the time of this writing.

Clifton Beverly Briley: Former county executive (judge) for Davidson County and Metro Nashville's first mayor. Based on his political acumen and vision, he was the catalyst for an impressive list of accomplishments for the city of Nashville as well as the new

Metro government. Briley also endured a number of personal scandals during his political career, and the fascinating book by James D. Squires, *The Secrets of the Hopewell Box*, is a great source of information about Nashville's colorful history, as well as its colorful mayor. Briley's involvement with two nurses and a hidden lifestyle in 1964 played a role in the Paula Herring slaying, as a ne'er-do-well named John Randolph Clarke was framed for Paula's murder, though Clarke was truly innocent of the crime. Five months after the Paula Herring slaying, Briley was chosen Outstanding Southern Mayor by the Suncoast League of Municipalities. He died in 1980 at age sixty-six.

Leslie Edward Jett: Elected sheriff, 1960. He studied law at night via the YMCA Law School in hopes of expanding his political career. Indicted and convicted for income tax evasion, he left politics and became a car salesman for a local dealership. He died in 1990 at age sixty-eight.

Hubert Otis Kemp: First chief of police, Metro Nashville Government, 1963–1972. Kemp maintained a file on the Herring case that became the catalyst years later in identifying the players involved with Jo Herring and their motivations for covering up the truth. Kemp died in 1992, aged eighty-four.

The "Vandy" Kids: Jerome Shepherd exited Vanderbilt University within days of his arrest in February 1964. He eventually earned a law degree from Emory University and began a very successful small town practice in East Tennessee. He is retired as of this writing. John Burwell Wilkes finished his undergraduate and law school degrees at Vanderbilt University and earned a Bronze Star for service in Vietnam with the United States Marine Corp. After clerking for Judge Charles Galbreath (yes, that Charles Galbreath), he became Nashville's first "Night Court Judge." Colonel Wilkes retired from the military in 1996, but continued careers in law and aviation. Among other hobbies he writes aviation adventure novels.

Nurse Evelyn: Decided to set the record straight on Paula Herring's behalf. The delightful Miss Evelyn is sadly deceased.

Nurse Amanda: She was a twenty-nine-year-old field nurse for Sumner County when she was recruited by Eva Jo Herring to go with her to the Noel Hotel to "discover" Wilmer Herring's body. Her public health service and Hollywood starlet good looks earned her extensive coverage in a 1954 *Nashville Tennessean Magazine* article. She still resides in Tennessee.

Eva Jo Herring: On a hot summer day in July, twelve years after her daughter's murder, Jo Herring was getting ready to attend a party in Waco, Texas. But her plans didn't work out, and while getting dressed for the event she fell against a wall at home, and then crumpled to the floor, dead. It was July 7, 1976, and she was fifty-two years old. Her remains are in a small remote cemetery in Limestone County, Texas, watched over by an old church chapel. Other residents include a few live oak trees and nearby gas wells. Her body lies next to a man she did or did not murder in September 1960. She never was formally arrested, indicted, or convicted of any crime, including the death of her husband or that of her only daughter.

Wilmer Herring: His remains are next to wife, Jo Herring. It is unknown as to his acceptance of this arrangement, given that she was buried next to him some sixteen years after his death or, as some might describe, after his murder. He preceded his daughter, Paula, in death.

Alan Herring: The author hopes that this work can provide answers to the little boy who slept through his sister's murder in February 1964.

Michael Bishop: He grew up on a small farm near Gadsden, Alabama. He is a graduate of Freed-Hardeman College/University and also earned a master's degree from the University of Tennessee. He is at work on his next book. His wife is hoping for a novel.

ACKNOWLEDGMENTS

This work also would not exist without the incredible patience and love of my wife, Anne, who fully supported the long journey to the truth. And with deep appreciation to my mother who helped me unravel the secrets of my vanishing Aunt Mae when I was six years old. Thanks also to my family members, especially those whose professional insights offered invaluable assistance: a minister, nursing home executive, nurse, lawyer, social worker, and more.

Immense gratitude is owed to my New York literary agent, Sharon Pelletier of Dystel, Goderich & Bourret. Sharon patiently helped shape the proposal into a readable tome and then provided her professional expertise in finding just the right publishing house for this project. An author should be so lucky as to be represented by Sharon Pelletier.

Which leads me to my editor, Steven L. Mitchell, of Prometheus Books. Steven Mitchell quickly recognized the potential of the story and took a chance on an unknown author from Tennessee. I am in his debt and can only aspire to his eloquence with word and pen. If this work finds commercial success in the marketplace of readers, it is in large part due to the wise counsel of Steven Mitchell and the talented staff at Prometheus Books: Hanna Etu, Sheila Stewart, Cate Roberts-Abel, Jackie Cooke, Jill Maxick, Jake Bonar, and others, and the distribution group at Random House. You are an amazing team. Thank you.

My humble gratitude also to the early readers of the manuscript and to my coworkers who found the story more intriguing than the mistakes so evident in the early versions they read. Their emotional response to the discoveries along the way kept me writing and rewriting in hopes that I could do justice to the story. And in that regard, a special note of thanks to Clayton Perkins, Friday Blackwood, Nichole Riley-Doud, and Katie Walton Lancaster for keeping the project on the right path.

To the world-class experts who so freely shared their insights with me, I am eternally grateful. The list is long and includes Dr. Al Harper, Dr. Klaus Neudecker, Dr. Andrew Hodges, Don Rabon, Mark McClish, and my good friend Richard D. Walter.

Thanks also to the amazing Beth Odle of the Nashville Public Library, Special Collections division and the gracious Ken Fieth of the Nashville Metro Archives. This book also would not exist were it not for the helpful staff at the Tennessee Supreme Court, the Tennessee State Archives, and the gracious assistance of Judge Alan E. Highers, retired, of the Western Division of the Tennessee Appellate Courts as well as Sue Roberts, former Chief Deputy Clerk.

I can only smile when I think of the "Vandy Kids" Jerome Shepherd and John Burwell Wilkes, IV and their willingness, decades later, to share their memories of their arrest experience at the time of Paula Herring's slaying. As highly successful lawyers in their own right, they were very encouraging of having the truth finally come to light.

I would be remiss if I did not express my humble gratitude to Paula Herring's classmates at John Overton High School, especially Bill Beasley Jr., Buzzy Neil, Richard Price, Paula's next-door neighbor Becky Wexler, and the amazing women who shared their all-too-brief experience with Paula at the University of Tennessee, Knoxville.

Kudo's as well to the leaders of Alpha Omicron Pi for their assistance in locating the student leaders who had planned to initiate Paula Herring into their sorority. Also to the members of the first Ski Club at the University of Tennessee, Paul Pharr, Susan Lackey, and others.

I don't know how to begin to describe my humble appreciation to the families of Wilmer Herring and John Randolph Clarke. They carried decades of emotional baggage that was undeserved, yet courageously spoke of forgiveness and their hope of future vindication for their lost family members.

Finally, to those citizens who lived through the events of 1964 and were willing to share their memories with me, I thank you.

Michael B. Bishop
June 12, 2017

NOTES

CHAPTER ONE: SATURDAY NIGHT SLAYING

1. James D. Squires, interview with the author, August 17, 2002.
2. Ibid.
3. Ibid.
4. Eva Jo Herring, testimony before Judge Andrew "Tip" Taylor, transcript, Tennessee's 12th Judicial Circuit Court of Madison County, September 21, 1964.
5. W. J. Core, medical examiner, testimony before Judge Andrew "Tip" Taylor, transcript, Tennessee's 12th Judicial Circuit Court of Madison County, September 21, 1964.

CHAPTER TWO: LEAVING TEXAS

1. "Cold to Stay Night in 20s Forecast," *Knoxville News Sentinel*, February 21, 1964, p. 1.
2. Gerald Henry, "We Loved Her," *Nashville Tennessean*, February 24, 1964, p. 1.
3. V. F. Hochnedel, interview with the author, July 3, 2000.
4. Julie Hollabaugh, "Paula Herring Full of Joy: Mother," *Nashville Tennessean*, March 15, 1964, p. 1.
5. James D. Squires, "Missing Book Killing Clue," *Nashville Tennessean*, February 24, 1964, p. 2.
6. *Mexia Weekly Herald*, June 23, 1944, p. 12.
7. "Anna Nicole Smith," *Wikipedia*, last modified February 21, 2017, https://en.wikipedia.org/wiki/Anna_Nicole_Smith (accessed March 12, 2017).
8. Florene Hines, interview with the author, September 10, 1997.
9. *Mexia Weekly Herald*, August 24, 1945, p. 9; *Mexia Weekly Herald*, January 2, 1942, p. 11.

10. *Mexia Weekly Herald*, June 23, 1944, p. 12.

11. Ibid.

12. "2nd Lt. Wilmer, Bomber Barons of the 13th AAF," *Mexia Weekly Herald*, August 24, 1945, p. 9.

13. "Herring Service Held at Waco," *Mexia Daily News*, July 9, 1976, p. 2.

14. "Noel Hotel" *Wikipedia*, last modified December, 2, 2016, https://en.wikipedia.org/wiki/Noel_Hotel (accessed March 12, 2017).

15. William Beasley Jr., interview with the author, September 22, 2013.

16. Ibid.

17. Sarah Taylor, "The Backward 'S,' A Dark Whodunit," *Nashville Tennessean*, September 22, 1962, p. 7.

18. Becky Wexler, interview with the author, November 18, 2005.

19. Hollabaugh, "Paula Herring Full of Joy."

20. Ibid.

21. John Hemphill, "Call Metro Police, Crieve Hall Urged," *Nashville Tennessean*, March 3, 1964, p. 1.

CHAPTER THREE: 1964 INVESTIGATION

1. James D. Squires, "Missing Book Killing Clue," *Nashville Tennessean*, February 24, 1964, p. 2.

2. Frank Ritter and John Hemphill, "Slaying Feared for Months," *Nashville Tennessean*, February 24, 1964, p. 1.

3. Ibid.

4. Ibid., p. 2.

5. John Hemphill, "Call Metro Police, Crieve Hall Urged," *Nashville Tennessean*, March 3, 1964, p. 1.

6. Jerry Thompson, "Police Retire 'Peeper' Count," *Nashville Tennessean*, March 1964, p. 1.

7. Al Baker, testimony before Judge Andrew "Tip" Taylor, transcript, Tennessee's 12th Judicial Circuit Court of Madison County, September 22, 1964.

8. Bob Wilson, "Sport Talk," *Knoxville News Sentinel*, October 26, 1947, p. B-2.

9. John Randolph Clarke, testimony before Judge Andrew "Tip" Taylor, transcript, Tennessee's 12th Judicial Circuit Court of Madison County. September 23, 1964.

10. Julie Hollabaugh, "Paula's Rites Marked by Dignity, Weeping," *Nashville Tennessean,* February 26, 1964, p. 2.

CHAPTER FOUR: THIRD BULLET

1. Larry Brinton, "Girl's Missing Book Found," *Nashville Banner,* February 26, 1964, p. 1.
2. *All The King's Men,* directed by Robert Rossen (California: Columbia Pictures USA, 1949).
3. Al Baker, testimony before Judge Andrew "Tip" Taylor, transcript, Tennessee's 12th Judicial Circuit Court of Madison County, September 22, 1964.
4. John Parish, "Prosecution Rests Case with Lab Report on Suit," *Jackson Sun,* September 23, 1964, p. 1.
5. Beverly Briley, 10:00 p.m. news broadcast, WLAC-TV, Nashville, TN, February 27, 1964, transcript from Criminal Court Records, Tennessee Supreme Court.
6. J. Edgar Hoover to Hubert Kemp and Harry Nichol, telegram, February 27, 1964, Hubert O. Kemp Collection, Metro Archives, Nashville, TN.
7. Wayne Whitt and James D. Squires, "Slaying Suspect Charged," *Nashville Tennessean,* February 28, 1964, p. 1.
8. "Resident of Crieve Hall Guns Down Mouse Prowler, Ruins Electric Stove," *Nashville Tennessean,* February 29, 1964, p. 1.
9. "2 Bar Groups Back Summers in Judge Race," *Nashville Tennessean,* March 16, 1964, pp. 1, 4.
10. Julie Hollabaugh, "Paula Herring Full of Joy: Mother," *Nashville Tennessean,* March 15, 1964, p. 6.
11. Frank Ritter, "Sherlock Flair Shown by Lawmen," *Nashville Tennessean,* March 1, 1964, p. 1.
12. Nellie Kenyon, "Donoho, Smith, Jett Hit on Taxes," *Nashville Tennessean,* March 18, 1964, p. 1.
13. Mickey Kreitner, interview with the author, April 18, 1998.
14. Ibid.
15. "It's a New Chapter for Ex-Police," *Nashville Tennessean,* March 18, 1964, pp. 1–2.
16. Nellie Kenyon, "Hoffa Guilty, Will Appeal," *Nashville Tennessean,* March 5, 1964, p. 1.

CHAPTER FIVE: CRIMINAL TRIAL

1. John Parrish, "Mrs. Herring Takes Stand In Murder Trial," *Jackson Sun*, September 21, 1964, p. 1.
2. "Andrew T. Taylor," Our Campaigns, last modified August 12, 2016, http://www.ourcampaigns.com/CandidateDetail.html?CandidateID=162011.
3. Parish, "Mrs. Herring Takes Stand."
4. Eva Jo Herring, testimony before Judge Andrew "Tip" Taylor, transcript, Tennessee's 12th Judicial Circuit Court of Madison County, September 21, 1964.
5. John Randolph Clarke, testimony before Judge Andrew "Tip" Taylor, transcript, Tennessee's 12th Judicial Circuit Court of Madison County, September 23, 1964.
6. Eva Jo Herring, testimony.
7. Ibid.
8. Ibid.
9. Alan Herring, testimony before Judge Andrew "Tip" Taylor, transcript, Tennessee's 12th Judicial Circuit Court of Madison County, September 22, 1964.
10. "Today's Television Schedule," *Nashville Tennessean*, February 22, 1964. p. 14.
11. Alan Herring, testimony.
12. W. J. Core, testimony before Judge Andrew "Tip" Taylor, transcript, Tennessee's 12th Judicial Circuit Court of Madison County, September, 21, 1964.
13. Albert Cason, "Wrecking Here Is Big Business," *Nashville Tennessean*, May 25, 1958, p. 3-A.
14. William Vanderpool, testimony before Judge Andrew "Tip" Taylor, transcript, Tennessee's 12th Judicial Circuit Court of Madison County, September 23, 1964.
15. A. J. Meadows Jr., testimony before Judge Andrew "Tip" Taylor, transcript, Tennessee's 12th Judicial Circuit Court of Madison County, September 23, 1964.
16. George Currey, testimony before Judge Andrew "Tip" Taylor, transcript, Tennessee's 12th Judicial Circuit Court of Madison County, September 22, 1964.
17. John Randolph Clarke, testimony.
18. Charles Galbreath, interview with the author, August 3, 1998.

19. John Parish, "Coed's Death Called Brutal in Clarke Case Arguments," *Jackson Sun*, September 25, 1964, p. 1.

20. Robert Kollar, "Clarke Gets 30-Year Term: 'Blackout' Follows Conviction," *Nashville Tennessean*, September 26, 1964, p. 1.

CHAPTER SIX: JO HERRING'S LETTER

1. "Aunts' $25,000 Bond Frees Clarke," *Nashville Tennessean*, October 1, 1964, p. 15.

2. Robert Kollar, "Clarke Gains Stay; Appeals to High Court," *Nashville Tennessean*, May 24, 1966, p. 1.

CHAPTER SEVEN: FORTY STORIES

1. Clayton Perkins, interview with the author, August 18, 1997.

2. Metropolitan Government Archives of Davidson County, Tennessee (Elm Hill Pike location, August 1997), available online at http://nashvillearchives.org/.

3. "Beverly Briley," *Wikipedia*, last modified December 28, 2016. https://en.wikipedia.org/wiki/Beverly_Briley (accessed May 23, 2017).

4. Clayton Perkins, interview with the author, August 22, 1997.

CHAPTER EIGHT: NEIGHBORS

1. "Wilmer Eugene Herring," *Nashville Tennessean*, September 4, 1960, p. 43.

2. Florene Hines, interview with the author, September 10, 1997.

3. "Herring Service Held at Waco," *Mexia Daily News*, July 9, 1976, p. 2.

4. Hines, interview with the author.

5. Alan Herring, interview with the author, September 18, 1997.

6. Ibid.

CHAPTER NINE: INMATE #62250

1. *The Green Mile*, directed by Frank Darabont (Blowing Rock, CA: Castle Rock Entertainment, 1999).
2. *The Last Castle*, directed by Rod Lurie (Nashville, TN: Blinding Edge Pictures, 2001).
3. Tennessee Department of Correction, Nashville, Tennessee, October 10, 1997, https://www.tn.gov/correction/.
4. Board of Paroles, State of Tennessee, Certificate 21746, John Randolph Clarke, No. 62250, October 1975.
5. Wanda Graham, interview with the author, October 14, 1997.
6. "Ray Blanton" *Wikipedia*, last modified February 12, 2017, https://en.wikipedia.org/wiki/Ray_Blanton (accessed March 11, 2017).
7. Graham, interview with author.
8. Charles Galbreath, interview with the author, August 3, 1998.

CHAPTER TEN: SOMETHING'S FISHY

1. Steven Dobbs, interview with the author, October 21, 1997.
2. Ibid.
3. "Lipscomb University," *Wikipedia*, last modified February 27, 2017, https://en.wikipedia.org/wiki/Lipscomb_University (accessed March 10, 2017).

CHAPTER ELEVEN: POLICE ARCHIVES

1. "Alan Highers," Ballotpedia, https://ballotpedia.org/Alan_Highers (accessed March 11, 2017).
2. Alan E. Highers, ed., "*The Spiritual Sword*," 2017, http://spiritualsword.org/ (accessed March 11, 2017).

CHAPTER TWELVE: SIX GIRLS

1. Julie Hollabaugh, "Paula Herring Full of Joy: Mother," *Nashville Tennessean*, March 15, 1964, p. 6.
2. V. F. Hochnedel, interview with the author, June 3, 2000.

3. Ibid.
4. Ibid.
5. V. F. Hochnedel, letter to the author, June 7, 2000.
6. Hollabaugh, "Paula Herring Full of Joy."
7. Susan Lackey, interview with the author, August 5, 2000.
8. Paul Pharr, interview with the author, June 28, 1999.
9. Claire Atkinson, interview with the author, August 21, 2000.
10. Kay Masterson, letter to the author, July 24, 2000.
11. John Marr, "The Long and Quiet Death of *True Detective* Magazine," Gizmodo, August 19, 2015, http://gizmodo.com/the-long-life-and-quiet-death-of-true-detective-magazin-1725094095.
12. "Robert Johnson," *Wikipedia*, last modified March 4, 2017, https://en.wikipedia.org/wiki/Robert_Johnson (accessed March 10, 2017).
13. "Mississippi State Penitentiary," *Wikipedia*, last modified March 6, 2017, https://en.wikipedia.org/wiki/Mississippi_State_Penitentiary (accessed March 10, 2017).
14. Dorothy Ellis, interview with the author, June 9, 2001.

CHAPTER THIRTEEN: TRIAL OF THE BLOODY MAN

1. Eva Jo Herring, testimony before Judge Andrew T. Taylor, transcript, Tennessee's 12th Judicial Circuit Court of Madison County, September 21, 1964.
2. "List of Justices of the Tennessee Supreme Court," *Wikipedia*, last modified November 2, 2016, https://en.wikipedia.org/wiki/List_of_Justices_of_the_Tennessee_Supreme_Court (accessed March 12, 2017).
3. George Currey, testimony before Judge Sam L. Felts, transcript, 5th Circuit Court of Davidson County, Tennessee, April 9, 1965.
4. Dana Ford Thomas, "Noisy Car Found in Coed Death," *Knoxville News Sentinel*, May 18, 1965, p. 1.
5. Sebastian Junger, *A Death in Belmont* (New York: Harper Perennial, 2007), p. 155.
6. Charles Galbreath, interview with the author, August 3, 1998.
7. Henry E. King, testimony before Judge Sam L. Felts, transcript, 5th Circuit Court of Davidson County, Tennessee, April 9, 1965.
8. Sam Carlton, testimony before Judge Sam L. Felts, transcript, 5th Circuit Court of Davidson County, Tennessee, April 9, 1965.
9. Ibid.

10. Board of Paroles, State of Tennessee, Certificate 21746, John Randolph Clarke, No. 62250, October, 1975.

11. Supreme Court of Tennessee, Jackson Division. John Randolph Clarke, Plaintiff-in-Error, #33338, August 26, 1965.

CHAPTER FOURTEEN: RED ACE

1. "Red Ace Gasoline," *Nashville Tennessean*, September 29, 1966, p. 63.

2. "Krystal," *Wikipedia*, last modified March 1, 2017, https://en.wikipedia.org/wiki/Krystal_(restaurant) (accessed March 12, 2017).

3. "Father Ryan High School," *Wikipedia*, last modified March 9, 2017, https://en.wikipedia.org/wiki/Father_Ryan_High_School (accessed March 12, 2017).

4. Jesse Henderson, interview with the author, March 3, 2000.

5. Jesse Henderson, interview with the author, March 16, 2000.

6. Jesse Henderson, interview with the author, March 23, 2000.

CHAPTER FIFTEEN: LAWYERS

1. John Hollins Sr., interview with the author, May 6, 1998.

2. Ibid.

3. John Seigenthaler, foreword, in *The Suspect: A Memoir*, by John Hollins Sr. and Jeffrey Womack (Nashville, TN: Eveready Press, 2012).

4. Ibid.

5. Hollins Sr., interview with the author.

6. State of Tennessee v. John Randolph Clarke, September 21–25, 1964, Tennessee's 12th Judicial Circuit Court of Madison County.

7. John Parish, "Prosecution Rests Case with Lab Report on Suit," *Jackson Sun*, September 23, 1964, p. 1.

8. Hampton Sides, *Hellhound on His Trail* (New York: Anchor Books, 2011), p. 387.

9. Charles Galbreath, interview with the author, August 3, 1998.

10. Ibid.

11. Ibid.

12. "Former Nashville Judge Charles Galbreath Dies at 88," WSMV, Meredith Corporation, March 21, 2013, http://www.wsmv.com/

story/21550330/former-nashville-judge-charles-galbreath-dies (accessed March 11, 2013).

13. Charles Galbreath, letter to the author, July 17, 1998.

14. Galbreath, interview with the author.

15. W. B. Hogan, interview with the author, June 11, 1998.

16. Mildred Carlton, interview with the author, August 19, 1998.

17. Deborah Carlton Glenn, interview with the author, August 19, 1998.

CHAPTER SIXTEEN: AUTOPSY REPORT

1. Dr. Ed Tarpley, interview with the author, April 11, 2000.
2. W. A. "Mickey" McDaniel, interview with the author, May 20, 1998.
3. Dr. Al Harper, interview with the author, April 7, 2004.
4. Dr. Al Harper, interview with the author, October 19, 2005.

CHAPTER SEVENTEEN: GIRL NEXT DOOR

1. Becky Wexler, interview with the author, November 18, 2005.

2. Becky Wexler, interview with the author, November 19, 2005.

3. "Gregg Allman," *Wikipedia,* last modified February 27, 2017, https://en.wikipedia.org/wiki/Gregg_Allman (accessed March 8, 2017).

4. "Allman Joys," *Wikipedia,* last modified February 27, 2017, https://en.wikipedia.org/wiki/The_Allman_Joys (accessed March 8, 2017).

CHAPTER EIGHTEEN: VANDY KIDS

1. Delta Kappa Epsilon Fraternity, http://www.dke.org/ (accessed March 11, 2017).

2. Tennessee Bar Association, Nashville, Tennessee, 2017, http://www.tba.org/.

3. Jerome Shepherd, interview with the author, June 13, 2001.

CHAPTER NINETEEN: BRIDGE CLUB

1. Hattie Morrison, interview with the author, March 3, 2001.
2. Oakes Cemetery, Fair Oaks, Limestone County, Texas.
3. Amanda Franks, interview with the author, June 4, 2001.
4. "Wilmer Eugene Herring," *Nashville Tennessean*, September 4, 1960, p. 43.
5. Amanda Franks, interview with the author, June 5, 2001.
6. Evelyn Johnson, interview with the author, June 10, 2001.

CHAPTER TWENTY: TRUE DETECTIVE

1. Kay Masterson, letter to author, July 24, 2000.
2. "True Detective Magazines," Patterson Smith, Morristown, NJ, http://patterson-smith.com/mags.htm.
3. John Marr, "The Long and Quiet Death of *True Detective* Magazine," Gizmodo, August 19, 2015, http://gizmodo.com/the-long-life-and-quiet-death-of-true-detective-magazin-1725094095.

CHAPTER TWENTY-ONE: RETURN OF JIM SQUIRES

1. James D. Squires, *Horse of a Different Color* (New York: Public Affairs, 2004).
2. James D. Squires, interview with the author, August 17, 2002.

CHAPTER TWENTY-TWO: GOT ANY VETERANS?

1. Jesse Henderson, interview with the author, May 5, 2000.
2. Charles Galbreath, interview with author, June 7, 2000.
3. "James Earl Ray," *Wikipedia*, https://en.wikipedia.org/wiki/James_Earl_Ray, last modified March 10, 2017 (accessed March 11, 2017).
4. Hampton Sides, *Hellhound on His Trail* (New York: Anchor Books, 2011), p. 294.
5. Jesse Henderson, interview with the author, July 12, 2000.
6. Gina DeVern, interview with the author, July 18, 2000.

CHAPTER TWENTY-THREE: PRESCRIPTION FOR MURDER

1. Gina DeVern, interview with the author, August 9, 2000.
2. Gina DeVern, interview with the author, August 25, 2000.
3. "'Lizzie Borden," *Wikipedia*, last modified March 11, 2017, https://en.wikipedia.org/wiki/Lizzie_Borden (accessed March 12, 2017).

CHAPTER TWENTY-FOUR: SINNERS

1. Jack Spence, interview with the author, February 1, 2001.
2. Ibid.
3. "Hartsville Nuclear Plant," *Wikipedia*, last modified September 25, 2015, https://en.wikipedia.org/wiki/Hartsville_Nuclear_Plant (accessed March 8, 2017).
4. Jesse J. Richmond, interview with the author, February 12, 2001.
5. Evelyn Johnson, interview with the author, September 20, 2001.
6. Biography of Mayor Clifton Beverly Briley, Briley Collection, Nashville Public Library, Special Collections/Nashville Room.
7. Beverly Briley, letter to Crieve Hall resident, March 2, 1964. [A copy of the letter has been included in the photo insert of this book.]

CHAPTER TWENTY-FIVE: RESEARCH OR REINVESTIGATION?

1. Patrick Keller, interview with the author, January 17, 2000.
2. Patrick Keller, interview with the author, February 1999.
3. "Little Green Army Men," Toy Hall of Fame, http://www.toyhalloffame.org/toys/little-green-army-men (accessed March 10, 2017).
4. Patrick Keller, interview with the author, March 21, 2000.

CHAPTER TWENTY-SIX: SHERLOCK HOLMES

1. Michael Capuzzo, *The Murder Room* (New York: Gotham Books, 2010), p. 2.
2. Ibid.
3. Ibid.
4. Ibid.

5. Richard Walter, interview with the author, September 15, 2011.
6. Alex McKechnie, "Jack the Ripper through a Wider Lens," Drexel University, September 15, 2011, http://drexel.edu/now/archive/2011/September/Jack-the-Ripper-Comes-to-Academia/October 2011.
7. Eva Jo Herring, testimony before Judge Andrew "Tip" Taylor, transcript, Tennessee's 12th Judicial Circuit Court of Madison County, September 21, 1964.
8. W. J. Core, testimony before Judge Andrew "Tip" Taylor, transcript, Tennessee's 12th Judicial Circuit Court of Madison County, September 21, 1964.
9. W. A. "Mickey" McDaniel Jr., interview with the author, May 20, 1998.

CHAPTER TWENTY-SEVEN: CONTROLLING THE VICTIM

1. Richard Walter, interview with the author, October 3, 2011.
2. John Randolph Clarke, testimony before Judge Andrew "Tip" Taylor, transcript, Tennessee's 12th Judicial Circuit Court of Madison County, September 23, 1964.
3. Paul Carden, "Clarke Freed Awaits Trial," *Nashville Tennessean,* April 10, 1964, p. 1.
4. Sebastian Junger, *A Death in Belmont* (New York: Harper Perennial, 2007), p. 195.
5. Robert D. Keppel and Richard D. Walter, "Profiling Killers: A Revised Classification Model for Understanding Sexual Murder," *International Journal of Offender Therapy and Comparative Criminology* 43, no. 4 (December 1999): 417–37.
6. Walter, interview with the author.

CHAPTER TWENTY-EIGHT: AMERICAN VETERANS

1. Betty Henderson, interview with the author, May 1, 2000.
2. Mary Henderson, interview with the author, July 17, 2011.
3. Jesse Henderson, interview with the author, July 24, 2011.
4. "AMVETS," American Veterans, http://www.amvets.org/ (accessed March 12, 2017).
5. "Beverly Briley," *Wikipedia,* last modified December, 28, 2016, https://en.wikipedia.org/wiki/Beverly_Briley (accessed March 12, 2017).

CHAPTER TWENTY-NINE: COACH AND PLAYER

1. Jody Ellis, interview with the author, June 9, 2001.
2. Dorothy Ellis, interview with the author, June 9, 2001.
3. Ibid.
4. Dr. Ed Tarpley, interview with the author, April 11, 2000.
5. Michael Bishop to Carmen Lee, letter, September 6, 2008.
6. Carmen Lee, interview with the author, June 25, 2010.

CHAPTER THIRTY: CLEAR BLUE SKY

1. Ben Raylee, interview with the author, November 11, 2011.
2. T. Ronald Vaughan, interview with the author, December 9, 2009.
3. Carl Raylee, interview with the author, November 11, 2011.
4. Jackie Fargo, interview with the author, July 13, 2009.
5. Jim Todd, Esq., interview with the author, September 26, 2000.

CHAPTER THIRTY-ONE: HOUSE FULL OF HELL

1. Evelyn Johnson, interview with the author, November 11, 2011.
2. Gerald Henry, "We Loved Her," *Nashville Tennessean*, February 24, 1964, p. 2.
3. Johnson, interview with the author.

CHAPTER THIRTY-TWO: GRAVEYARD DEAD

1. Gina DeVern, interview with the author, December 2, 2011.
2. "Onsite Workshops," 2017, https://www.onsiteworkshops.com/ (accessed March 10, 2017).

CHAPTER THIRTY-THREE: SHERLOCK IN ATLANTA

1. "2012 64th Annual Scientific Meeting," American Academy of Forensic Sciences, Atlanta Marriott Marquis, Atlanta, GA, 2017, https://www.aafs.org/.

2. Michael Capuzzo, *The Murder Room* (New York: Gotham Books, 2010), p. 2.

3. Richard Walter, interview with the author, February 15, 2012.

4. Furrah Qureshi, "Jack the Ripper through a Wider Lens," Drexel University, May 12, 2011, http://drexel.edu/coas/news-events/news/2011/May/Jack-the-Ripper-Through-a-Wider-Lens/.

5. "Montague Druitt," *Wikipedia*, last modified June 22, 2016, https://en.wikipedia.org/wiki/Montague_Druitt (accessed March 12, 2017).

6. Alan Herring, interview with the author, September 18, 1997.

CHAPTER THIRTY-FOUR: BAD NIGHT IN NASHVILLE

1. "Cold to Stay Night in 20s Forecast," *Knoxville News Sentinel*, February 21, 1964, p. 1.

2. Julie Hollabaugh, "Paula Herring Full of Joy: Mother," *Nashville Tennessean*, March 15, 1964, p. 1.

3. Kathryn Ann Capps, testimony before Judge Andrew "Tip" Taylor, transcript, Tennessee's 12th Judicial Circuit Court of Madison County, September 21, 1964.

4. Carmen Lee, interview with the author, June 25, 2010.

5. Dorothy Ellis, interview with the author, June 9, 2001.

6. Gerald Henry, "We Loved Her," *Nashville Tennessean*, February 24, 1964, p. 1.

7. Al Baker, testimony before Judge Andrew "Tip" Taylor, transcript, Tennessee's 12th Judicial Circuit Court of Madison County, September 22, 1964.

8. John Randolph Clarke, testimony before Judge Andrew "Tip" Taylor, transcript, Tennessee's 12th Judicial Circuit Court of Madison County, September 23, 1964.

9. Carl Raylee, interview with the author, November 11, 2011.

10. Gina DeVern, interview with the author, December 2, 2011.

11. Eva Jo Herring, testimony before Judge Andrew "Tip" Taylor, transcript, Tennessee's 12th Judicial Circuit Court of Madison County, September 21, 1964.

12. A. J. Meadows Jr., testimony before Judge Andrew "Tip" Taylor, transcript, Tennessee's 12th Judicial Circuit Court of Madison County, September 22, 1964.

13. Evelyn Johnson, interview with the author, November 11, 2011.

14. Reta Howze, interview with the author, December 12, 2016.

15. Richard Walter, interview with the author, October 3, 2011.

16. John Parish, "Clarke Flatly Denies Slaying UT Coed," *Jackson Sun*, September 24, 1964, p. 1.

17. Raylee, interview with the author.

18. Evelyn Johnson, interview with the author, June 10, 2001.

19. Ibid.

20. A. J. Meadows Jr., interview with the author, October 1999.

21. James D. Squires, *The Secrets of the Hopewell Box* (New York: Time Books, 1996), p. 242.

22. Jerome Shepherd, interview with the author, June 13, 2001.

CHAPTER THIRTY-FIVE: QUEEN OF METRO

1. Robert Penn Warren, *All the King's Men* (New York: Harcourt, Brace, 1946).

2. Julie Hollabaugh, "Paula Herring Full of Joy: Mother," *Nashville Tennessean*, March 15, 1964, p. 1.

3. James D. Squires, "Missing Book Killing Clue," *Nashville Tennessean*, February 24, 1964, p. 1.

4. William Beasley Jr., interview with the author, September 22, 2013.

5. "Nichol Plans to Take Part in Clarke Trial," *Nashville Tennessean*, March 1, 1964, p. 1.

CHAPTER THIRTY-SIX: CLASS OF 1963

1. Joshua Prince, interview with the author, September 17, 2013.

2. William Beasley Jr. interview with the author, September 22, 2013.

3. Beverley Beasley, interview with the author, September 22, 2013.

CHAPTER THIRTY-SEVEN: FINAL RESTING PLACE

1. "Former Resident of Shiloh Buried in Fairoaks Today," *Mexia Daily News*, September 6, 1960, p. 1.

2. "Herring Service Held at Waco," *Mexia Daily News*, July 9, 1976, p. 2.

INDEX